Practical
CONSERVATION

Practical
CONSERVATION
Site Assessment and Management Planning

By Joyce Tait, Andrew Lane and Susan Carr

The Open University in association with the Nature Conservancy Council

Foreword by HRH The Prince of Wales

CONSERVATION

Open University course team

Joyce Tait (Chairperson)

Andrew Lane (Lecturer)

Graham Turner (BBC Producer)

Susan Carr (Course Manager)

Dee Marshall (Editor)

Lesley Passey (Designer)

Roy Lawrance (Graphic artist)

Julie Lane (Research Assistant)

Sue Snelling (Secretary)

Angela Walters (Secretary)

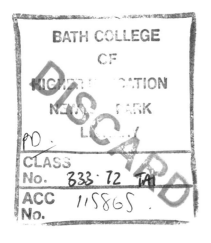
British Library Cataloguing in Publication Data

Tait, Joyce
Practical conservation: site assessment
and management planning.
1. Natural resources. Conservation &
exploitation. Planning
I. Title II. Lane, Andrew III. Carr, S.
(Susan)
33.7'2

ISBN 0–340–49003–9

First published 1988

Typeset by Taurus Graphics Abingdon
Printed in Great Britain for Hodder and Stoughton Educational,
a division of Hodder and Stoughton Ltd, Mill Road,
Dunton Green, Sevenoaks, Kent
by Thomson Litho Ltd, East Kilbride

Contents

Foreword

There has been a long-running campaign to make people more aware of the need to consider conservation alongside other uses of the land, such as farming, forestry, recreation and the management of waterways and roadside verges. Its success is measured by the fact that people are no longer asking "Why should I do it?" but "How should I do it?", creating an unprecedented demand for training and advice.

Now, for the first time, practical information on how to assess the conservation value of a piece of land, and how to draw up a management plan to maintain or improve it, is available within the covers of one book. This will form the foundation for a series of Open University teaching packs dealing with: Woodlands; Boundary Habitats; Wetlands; Grasslands, Heathlands and Moorlands; Coastal Habitats; and Urban Habitats.

The existence of agricultural surpluses and the resulting pressures for land use diversification are creating new opportunities to improve our landscapes and wildlife habitats. But unless we have a well trained body of land managers and advisers, knowledgeable and imaginative, and able to cope with the greater complexity introduced by these new opportunities, there is a danger that the countryside will change for the worse, rather than for the better.

The book will teach how to work with nature, rather than against it, without unduly affecting the non-conservation aspects of land use. It approaches this from the viewpoint of the land manager, or owner, who has the power to take decisions about the land in question and whose long-term commitment will be needed if conservation decisions are to be put into practice. In other words it really means sensitive *stewardship* of the land as it was always practised before there was such pressure to maximise production from the land; to drain every wet area and to remove the hedgerows in order to squeeze every last intensive drop out of our natural resources.

This book has benefited from the expertise of many of the organisations concerned with conservation and land management in Great Britain. The result is an authoritative guide, relevant to all the major habitats and land uses from the north of Scotland, through Wales to the south of England.

This publication is simple enough to be understood by those with no previous training in the subject, but at the same time incorporates the latest ideas on land use management planning so that experts will also find it useful.

The widespread adoption of the ideas and methods explained here could contribute greatly to the improvement of our environment.

CONSERVATION:

*A continuing education teaching programme
from The Open University*

This book, *Practical Conservation: Site Assessment and Management Planning*, has been published for the Open University as the foundation text for a teaching programme developed as part of its Scientific and Technical Updating Programme. The book is complete in itself and introduces and explains the process of land use management planning, showing how to integrate conservation with business and other activities. A complementary 50 minute television programme, *Practical Conservation: Working Wildlife into our Environment*, will be broadcast twice yearly. Marginal flags ◲ throughout the book refer to topics that are illustrated further in the television programme.

The complete teaching programme consists of six modules, suitable for individual or group use.

The first module is a foundation module and includes:

▶ this book;

▶ a video cassette of the television programme;

▶ two supplementary booklets describing sources of advice and grants and legislation relevant to practical conservation;

▶ an audio cassette;

▶ a study guide to the full programme.

The other five modules deal with the practical knowledge and techniques necessary to understand and manage particular types of habitat, namely:

▶ Woodlands;

▶ Boundary Habitats (e.g. hedgerows, roadside verges, ditch and river banks);

▶ Wetlands;

▶ Grasslands, Heathlands and Moorlands;

▶ Urban Habitats.

Each habitat module includes a book and a 30 minute video cassette.

For those who would like to gain practical experience or a qualification in this subject, the Open University teaching programme is being incorporated into courses offered by colleges, field centres and other training bodies. In some cases, a joint qualification of the Open University, the Nature Conservancy Council and the training body may be available.

For further information please write to:

Learning Materials Service Office
The Open University
P O Box 188
Walton Hall
Milton Keynes MK7 6DH

Chapter 1

INTRODUCTION

1.1 Conservation and land use management planning

Conservation is only one of many possible land uses and like others it depends on good management. However, its importance has greatly increased as the environmental impact of human activities has grown. Reserves and other specially designated areas of land are protected to help conserve the rarest species, the most fragile and threatened habitats, the most precious landscapes, and important archaeological sites, but they cannot do an effective job on their own. They need to be backed up by a wider environment that integrates conservation into the everyday, working aspects of land use.

The approach to conservation advocated here involves the wise use of resources to achieve, as far as possible, the best of both worlds: profitable and efficient use of the land, along with enhancement of its wildlife, its appearance and its historical and cultural associations. This is not the same as preservation and does not necessarily mean putting a stop to changes in land use or avoiding managing the land; on the contrary, many new land use developments could have considerable conservation benefits and most areas, if left unmanaged, would deteriorate.

The total area of Great Britain is approximately 23 million hectares and as you can see from Figure 1.1 (overleaf) only a small proportion has specific protection of wildlife or landscape. The rest is managed primarily for other purposes. It provides the environment in which most people live and also a home for most of our wild plants and animals, often common species, which give a great deal of pleasure. This book deals primarily with management planning for this large body of land, which has the potential to make such a significant impact on the quality of our lives.

What England (GB) land is managed for

Management planning is becoming routine for those who make a living from the land, replacing the previous approach where a vague and intangible plan for the business as a whole was stored in the manager's head. One reason is that running a business is much more complicated than it used to be: if you are a manager, you will have to take account of a wide range of factors that affect your work, including, for example, government regulations, markets for your product, prices and competition, public attitudes, new technological developments, the availability of grants for specific purposes or a range of new proposals for diversification of land uses. In addition, if you go to your bank manager for a loan or an extension to an overdraft, or to some other body for a grant for a specific purpose, they will probably want to see this justified in relation to a carefully thought-out plan for the business as a whole.

An expansion in management planning for landscape and wildlife conservation has also been taking place as a way of ensuring continuity of management for such long-term activities, to identify priorities and to help in the allocation of labour and money. The need now is to integrate the two strands, business and conservation, so that full account is taken of the

Integration

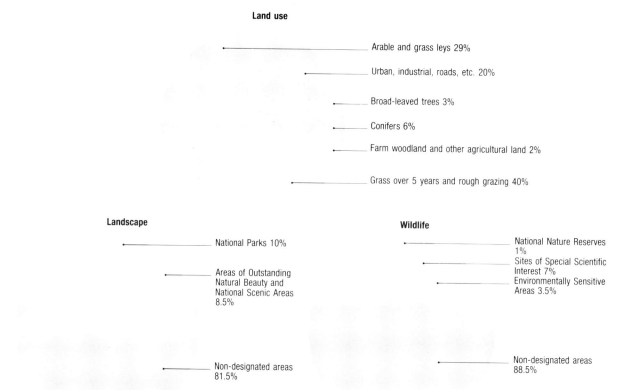

Land use

Arable and grass leys 29%

Urban, industrial, roads, etc. 20%

Broad-leaved trees 3%

Conifers 6%

Farm woodland and other agricultural land 2%

Grass over 5 years and rough grazing 40%

Landscape

National Parks 10%

Areas of Outstanding Natural Beauty and National Scenic Areas 8.5%

Non-designated areas 81.5%

Wildlife

National Nature Reserves 1%

Sites of Special Scientific Interest 7%

Environmentally Sensitive Areas 3.5%

Non-designated areas 88.5%

Figure 1.1 The major land uses and the extent of designated landscape and wildlife areas in Great Britain (total area 23 million hectares). Note: some areas may be included in more than one category

impacts of each on the other. This will improve public relations and make it easier for the manager to run the business smoothly and without interruptions. It will also help to create or maintain a more pleasant environment for those who live in or visit the countryside and can add considerably to the market value of a property.

It is possible that current pressures for rapid change in many land uses will lead to hasty and ill-considered actions that will, in the end, be regretted. Ploughing herb-rich grassland, or draining marshland to plant trees or to grow organic crops, or setting land aside for a fallow period of one or two years, will not benefit conservation. Incorporating conservation alongside a range of other land uses is not difficult, but it does require a basic understanding of the processes that have shaped, and will continue to shape, our environment, and the ability to draw up management plans that take account of the interactions among the various interests in the land. Unless we have a well-trained body of land managers, workers, advisers and helpers, backed up by adequate resources, the conservation value of the majority of British land will remain very vulnerable.

1.2 Who should read this book?

This book should be used by all those with an involvement or interest in the management of the countryside or urban open land. Farmers, foresters, estate managers, water authorities, local authorities, managers of country and recreation parks are all under increasing pressure to consider wildlife and landscape conservation alongside their other objectives. Many managers are enthusiastic about encouraging conservation on their land but are not sure how to go about it or are nervous of making mistakes.

There is an increase in demand for advice from the Agricultural Development and Advisory Service (ADAS), the Welsh Office of Agricultural Development (WOAD), the Scottish Agricultural Colleges, the Farming (Forestry) and Wildlife Advisory Groups (FFWAG), local authority staff and private consultants. As a result there is a need for more and better trained advisers.

An increasingly important role is being taken in countryside and urban land management by voluntary organisations and their members will need a better understanding of the background to land management if they are to give the best possible service to the community.

Many members of the general public are also interested in conservation and would like to understand more about the pressures leading to changes in patterns of land use, and how they can influence them in their local area. The subject is also a fruitful source of project material for school teachers, as it can introduce biological concepts in ways that also enhance the pupils' understanding of practical decision-making and land management.

Some of the instructions and suggestions throughout the book will be most relevant to people who actually have the power to take decisions about the land in question. If this does not apply to you, it should not make any difference to your understanding of the book; being encouraged to think things out from the position of the manager should give you a better appreciation of the practical aspects of the situation.

Given such a varied target audience, readers will want to use the book in different ways. If you are an adviser or consultant, or are training to be one, or are involved in management planning on behalf of a large organisation or public body, you will need to understand most of the topics dealt with here, even though you may not use all of them regularly in your work. If you are a landowner or manager, you will probably want to prepare only one management plan for your own land, which will be updated from time to time. You can therefore select the sections that are most relevant to your own needs. Although you will inevitably be a busy person, you may not be preparing your plan to any particular deadline, in which case you would have the flexibility to give more attention to those aspects of the plan that interest you most. School teachers, volunteers and members of the public will probably want to take at least a superficial interest in most of the topics covered, but to concentrate on particular sections.

1.3 How to use this book

The chapters of this book are based on a series of stages in the development of a management plan, as outlined in the next section. Part of the first stage is the assessment of the conservation value and potential of an area of land from its landscape and habitat aspects and this is explained in Chapters 2 and 3. The following chapters take you through each of the stages of management planning in sequence. They explain what the stages involve and illustrate how they can be carried out using examples from a range of different areas and types of land use. To provide continuity, one case study is carried through all the stages of management planning in sections at the end of each chapter: these pages are marked with a green strip at the top outer corner. Shorter and more varied examples are also included in each chapter. A book of this scope cannot cover any single topic in great detail, but a bibliography and a list of suggestions for further reading are included in Appendix I. Appendix II contains a glossary of terms for reference; each term is printed in bold type the first time it occurs in the text.

As the book is intended to give practical instruction, you are encouraged to develop a management plan for a piece of land to which you have legitimate access, as you work through the chapters. Your instructions are printed on a green background. Refer to the case study for guidance at each stage.

At the beginning of each chapter there is a summary of its contents. This will help you to be selective in your reading, either by skipping topics about which you already know or in which you are not interested, or by using the book regularly for reference purposes.

1.4 The process of management planning

Management plans are made in a series of stages, carried out in a logical order, as shown in Figure 1.2. There are formal names attached to each stage, but the underlying logic is really very simple. The planning process begins with a desire to change your present situation, either because you have a problem or because you see an opportunity.

Stage 1, Integrated Assessment, helps you to understand your present situation better and to describe it clearly, both for your own benefit and to help you to communicate it to others. It emphasises the need to integrate habitat and landscape assessment with the working aspects of the present land management and to show how they interact. Stage 2, Identifying Objectives and Constraints, considers the future state of affairs that you would like to achieve and any factors that might prevent you achieving it. The many ways in which these objectives could be attained are considered in Stage 3, Exploring and Choosing the Management Options, and the most promising options are chosen to be incorporated in the final plan.

In Stage 4, Drafting a Formal Plan of Action, a written plan is prepared to put into practice the options you selected at Stage 3. Stage 5, Implementing the Plan and Monitoring Progress, involves carrying out the proposed actions and comparing your progress with the situation as it was at the beginning (Stage 1). Implementation is a long-term, continuing process, and the extent to which a plan's recommendations are put into practice is the ultimate test of its value.

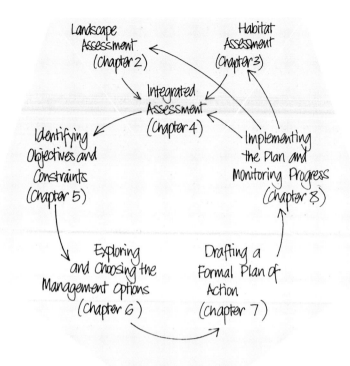

Figure 1.2 The process of land use management planning

The arrows leading from Stage 5 back to Stage 1 indicate that conservation, like any other management job, is never 'finished', and you need to update the plan at regular intervals, making minor adjustments on a yearly basis with a major revision every five years. Once you have become expert at drafting plans, you will find that you can skip stages or jump around in a different sequence from that recommended, but to begin with, until you understand clearly how it works, it is better to follow the textbook version.

It is easy to fall into the trap of thinking that *real* management planning only begins at Stage 4 and that the rest is some irritating preliminary, to be got out of the way as quickly as possible. However, what goes into the final plan at Stage 4 is the direct outcome of the earlier stages and it will reflect the amount of effort put into them. The more complex the situation, the more important it is to cover the earlier stages fully and thoroughly.

Managers and their advisers are busy people and often cannot afford to spend as much time on planning as they would like. However, it should never be allowed to become a routine, reflex activity. Each land use situation will be unique in many ways, and will change from year to year and unless this is recognised in the early stages, there will be little chance of the management plan being put into practice consistently.

The final written plan need not be long and technical. In many cases, a short guide to future management actions, as shown in Chapter 7, and a map summarising them, as shown in Figure 1.3, will be all that is needed. It should be a practical document that you consult regularly to show where and when resources and labour are needed.

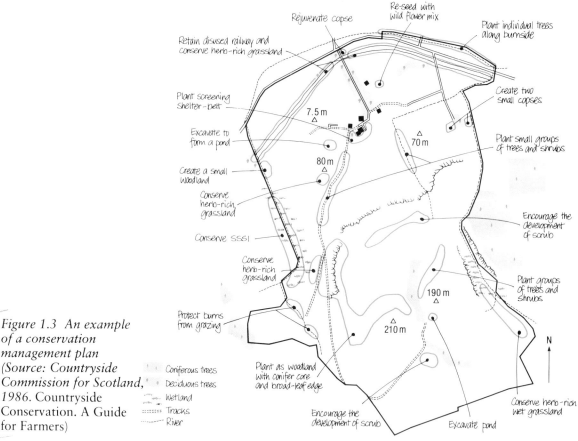

Figure 1.3 An example of a conservation management plan (Source: Countryside Commission for Scotland, 1986. Countryside Conservation. A Guide for Farmers)

The time taken to develop a plan will vary according to the complexity of the site and pressures on the planner, but the following is a rough guide:

▶ Integrated Assessment: between 4 hours and 10 days
▶ Identifying Objectives and Constraints: 2–4 hours
▶ Exploring and Choosing the Management Options: between 2 hours and 3 days
▶ Drafting a Formal Plan of Action: between 4 hours and 10 days
▶ Implementing the Plan and Monitoring Progress: seasonal activities over a period of months or years.

Thus, on a small, fairly simple site, preparing a management plan would take a minimum of twelve hours.

There is not space here to explain how to devise a full *business* management plan. If you already have one, this book will help to integrate conservation into it. If not, then the plan you produce will be mainly directed towards conservation. However, the basic principles described here are relevant to all types of management planning and you should find it easy to extend your knowledge to other areas.

The first stage of management planning, Integrated Assessment, involves learning how to look at wildlife habitats and the landscape, recognising the most important basic features, deciding what is good and what is bad, understanding where personal opinions and attitudes come into your assessment and predicting what will happen to the land if you manage it in various ways, including doing nothing and letting nature take its course. The next two chapters deal first with landscape assessment and then with wildlife habitat assessment, and Chapter 4 links these with the working aspects of land management.

1.5 Case study: The manager's problem

At the end of each chapter there is an example showing how the relevant stage of management planning can be applied in practice. To provide continuity, the same case study has been used throughout. It could be described as either a large mixed farm or a small estate, which seemed an appropriate choice as the majority of land use management plans will be prepared for farms and estates. However, the principles will be just as applicable to forest management, to local authorities and water authorities, or in an urban context.

The farm is in a **Less Favoured Area** in the Tayside Region of Scotland and includes hill grazing, arable land on the gentler south-facing slopes of the hill, permanent pasture and coniferous woodland, some of it approaching maturity. The photographs in Plates 1 to 4 were taken there recently.

The farmer inherited the farm a few years ago with a fairly heavy burden of debt, but this situation is gradually improving. Because of a lack of intensive management in the recent past, many parts of the farm are already quite rich in wildlife habitats and the landscape is varied and interesting.

The farmer must improve the income from the farm to help pay off the debt, but would like to do this without having an adverse impact on the wildlife and landscape and, if possible, to create some improvements. This is his starting point for the preparation of a conservation management plan, as described in the previous section — his sense of dissatisfaction with the present situation, and need or desire to see some changes in the future.

This farm was chosen because it offers a very wide range of landscape and wildlife features and thus a wide range of management options. As you work through the case study, do not be discouraged by the amount of work involved. By the end of the exercise you will have a comprehensive set of techniques and tricks of the trade that will help you to deal with almost any problem that may arise.

Chapter 2

LANDSCAPE ASSESSMENT

Summary

This chapter is about the appearance of the land, the factors that have contributed to this in the past and are likely to affect it in the future. After reading it you should understand which landscapes are highly valued and why, and which are less valuable and could be improved. Landscape assessment involves consideration of the landform, vegetation and structures that reflect long-term climatic influences and also the influence of people on the land. It also reflects attitudes and social influences. Landscape is a valuable public resource and should be assessed and planned with this in mind. Viewpoints should be selected for a site and the landform, vegetation, structures and landscape perceptions recorded. The map of the area in question is then partitioned, if necessary, into distinctive landscape zones.

2.1 Understanding landscapes

The word 'landscape' is used to mean 'the overall impression of the land' — not just the fine detail of the components of any scene, but also how these details fit together to make up the whole picture, which may, or may not, be considered beautiful. Included in this concept are: the underlying skeleton of rocks and soil (the **landform**); the covering of vegetation; buildings, historical and archaeological features (structures) and their cultural associations.

You may not be in the habit of paying attention to your surroundings in a critical way, except perhaps when you are on holiday or visiting somewhere new. To begin making a formal assessment of a familiar landscape, a conscious effort is needed to think about what you like or dislike and why, what has influenced your taste, and how the present landscape evolved. However, this is only part of the exercise: to contribute to a management plan, the assessment must be recorded so that you can communicate it to others, and so that it can act as a long-term bench mark against which to measure your progress.

When you are assessing a landscape it will probably seem natural to begin thinking about how you might make improvements. However, in the context of our *integrated* land use management plan, this would be premature. By all means keep your ideas for future reference, but do not make any decisions until after you have done the integrated assessment stage (Chapter 4).

The variety of landscapes that make up our countryside depend, at the most basic level, on the kinds of rock underlying the soil or exposed at the surface, their height above sea level, the way they have been weathered and eroded over the centuries, the climate to which they are now exposed and the types of soil they have formed. However, if these had been the only factors influencing our countryside, it would look very different from today's mosaic of fields, hedges, ditches, grasslands, moorlands, lowland heaths and coniferous, broad-leaved and mixed woodlands.

In the absence of human influences, a large proportion of the country would be covered in trees, mainly broad-leaved except in some northern upland areas where Scots pine and juniper would be most common. There would be much more marsh than there is today and less grassland and moorland. People have been influencing this 'primeval' landscape at least since Neolithic tribes first began to clear the forest around five thousand years ago and there are few identifiable remnants of this original forest cover left. However, it would be a mistake to assume that people are now the only major influence on landscape. The severe storm in the south-east of England in October 1987 felled over fifteen million trees in one night and completely changed many landscapes. Slower, but just as devastating, was Dutch elm disease, spread by the elm bark beetle, which has killed almost as many trees since the 1960s.

It is easier to understand a landscape if you first think about it in terms of three types of feature: (1) landform or physical features, (2) vegetation and (3) structures, as described below. However, it is the way these factors interact to make up the complete picture that is most important. What we see, and how we react to it, are influenced by our upbringing and past experiences, by economic necessity, by fashion and by personal preferences.

Landform

The landform has a major influence on the character of the landscape. The underlying rocks and soil and the climate to which they are exposed dictate the landform — whether it is hilly or flat, with steep crags or rounded tops to the hills, whether valleys are wide and shallow or narrow and steep, whether the land surface is dry, waterlogged or completely covered by water.

The soil itself can vary in colour, depending on the nature of the underlying rocks and the amount of water it contains. The colour of the soil is often a regional characteristic and can contribute to the landscape quality. For example, reddish soils are found in Devon and parts of southern Scotland, black soils in the East Anglian fens, chalky soils on the downs and slate soils in Wales. Black soil is probably peaty, dark brown indicates a high **humus** (organic matter) content, blue-green soil is often waterlogged and lacking in oxygen.

The most important soil characteristics, texture, wetness and **pH**, are described in Box 2.1 (overleaf).

Vegetation

The physical features of a landscape will have a major impact on the types of vegetation that can grow there. Deep soils or flat land will be mainly in agricultural use, growing crops on the drier, eastern side of the country and grass for animal rearing in the west.

Trees need large amounts of moisture to grow well and will not normally thrive on thin soils or steep well drained slopes unless rainfall is high. Rhododendron and some species of heath prefer acid soils. **Alkaline** chalk soils, if managed as grassland and not treated with fertiliser, will grow a wide range of specialist and very colourful wild flowers.

Often the type of vegetation that grows naturally in an area will be one of the main clues to the soil type. This is useful information at a later stage of management planning as it helps you to decide what are viable options for

Box 2.1 Soil characteristics

ing soil characteristics will affect the
a by influencing the vegetation cover.

. The texture or 'feel' of the soil depends on
the relative proportions of sand, silt and clay that it
contains. The largest soil particles — sand — feel
gritty when rubbed between the fingers. Silt tends
to feel smooth and slightly soapy when wet, while
clay — with the smallest soil particles — feels
sticky. As the size of the soil particles decreases,
the soil becomes very difficult to work and more
prone to waterlogging in wet weather. Very sandy
soils tend to dry out quickly and are easy to work
but very prone to drought.

Wetness. Soil wetness is determined partly by its
texture, as described above, and also by the local
rainfall and the position of the water table.
Figure 2.1 shows how these factors influence soil
wetness and the erosion and deposition of soil. On
the crest of the hill the soil is well above the water
table and water percolates through the soil. Further
down the slope, eroded soil from above
accumulates, but it is still well drained until near

the valley floor where the water table is close to the
surface. Here the deeper soil may be waterlogged.

pH. This is a scale indicating the extent to which a
soil is acid or alkaline. Soils often become acid
when they are waterlogged for long periods of
time. At the opposite end of the scale, soils are
alkaline when the parent rock is chalk or limestone.
Soils that are neither acid nor alkaline are known
as neutral.

In many places modern agriculture has ironed out
the original patterns of wetness and acidity by
drainage and the use of lime. However, as
explained in Chapter 6, it can be important to
understand the underlying characteristics of the
soil before you undertake activities such as
creating a footpath or car park, removing a hedge,
planting a wood or digging a pond. Detailed maps
(Plate 5) and other information can be obtained for
most parts of the country from the Soil Survey and
Land Research Centre (for England and Wales)
and the Soil Survey of Scotland.

Figure 2.1 Soil wetness and erosion

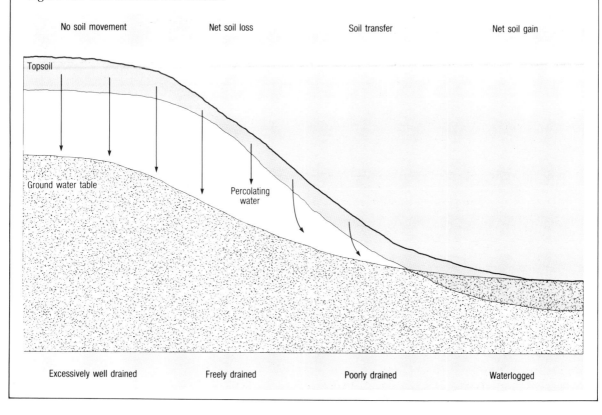

| No soil movement | Net soil loss | Soil transfer | Net soil gain |

Topsoil

Ground water table

Percolating water

| Excessively well drained | Freely drained | Poorly drained | Waterlogged |

Box 2.2 Unstable landscape

Plate 7 from the Brecon Beacons National Park shows a lowland area of small fields, bounded by hedgerows, and interspersed with small woods, creating an intricate pastoral landscape. You may think that this landscape would be protected because it is part of a National Park, but it is seriously threatened and could change drastically if land management practices in the area are not changed.

There are two main causes of the problem. First, the lack of spare labour on the farms has meant that hedges are no longer managed in the traditional way, by laying and regular trimming. There are many examples where they have been laid in the past, about twenty years ago, and then they have grown straight again. These hedges are rather unsightly when seen close up, although they are still contributing to the distant landscape, and they are in danger of being blown over by the wind.

The other main threat to the woodland and hedgerows is from grazing animals. Plate 8 shows what happens when sheep graze heavily around the base of trees and shrubs, often completely debarking them and killing them. Under these circumstances, there will certainly be no regeneration as all seedlings will be eaten by the animals. From the farmer's point of view, the trees provide valuable shelter for stock, particularly in winter, but unless this is controlled, the trees and hedges will eventually die and there will be no new growth to replace them.

Thus, although the landscape in Plate 7 looks traditional and is protected from deliberate destruction by being in a National Park, the hedges and woods that give it its character could disappear in a short space of time as they all become over-mature and die. Constructive management is needed to keep this landscape in its traditional form and this costs money. Some hedges will need to be cut down to their stumps and allowed to regenerate then laid in the traditional way; others will have to be grubbed out and re-planted. In both cases, the young hedge will need to be protected from grazing animals, sometimes by double fencing. Some of the woodlands can also be regenerated by going back to a **coppicing** regime, where most of the trees are cut back regularly on a rotation of about twenty years, with good specimen trees being allowed to grow to maturity. The benefits of shelter for stock can be achieved by fencing off sections of the woodland, again on a rotation of about twenty years, to allow natural regeneration to take place, and by keeping a close watch on the animals to make sure they do not get hungry enough to remove the bark from the trees.

---

the land management. The present pattern of vegetation cover and its future stability often depend on past and present land use systems, as illustrated in Box 2.2.

When looking at vegetation as part of landscape assessment, you should be paying attention to factors such as its colour and texture and how they vary with the seasons, the extent to which vegetation masks the underlying landform, obscures a view or hides an eyesore, the degree of permanence or vulnerability of a feature. (Chapter 3, 'Habitat Assessment', looks at vegetation from the point of view of the plant communities and the role they play in supporting other wildlife species.)

Structures

Buildings and other structures can be conspicuous or inconspicuous and can complement the landscape or detract from it. Many landscapes will include buildings serving a variety of purposes, some old and some new. Older buildings usually blend more harmoniously into a landscape and have a stronger sense of regional character than new buildings that are less likely to be constructed from traditional materials. However, a well-designed modern building can still be a positive feature in the landscape.

Because of a long history of human settlement our countryside is particularly rich in recent and ancient archaeological remains. They can be classified into three general types by their appearance:

▶ standing remains, including the walls of old buildings or field boundaries, stone circles, standing stones, burial chambers;

▶ **earthworks**, or soil-covered remains, visible as undulations on the land surface, including the remains of ruined buildings or their foundations, banks, mounds, **ramparts** and **lynchets**;

▶ buried features, soil covered remains with no visible trace at ground level. (These often come to light only by accident, e.g. during ploughing, but they can also be detected using aerial photography as shown in Plate 6.)

The rate at which a structure passes through these stages of decay will depend on the type of site, the materials used in its construction, natural erosion, human activities and the type of land use that now surrounds it. Understanding the nature and importance of archaeological features, even fairly recent ones, requires specialist knowledge and if you think there may be something interesting on your land, try to get expert advice about it, beginning with your local authority.

Landscape perception

The landscape is continually changing, not just with the seasons but from year to year. The early inhabitants who left the remains of their structures in the landscape have also influenced it in other ways. For example, as Figure 2.2 shows, the main visual change on a farm in the south of England from Saxon times to the middle of the eighteenth century was the gradual enclosure of the land into approximately 16 'fields'. In 1766 there were a few internal hedges with many more being added in the next 40 years. Since 1806 there has been a gradual removal of boundaries such that by 1883 the layout of the southern half of the farm resembled that of 1766. Between 1883 and the beginning of the present farmer's tenancy in 1968 the farm passed through several ownerships and several types of farm system including market gardening, intensive cereals and outdoor pigs. The present farmer has added and removed hedges and fences.

Enclosure of fields and removal of field boundaries were widespread and both were perceived at the time as disastrous. The fact that people complained in the eighteenth century about the *planting* of hedgerows and complained again in the twentieth century about their *removal* has been cited as an example of the fickleness of our perceptions, and our in-built resistance to change. Fashion certainly plays some part in landscape perception but there is more underlying consistency than this interpretation suggests. Both changes were regretted partly because they were seen as causing a decline in the natural elements of the countryside. During the enclosures, the land that had been held in common, which tended to follow the natural contours of the land and to be rich in wildlife, was replaced by a rigidly defined grid of field boundaries enclosing more intensively farmed land. Eventually, as the hedgerows grew they created an intricate pattern of new natural areas in the countryside. When these were removed in recent years people saw the change as a further large net loss of natural elements in the landscape.

Personal tastes

Your perception of the landscape, whether you like or dislike what you see, will have a major impact on any decisions you may make or advice you may give about future land use. It is therefore not enough merely to record the

18

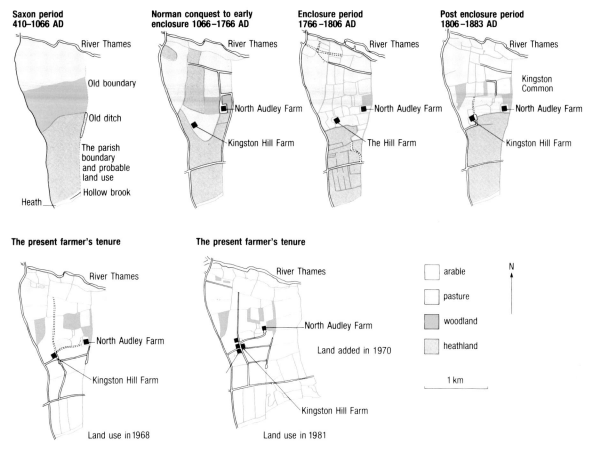

Figure 2.2 Changes in land use on the Countryside Commission Demonstration Farm at Kingston Bagpuize, Oxford (Source: Countryside Commission, 1986. Demonstration Farms Project. Kingston Hill Farm)

presence or absence of particular types of feature in a landscape, it is also important to record how you perceive them. The following criteria seem to reflect generally highly valued properties of landscape:

▶ wilderness, large scale, **naturalness**, a sense of being unaffected by human activity, particularly in upland areas;

▶ diversity, intimacy, small scale, particularly in lowland farming areas;

▶ familiarity and surprise, a fondness for the familiar but at the same time delight at being surprised by the unexpected;

▶ historical and cultural association, a sense of regional diversity and appropriateness to the local landscape and an understanding of previous influences reflected in the landscape.

The criterion 'naturalness' should perhaps always be placed in quotation marks as there is little truly natural countryside left in Britain. The lowland heaths were probably created by pre-historic tribes who cut and burned the woodland and temporarily cultivated the soil, resulting in rapid loss of fertility. Many upland bogs and moors were probably beginning to form as a result of an increase in rainfall around 5000 years ago, but human interference through grazing and burning may have tipped the balance towards blanket bog formation, rather than continuing regeneration of the woodland. Most chalk grasslands and flower-rich meadows owe their existence to the grazing regimes of earlier farming systems and the introduction of the rabbit by the Normans.

Bodies of water, moving or still, large or small, act as a focal point in any landscape. They draw the eye towards them and everything else tends to be viewed in relation to them. Their treatment is therefore particularly important and yet they are often abused as dumping grounds for rubbish or managed, for convenience, in ways that detract from their visual impact, for example by straightening the course of a stream to smooth the flow of water and simplify maintenance of the banks.

Landscape perception is not restricted to what can be seen. Sounds and smells can be just as important in creating an overall impression. Many people feel that their visits to 'peaceful' mountainous areas in Wales, the Lake District and Scotland are spoiled by the noise of low-flying aircraft. Background sounds of birdsong are pleasant; traffic noise from a road is unpleasant. Your appreciation of a landscape will also be affected by elements such as the smell of honeysuckle in a hedgerow or air pollution from a local factory.

Other commonly agreed criteria, less easy to summarise, relate to the general principles of good design, the relative size, proportion and colour of various elements of the landform, their relationship to one another and the overall unity of the whole scene that they create, as illustrated by the written comments on Figure 2.3.

Figure 2.3
Landscape assessment:
design criteria

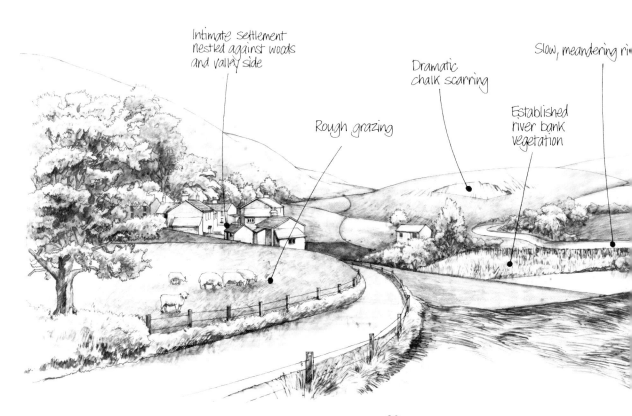

Intimate settlement nestled against woods and valley side

Dramatic chalk scarring

Slow, meandering ri[ver]

Rough grazing

Established river bank vegetation

20

One of the things most people seem to dislike about many forestry developments planted before the 1970s is the way they are laid out in square blocks or rectangles, with no regard for the natural shapes of the hills or river valleys they are invading. Nowadays, people seem less averse to square or rectangular fields, perhaps because their scale is more in keeping with the intimate lowland landscape, and where hedges are the boundary feature they add naturalness and diversity to the landscape. Most people would thus rate more highly landscape that has irregular boundaries, provided these are well designed and in keeping with the landscape scale. Straight lines and abrupt changes from, say, woodland to grassland are seen as negative landscape features — as much a blot on the landscape as an ugly building.

There are also landscape qualities about which there is less agreement. For example, some people adopt a landscape gardening approach to the countryside and to parks and open spaces in towns. Where there are hedges, they are kept small and neatly clipped; areas of grass are regularly mowed and even fertilised or treated with herbicide to remove 'weeds'. In strictly landscape terms, there is no reason why this should be discouraged, but it does have an adverse affect on wildlife, and it can also cost more than creating a more natural effect. One of the reasons for integrating landscape and habitat assessment is to help you to design a landscape that looks well maintained without over-managing it in ways that are detrimental to wildlife.

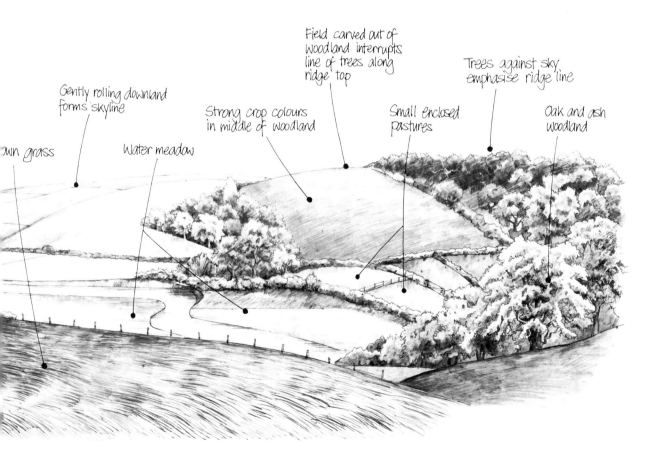

Field carved out of woodland interrupts line of trees along ridge top

Trees against sky emphasise ridge line

Gently rolling downland forms skyline

Strong crop colours in middle of woodland

Small enclosed pastures

Oak and ash woodland

own grass

Water meadow

Many recent landscape changes have been made with the intention of increasing the economic returns to the land, but they have also had the undesirable effect of creating a much more uniform countryside and a loss of the sense of place at a small scale which is one of the attractions of British scenery. It used to be possible to tell which part of the country you were in from the way hedges were laid or trimmed, from the style of the buildings, from the type of field and roadside boundary, or the style of woodland management. The places that retain this kind of local character are rapidly becoming tourist attractions, so it is undoubtedly something that people like to experience and would want to keep if possible. Some of these regions have already been designated **Environmentally Sensitive Areas** and financial support is available for their maintenance. In other areas we should be looking actively for ways to improve the landscapes we have inherited and, if possible, to restore a sense of local character. No landscape will be perfect, but even the worst will probably have a few redeeming features to form a basis for future improvements.

2.2 Public and private aspects of landscape

Landscape and wildlife features can take more than a lifetime to develop to maturity, but they can be destroyed in weeks or even hours, so the manager should take responsibility for long-term stewardship of the land. On most farms and other types of land, there will be public access to parts of it or to land nearby. This will mean that some features are highly valued by people who have no say in its management. Some attempt should be made to find

Box 2.3 Strategic landscape

The hills above the small town of Dunkeld in Tayside border one of the main tourist routes to the north. The land on both sides of the road is managed largely as commercial forest. To the east of the road is a large private estate (Plate 9) and to the west is Forestry Commission land (Plate 10).

On the estate land the forest is mature and ready for felling and the manager wanted to create as little disturbance to the landscape as possible, being well aware of its strategic nature. He took a colour transparency of the hillside, projected it onto a large sheet of paper and then drew over the projection a plan of the **coupes** (areas to be cut) over a long-term rotation. All the coniferous trees on the hillside will be cut and re-planted in large irregular blocks, following the lie of the land, over a period of many years. As you can see from Plate 9, some of the trees have already been cut and the disruption to the landscape is not serious. The large block of broad-leaved trees in the foreground helps to screen the commercial activities from the public view, and the manager also plans to leave untouched the trees on the knoll to the far left of the hillside, closest to the road.

The Forestry Commission land was planted an average of forty years ago, at a time when their remit was to maximise the production of timber with little or no concern for the landscaping of their forests. The **stand** is almost entirely sitka spruce with a sprinkling of larch along the edge, following the line of a small stream. (The larch contrasts more effectively with the sitka spruce in autumn, winter and spring than in the summer when the photograph was taken.) The uneven edge of the forest planting along the valley floor also helps to avoid monotony.

This timber is approaching maturity now and much of it is ready for felling. However, the Forestry Commission will delay cutting some trees for up to twenty years and will harvest others before they are quite mature, giving up some of the potential profit to improve the landscape value of the area. The coupes will be large, but irregular, following the lie of the land. The large scale of this landscape can easily accommodate large coupes and they are more efficient financially. Firebreaks will be similarly irregular. Re-planting will be done with a mixture of commercial coniferous species, and native broad-leaved trees will be encouraged to establish themselves at the margins of the forest. In future plantings, the margins of the stream will also be kept clear of conifers, although broad-leaved trees will be encouraged (see Box 4.1).

out what they like and dislike, and whether there is anything that has local historical or cultural associations. In most cases this can be managed through informal local contacts. However, for particularly important landscape areas more formal arrangements have been made, such as designation as an **Area of Outstanding Natural Beauty** or a **National Scenic Area**. On a smaller scale, individual trees may be subject to **Tree Preservation Orders**. These should be recorded in the landscape assessment.

For some strategically important landscapes in major tourist areas, the Countryside Commissions take an active role in landscape assessment and management planning. Box 2.3 gives an example of the management of strategic landscape in Scotland, showing the need to think about its long-term future over a very wide area, the importance of understanding its history and the public perception of the area, how it is being managed now and how it can be improved in future. Although this example deals with rather special circumstances, the principles should be the same for all landscape management.

2.3 Landscape assessment methods

As implied in Section 2.1, the assessment of landscape quality has two main perspectives: the first directed towards the landform (or physical features), vegetation and structures, recording the nature and extent of various types of landscape feature; the second concentrating on perception of the landscape, taking account of general and personal taste and attitudes. This section shows you how to carry out the assessment and how to record your impressions.

Background information

Before going out to look at the site in which you are interested, it can be helpful to have some information on the local history of the land and buildings, and their uses. If you know the area well, you may have some of the necessary information already, but there will also be some gaps to be filled.

Try to identify any recent changes in the landscape: for example, trees lost due to Dutch elm disease or changes caused by agricultural or forestry activity, road construction, the abandonment of railway lines, gravel extraction, filling in of ditches and ponds, or straightening of the course of streams. People who have lived in the area for a long time are a useful source of this kind of information. Try also to find out something about the local geology, soils and climate.

Old records

If there are records available, you may be able to go back quite a long way. Title deeds, maps or photographs can tell you a great deal. Old paintings can be helpful but will give a very subjective impression. Some regions will have Archaeological Survey Reports. Local libraries and local authority archives are excellent sources of historical information and they will have collections of old maps, aerial photographs and papers.

Statutory designations

Find out also from your local authority about any legal, regulatory or other obligations related to the land. There may be public rights of way, tree preservation orders, or it may be designated a scenically important area. Many historic buildings and most features of archaeological interest are protected in some way.

The amount of effort you put into this should be related to the time you have available for the whole management planning exercise. If you are interested in this subject or if you are doing the assessment for your own land, you may be happy to spend several days on it. Otherwise you may have to limit your time.

The historical and archaeological information you collect can be marked on a map, as shown in Figure 2.4. This background information will give you a useful perspective of the land when you assess its present landscape quality. It will help you to appreciate the rate and extent of changes that have taken place in the past and the reasons for the present state of the landscape. It will also forewarn you of any possible constraints on the future management of the land.

Selecting viewpoints

For a formal landscape assessment you will need a set of carefully selected viewpoints, both to provide continuity, so that your assessment can be useful as a long-term record, and as a basis for communicating your impressions to someone else.

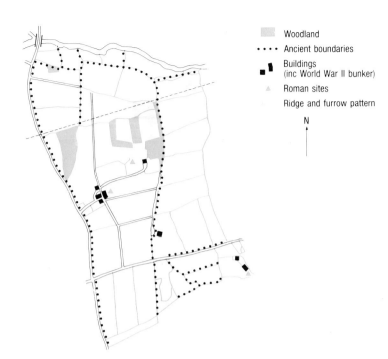

Figure 2.4 Historical features of interest on the Countryside Commission Demonstration Farm at Kingston Bagpuize, Oxford (Source: Countryside Commission, 1986. Demonstration Farms Project, Kingston Hill Farm)

Views of the land area from within its boundaries and looking out to the surrounding countryside, especially those from around people's homes, are most important from the land manager's point of view. The perspectives of people outside the boundaries of the land looking in on it should also be considered and if there is public access to the land or if a busy road runs past it, then public viewpoints should be given particular attention. If possible, there should also be one or two vantage points that will give an overview of the total land area to help you to see it as a whole and appreciate the need for design changes and their impact. Such 'designer viewpoints' may not be generally very accessible: on hilly land, they may be at the top of a hill; on flat land, the top floor of a building may be the best that is available.

Select your viewpoints by driving, cycling or walking around the land in question and the surrounding area. The number of viewpoints you need will depend on the size of the land area, the openness of the landscape and the number of different types of landscape in the area. It is impossible to provide general rules for this: on a small farm with an uncomplicated landscape, two viewpoints may be enough; a large estate with a varied landscape may need a minimum of twenty and even up to fifty, although in this case the assessment would probably be done by a team of people. As a general rule, if any two viewpoints give very similar impressions, one of them could probably be rejected.

Mark your chosen viewpoints on a blank map, number them and use this map to record the landscape features you can see from the viewpoints as shown in Figure 2.5 for the case study farm. Section 2.5 shows how the landscape was assessed, as described below, for the case study farm.

From each viewpoint, the landscape should be described in terms of:
- ▶ the landform, vegetation and structures
- ▶ your own and other people's perceptions of the landscape.

Landform, vegetation and structures

To describe the landform, vegetation and structures, begin with a short statement about the landscape as a whole, based on your impressions while you were setting up the viewpoints. Note the nature and extent of various features, as viewed from the approaches to the land area and from the land itself: is the land flat or sloping; if the latter, are the slopes steep or shallow; which crops are grown; what size are the fields; what are the field boundaries like; what kinds of trees are there and how do they fit into the landscape; are there ponds or rivers and what are their characteristics? How does your land fit into this general pattern?

Next, carry out a more detailed landscape assessment from the viewpoints you selected. (Be prepared to change a viewpoint or to add a new one if you think you need to.) Table 2.1 gives a useful checklist of landscape features you are likely to come across, but it probably does not cover every situation and you may need to add to it. As well as recording the presence or absence of a feature, it is important to grade its contribution to the overall landscape impression, as inconspicuous, noticeable or conspicuous.

Seasonal changes

Try to take account of the fact that landscapes change with the seasons. Heather moorland is purple in August but a drab brown in winter. Gorse (whin), one of the earliest spring flowers, brightens up many hillsides and railway embankments, as does the golden brown of bracken in autumn. Deciduous trees can conceal an eyesore in summer, but it will be visible in winter. On the other hand, when they shed their leaves, they may open up a beautiful view. A meadow full of wild flowers in summer will be plain green at other times of the year. If you know the land well, you will be aware of all these factors, but if you do not, you will need to be careful to think in these terms and you should visit the viewpoints at different times of the year if possible.

Landscape perception

You could use a separate photocopy of the checklist in Table 2.1 for each viewpoint and mark your assessment on it as you go along. Alternatively, have one copy of the checklist to remind you what to look for and write a brief statement describing the landscape from each viewpoint. You should also take one or more photographs from each viewpoint and annotate them, or make some simple sketches. Then add the major landscape features to your site map.

As noted already, the attractiveness or otherwise of any landscape is partly a personal matter, although there are also many areas of agreement over what is good and what is bad. You therefore need to record your own feelings about the landscape in question, what you like, what you dislike, and why, and also those of other people whose opinions might be relevant. In many cases, the opinions of the landowner or manager will carry most weight. Table 2.2 (overleaf) gives a checklist of some of the words you could use to describe your area. (This list is intended as an example only so do not feel restricted by it — use the words that come most naturally to you.)

Look at the shapes and colours that make up the whole scene, the length and breadth of views, the proportion of land to sky, the presence of features that attract the eye. Note whether the most obvious features are characteristic of

Table 2.1 Checklist of landscape features: landform, vegetation and structures

Grade the relative contribution of each feature as follows: *inconspicuous;
**noticeable; ***conspicuous.

Land holding .... Viewpoint no. ....

Date .... Time of day ....

Weather ....

Plain	Coast	Marsh	Lake
Lowland	Estuary	Mudflat	Pond
Plateau	Broad valley	Dune	River
Hill	Narrow valley	Beach	Stream
Crag or cliff	Deep gorge		Canal
Mountain			Ditch

Slopes

Vertical	Steep	Gently sloping
Undulating	Flat	

Vegetation

Woodland
Broad-leaved woodland   Mixed woodland
Coniferous woodland   Scrub

Heathland and grassland
Heather moorland   Bracken
Upland grass moor   Lowland heath
Peat bog   Lowland unimproved grassland
Water meadow

Cultivated land
Arable land   Market gardens and orchards
Improved pasture   Parkland

Linear features
Hedgerows   Roadside verges
Woodland fringe   Railway embankments
River banks

Small isolated features
Isolated trees   Small shelter-belts
Groups of trees, mainly broad-leaved   Copses and spinneys
(less than 0.25 ha)   Small gardens
Groups of trees, mainly coniferous
(less than 0.25 ha)

Structures

Buildings	Fences
Farmyards	Walls
Camp sites	Telephone wires
Car parks	Electricity pylons
Quarries	Rubbish dumps
Industrial land	Derelict land

Table 2.2 Landscape perception

Criterion	Suggested descriptions*
Scale	intimate, small, large, vast
Enclosure	tight, enclosed, open, exposed
Variety/diversity	uniform, simple, varied, complex, surprising
Harmony	well balanced, harmonious, discordant, chaotic
Movement	dead, calm, lively, busy, frantic
Texture	smooth, rough, coarse-grained
Naturalness	wild, unmanaged, remote, undisturbed
Tidiness	untidy, neat, over-managed
Colour	monochrome, subtle, muted, colourful, garish
Smell	pleasant, unpleasant, obnoxious
Sound	intrusive, noisy, quiet
Rarity	ordinary, unusual, rare, unique, familiar
Security	comfortable, safe, intimate, unsettling, threatening
Stimulus	boring, monotonous, bland, interesting, surprising, invigorating
Beauty	ugly, uninspiring, pretty, attractive, majestic, picturesque

(Source: adapted from Countryside Commission, 1987)

* The lists in this column are not intended to imply a scale of values, from good to bad, and the words are not arranged in any particular order.

the area, whether they give a particular quality to the scene, and the extent to which they dominate the view. Decide whether the land you are concerned with fits well into the surrounding area or is different in some way. Does it have less tree cover and fewer hedges or is it an oasis of variety in an otherwise featureless landscape? Are there any particular 'blots' on the landscape, such as a badly sited grain silo that stands out from miles around?

As before, you can either prepare a copy of the checklist for each viewpoint, or use one copy to remind you what to look for and write a brief statement describing your perceptions of the landscape from each viewpoint. Annotate the photographs or sketches from each viewpoint, and add any relevant comments to your notes or the landscape assessment map.

Landscape zones

On most land areas of any size, after you have recorded the landform, vegetation and structures, and perceptions of the landscape, you will be able to divide the land area into landscape zones that differ in appearance or 'feel'. This will be useful later when you want to adopt different management tactics to improve the landscape in each zone.

Give each landscape zone on your map a short title that defines its major quality, such as: 'farmhouse and surroundings'; 'hilltops'; 'steep slopes'; 'centre of arable production'. Note the nature of the boundaries between zones and any features that form links across them. Note also the features in each zone that should be preserved, for example because of historical associations, public interest or personal preferences, or perceived high landscape value. Also note features that need to be improved.

Table 2.3 overleaf suggests a format for summarising your landscape assessment to show:

▶ background information including historical aspects, public access and interests, and any statutory obligations and constraints;

▶ the overall impression of the land and its surroundings;

▶ the landform, vegetation, structures and landscape perception from a range of viewpoints;

▶ landscape zones.

2.4 Making your own landscape assessment

It is much easier to understand a practical subject like landscape assessment if you do it yourself, rather than reading about it. Your first attempts may not be very professional, but you will learn quickly with practice.

If you are a land manager or adviser, carry out a landscape assessment on the area of land where you are interested in incorporating conservation into its overall management. If you do not have an area of land where you can have some say in its management, choose a site you are moderately familiar with and to which you can have access (for example, it could be a farm, a nearby park, roadside verge or river bank). To make the exercise more realistic, imagine yourself in the position of a land manager or adviser. Observe the area carefully. Take account of what you have learned from the previous sections of this chapter and think about it in relation to your land.

You will need the following:

▶ blank sheets of paper for making notes and sketches;

▶ copies of the checklists in Tables 2.1 and 2.2;

▶ Ordnance Survey maps showing your area and some of the surrounding countryside. (The scale of the maps is a matter of personal judgment: the important points are that the size of the piece of paper you are dealing with is manageable out of doors and that the level of detail, which depends on the scale, should be suitable for the nature of the land. An intricate lowland site will need a large scale map while an extensive upland estate could be covered adequately by a smaller scale map. If necessary, a large sheet covering the whole area can be split up into smaller sections. As a general rule, for a large property, use a map on a scale of 1:10 000, and for a smaller area, a scale of 1:2500. Additionally, a map on a scale of 1:50 000 or 1:25 000 is useful for establishing viewpoints, contour lines and rights of way.) If you cannot find an Ordnance Survey map of your land, a hand-drawn sketch map would be satisfactory, but not ideal;

▶ a clipboard to hold your papers together;

▶ a camera and binoculars if you have them.

First, find out what you can about the history and general background of the area and of your land. Check, for example with your local authority, on the existence of any regulations governing landscape aspects of the land use.

Select several viewpoints both inside and outside the land area from which to view the landscape; note the viewpoints on your map and number them; note any areas to which there is public access, or which would be particularly visible from a public viewpoint. Describe your overall impression of the landscape in a few brief notes.

Describe the landform, vegetation and structures, and your own and other people's perceptions of the landscape with the help of the checklists in Tables 2.1 and 2.2. Note the position of important landscape features on one of your maps. If you have a camera, take some photographs from each viewpoint, and make a note of which viewpoint they were taken from; also, if possible, make a quick sketch of the view from each viewpoint.

Mark any distinctive landscape zones on your landscape assessment map.

Your notes at this point will be fairly crude and untidy. Tidy them up and summarise your landscape assessment as suggested in Table 2.3.

Table 2.3   Format for landscape assessment summary

(Note: This format is merely a list of relevant headings. You will need to write them out on several sheets of paper with space between headings for your notes.)

Site ....   Date ....

Background information

Including historical aspects, public access and interests, statutory and customary obligations and constraints, and any relevant maps.

Overall impression

Viewpoints

For each viewpoint, a brief description of the landform, vegetation, structures and landscape perception, including any maps, sketches and photographs.

Landscape zones

Landscape assessment map indicating the landscape zones, a brief description of each zone, the nature of the boundaries between them and links across them.

2.5 Case study: Landscape assessment

(This overview is formatted as suggested in Table 2.3.)

Site: Case Study Farm, Tayside, Scotland   Date: 14 July

Background information

The geology of the area is rock of Lower Old Red Sandstone giving rise to well drained, relatively fertile, brown forest soils.

The valley, 200 m above sea level, contains good arable land bordering a line of hills, up to 400 m above sea level (Figure 2.5).

The slopes are south facing. The average annual rainfall is 30 inches. The area is very cold, bleak and windswept in winter, but warms up quickly in spring, producing lush vegetation in summer.

Many of the fields in the fertile valley floor have been enlarged in recent years, emphasising the openness of the landscape. Eighty years ago, the hills were all forested right to the tops, and tree stumps can still be seen in places. Most were blown down in storms in 1893 and 1926 and the rest were felled during the Second World War.

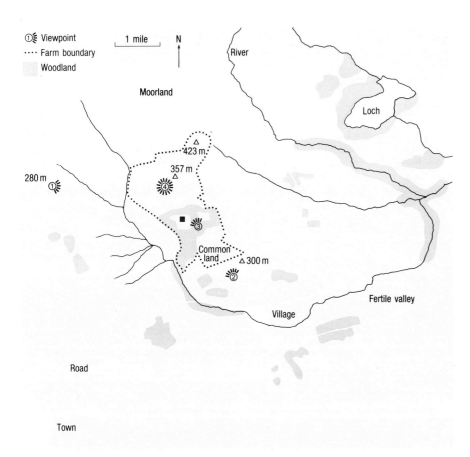

Figure 2.5 Case study farm: landscape assessment

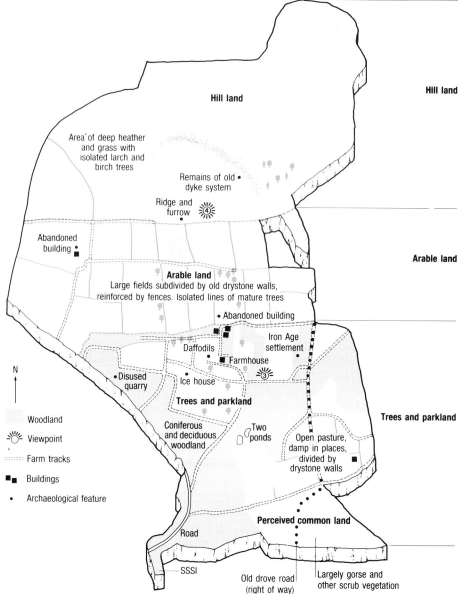

Figure 2.6 Case study farm: detailed landscape assessment

The farm has a rich historical background and there are many features providing a record of past land use and occupation. The following are marked on the map in Figure 2.6:

▶ a possible Iron Age settlement with evidence of an earth rampart in an area of sycamore woods (the farmer had sought expert advice about this and was told that it could be either Iron Age or medieval, i.e. between 800 BC and 1200 AD);

▶ a regular pattern of ridges and furrows visible in the close-cropped grass of the hillside, showing that the area was cultivated, probably several hundred years ago;

► an old ice house built in the late eighteenth century (ice which formed in winter would be broken up and stored there, lasting through most of the summer);

► a long, rectangular ridge (possibly an old **dyke** system) with a trough on one side, running round the hillside;

► an old drove road, now a public right of way (the local town was a centre of the cattle trade up to the late 1930s and the road is described in old records);

► several old abandoned farm buildings, one of which has been partially renovated;

► two parallel lines of daffodils that appear in spring on what is now parkland, marking the old approach to the house (this road is shown on a map of Perthshire of 1783).

As regards statutory or customary obligations, there is a low hill to the south of the farm, on which the farmer has grazing rights. This has been taken over by whin and its grazing value is low over much of its area. This land is perceived by local people as 'common land' and is used regularly for walking and sometimes motor cycling. There is a potential conflict here, but the farmer has sympathy for the desire of the local people to use the area recreationally and does not want to antagonise anyone. Sheep from his farm have not grazed the area since 1973.

Many of the tracks and paths shown on Figure 2.6, particularly the network to the south and east of the farm house, are used regularly for country walks by local people from the small town to the south of the farm.

Overall impression

See the map in Figure 2.5.

Area of fairly large farms.

Pleasant sense of openness and good long-distance views from the hills, contrasting with the often wooded valleys. As seen from the hillside, the valley is undulating, with hummocks and depressions due to glacial deposits adding diversity to the landscape.

The valley floor supports a mixture of coniferous and broad-leaved woodland, permanent pasture, fields with mature parkland trees, and arable crops on the lower slopes of the hill. The landscape here is a patchwork of fields divided by drystone walls and lines of mature broad-leaved trees.

Viewpoints

Four viewpoints were chosen, as indicated in Figure 2.5. The checklists in Tables 2.1 and 2.2 have been filled in for the first viewpoint only (see Tables 2.4 and 2.5 overleaf). The following notes give brief descriptions of the landform, vegetation, structures and landscape perception from each viewpoint.

1 This is an excellent spot from which to view the whole of the main valley with the farm in the foreground. The range of hills to the north of the farm forms part of the Highland Boundary Fault. The viewpoint is beside a narrow country road which sees little traffic and is a very peaceful spot on a pleasant day in summer. However, it is also quite high and would be very cold and exposed in winter. The case study farm stands out as being more diverse in terms of both landscape and habitat than neighbouring farms.

Table 2.4   Checklist of landscape features: landform, vegetation and structures

Grade the relative contribution of each feature as follows: *inconspicuous; **noticeable; ***conspicuous.

Land holding *Case study farm*   Viewpoint no. *1*

Date *July 1987*   Time of day *Afternoon*

Weather *Patchy cloud, light breeze, warm*

Landform

Plain	Coast	Marsh	Lake ✳
Lowland	Estuary	Mudflat	Pond ✳
Plateau	Broad valley ✳✳✳	Dune	River ✳✳
Hill ✳✳✳	Narrow valley ✳	Beach	Stream
Crag or cliff	Deep gorge		Canal
Mountain			Ditch

Slopes

Vertical   Steep   (Gently sloping)
(Undulating)   Flat

Vegetation

Woodland
Broad-leaved woodland ✳✳✳   Mixed woodland
Coniferous woodland ✳✳✳   Scrub ✳✳

Heathland and grassland
Heather moorland ✳✳✳   Bracken
Upland grass moor ✳✳✳   Lowland heath
Peat bog   Lowland unimproved grassland
Water meadow

Cultivated land
Arable land ✳✳   Market gardens and orchards
Improved pasture ✳✳   Parkland

Linear features
Hedgerows ✳   Roadside verges ✳
Woodland fringe ✳✳   Railway embankments
River banks ✳✳

Small isolated features
Isolated trees ✳   Small shelter-belts ✳✳
Groups of trees, mainly broad-leaved   Copses and spinneys
(less than 0.25 ha) ✳✳   Small gardens
Groups of trees, mainly coniferous
(less than 0.25 ha)

Structures

Buildings   Fences
Farmyards ✳   Walls ✳✳
Camp sites   Telephone wires
Car parks   Electricity pylons
Quarries   Rubbish dumps
Industrial land   Derelict land

Table 2.5 Landscape perception

Criterion	Suggested descriptions*
Scale	intimate, small, large, vast
Enclosure	tight, enclosed, open, exposed
Variety/diversity	uniform, simple, varied, complex, surprising *patchy*
Harmony	well balanced, harmonious, discordant, chaotic
Movement	dead, calm, lively, busy, frantic
Texture	smooth, rough, coarse-grained
Naturalness	wild, unmanaged, remote, undisturbed
Tidiness	untidy, neat, over-managed
Colour	monochrome, subtle, muted, colourful, garish
Smell	pleasant, unpleasant, obnoxious
Sound	intrusive, noisy, quiet
Rarity	ordinary, unusual, rare, unique, familiar
Security	comfortable, safe, intimate, unsettling, threatening
Stimulus	boring, monotonous, bland, interesting, surprising, invigorating
Beauty	ugly, uninspiring, pretty, attractive, majestic, picturesque

(Source: adapted from Countryside Commission, 1987)

* The lists in this column are not intended to imply a scale of values, from good to bad, and the words are not arranged in any particular order.

2 The second viewpoint, at the top of the low hill to the south of the farm, overlooks the area of grazing land used by the local villagers. This is dominated by whin which gives the landscape a rather unkempt appearance, although it looks very colourful in spring. Beyond this there is an excellent view of the whole farm. The land slopes steeply down to the road from this viewpoint and the farmhouse, farm woods and pastures are in an offshoot of the main valley floor, from where the land rises again more gently to the hilltops behind. On the hill land, there is a very obvious demarcation between the case study farm, which is still heather-covered with isolated trees, and the neighbouring farm, which is now largely grass.

The farm woods, pastures and parkland lie spread out below this point. The farmer likes the fact that his farm is much more heavily wooded than most of the neighbouring farms, but would prefer a balance that is more biased to broad-leaved trees than at the moment. The trees in the wooded valley to the south-west of the farm are entirely broad-leaved, including oak, beech, ash and elm. Two areas of woodland, can just be seen on the arable land area of the farm. The area to the east is mainly mature with a section in its southern tip that is about 10 years old. The western block is only 2 years old and still looks like an area of pasture that is slightly less green.

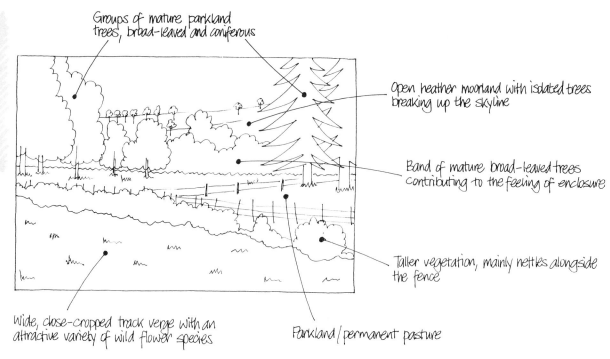

Groups of mature parkland trees, broad-leaved and coniferous

Open heather moorland with isolated trees breaking up the skyline

Band of mature broad-leaved trees contributing to the feeling of enclosure

Taller vegetation, mainly nettles alongside the fence

Wide, close-cropped track verge with an attractive variety of wild flower species

Parkland/permanent pasture

Figure 2.7 A section of the landscape from viewpoint 3 on the case study farm (see Plate 1)

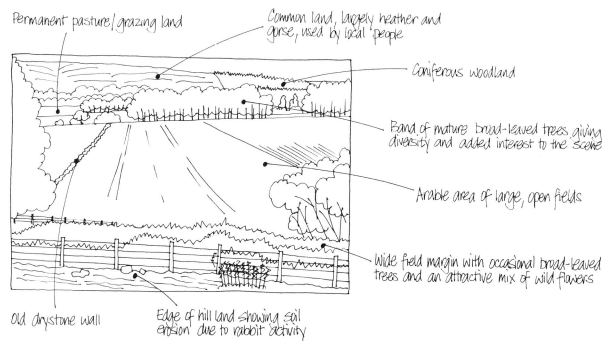

Permanent pasture/grazing land

Common land, largely heather and gorse, used by local people

Coniferous woodland

Band of mature broad-leaved trees giving diversity and added interest to the scene

Arable area of large, open fields

Wide field margin with occasional broad-leaved trees and an attractive mix of wild flowers

Old drystone wall

Edge of hill land showing soil erosion due to rabbit activity

Figure 2.8 A section of the landscape from viewpoint 4 on the case study farm (see Plate 2)

3 The view from here has a much more enclosed feeling than from the other viewpoints. The grazing sheep on open parkland in the immediate foreground (Plate 1 and Figure 2.7), and the farmhouse with its rather overgrown garden, give an air of domestication and flourishing vegetation to the scene in contrast to the open hill land just visible beyond the belt of trees. The parkland trees are all mature.

4 Like the first viewpoint, this spot is pleasantly open on a summer day, but could be very bleak and inhospitable in winter (Plate 2 and Figure 2.8). The fields on the arable land are separated mainly by rather dilapidated drystone walls with lines of mature trees in many places. The surrounding hill land has isolated trees, mainly Scots pine, larch and birch, among the heather. The very large number of rabbits on this part of the farm are causing erosion problems on the hillside and serious crop losses on the arable area as can be seen in the foreground.

Landscape zones

As shown in Figure 2.6, the land divides very clearly into three zones: hill land, arable land, and trees and parkland.

1 *Hill land.* In summer this is a pleasant area of deep heather and grass with isolated larch and birch trees. In winter it can be very bleak and exposed, with little shelter except on the western edge.

2 *Arable land.* This is an area of fairly large fields, bounded by drystone walls, reinforced by fences, and emphasised in places by lines of mature broad-leaved trees. These and the occasional thick hedge beside a farm track form a link between the arable area and the area of trees and parkland around the farmhouse. Some of the walls are now in disrepair and no longer stock-proof. Several have fences alongside and in some cases the field boundaries have been eliminated.

3 *Trees and parkland.* This is an area of fairly mature stands of coniferous woodland bordering open patches of parkland. Along farm tracks and to the north-east of this area there is a high proportion of broad-leaved trees, including ash, beech, sycamore, oak and wild cherry (gean). Mature trees, isolated and in small groups, are an important feature of the parkland.

The isolated trees and small groups of trees that are such important features of the landscape in all three zones are all mature or over-mature, with no natural regeneration and no re-planting having taken place. They will therefore be gradually lost over the next 20 years or so.

Chapter 3

HABITAT ASSESSMENT

Summary

This chapter describes the ecological concepts of habitat and niche and the underlying processes of nutrition and feeding, population change, competition and succession, distribution and dispersal. Brief descriptions are given of the major habitat types that have resulted from these processes, including woodlands, wetlands, boundary habitats, grasslands, heathlands, moorlands, urban and coastal habitats. Their value can be assessed using the criteria of naturalness, diversity, rarity and area, as illustrated for the case study.

3.1 Habitats and niches

To assess the conservation value of habitats you will need to understand the processes that have created them and will continue to affect them in future. The type of habitat that evolves in a particular place will result from a complex web of interactions among various plants and animals in the habitat, competing for light and space, feeding on or providing food for one another, opening up new opportunities for some species and closing down possibilities for others.

The concept of **habitat** is difficult to define but very widely used in relation to conservation. It is often used, at the simplest level, to mean the place where an organism lives, for example the habitat of the red grouse is heather moorland. However, the use of the word has been extended to cover identifiable types of countryside, each of which supports a characteristic range of species. The nature of the dominant vegetation in any area depends, in the absence of human interference, mostly on soil and climate, and the dominant vegetation will in turn have a major influence on the other plants and animals that can live there. Thus, in the extended meaning of the word, the vegetation gives the habitat its name, for example heather moorland, chalk grassland, broad-leaved woodland.

Some **species** are very restricted in their range and will be found only in rare or very specialised habitats while others will be found in a wide variety of habitats. The red grouse, for example, is restricted to heather moorland, so this is its habitat in both senses of the word. The fox, on the other hand, is found in woods, on open moorland, on farmland and even in cities, and its range therefore covers several different 'habitats' in the extended definition of the word. Another way of looking at this is to describe the fox as a **generalist species** and the grouse as a **specialist species**.

The human race is hardly constrained at all by habitat requirements. We have the ability to adapt habitats to our own needs and are not accustomed to thinking in these terms. However, for wildlife, a reduction in area of the appropriate habitat often means a reduction in numbers of the species that it can support, particularly for specialists adapted for that habitat only.

The previous chapter described various features of the countryside in terms of how they looked. In landscape terms you may be interested in a wood because of its colour, texture, variation with the seasons, the way it blocks out a beautiful view or conceals an eyesore. From a habitat point of view you will be interested in the plant and animal species that live there and their relationships.

Feeding strategies

The other key concept for this chapter is that of an ecological **niche**, which is a short-hand term for the totality of factors that specify how a species makes its living in the world. It describes how it feeds, behaves, responds to and modifies its environment, and interacts with the other species in the community. To take the simple example of **herbivores** feeding on oak leaves: deer will occupy the niche of 'large herbivores feeding on oak leaves'; caterpillars will occupy the niche of 'small herbivores feeding on oak leaves'; and greenflies will occupy the niche of 'sap feeders'. As noted above, some species are generalists and others are specialists: for example, deer will eat the leaves of most tree species as well as grass and smaller plants, while many caterpillars are restricted to feeding on one type of plant. Herbivores in their turn provide niches for **carnivores** and also for **omnivores**.

There is rarely room for more than one species in the same niche. For example, when the grey squirrel was introduced to Britain, it was blamed for ousting the native red squirrel from its niche in broad-leaved woodland. Sometimes a species can exploit a niche that is not already occupied. The collared dove, now common in parks and gardens throughout the country, began spreading across Europe from the Balkans in the 1930s, without having to compete significantly with any other species. However, once a niche has been occupied in this way, it will have knock-on effects on other niches that are related to it and on the host habitats.

The habitat can be said to be the 'address' of the species, while its niche describes its 'lifestyle'. As in human affairs, there is often a strong correlation between the two, but they are by no means the same thing. Both habitat and niche are central concepts for the subject of **ecology**, which studies the relationships between plants and animals and their **environment**.

The present range of wildlife habitats and niches found in this country is the result of a long process of natural **succession** and human exploitation and is still changing. The stimuli for change are similar to those described in the previous chapter, but here we are concerned with the effects of change on wildlife, rather than the landscape.

3.2 The history of wildlife habitats

By the end of the last Ice Age about 10 000 years ago, much of the country had been covered in ice and the rest consisted of **tundra** vegetation now found much nearer the Arctic Circle. As the ice receded, the bare earth it exposed was quite unlike the bare soil found on agricultural land or in a garden. It was very low in the nutrients needed to support plant life and only specially adapted species were able to exploit this niche.

Colonisation

The first colonists of the bare soil were low plants and shrubs with small leaves, such as thrift, mountain avens and dwarf birch. The remains of dead plants gradually built up the levels of **organic material** in the soil and provided niches, allowing larger trees such as birch, juniper and aspen to become established. These woods provided habitats for a range of plant and animal species, but destroyed the conditions favourable to the growth of the original colonisers which then disappeared from such areas.

During the first 5000 years after the Ice Age there were many invasions and retreats of trees and other species as conditions fluctuated between warm and dry or wet and cold. Thus, pine, hazel, oak and elm trees replaced birch as mixed woodland became established. In wetter periods, pine declined and alder became more common, and peat bogs became more widespread along with their covering of bog moss and cotton grass. In warmer periods, lime trees flourished. During this period, about 5000 BC, the English Channel formed, preventing some continental species from spreading to this country.

Forest clearance

By around 3000 BC, most of Britain was covered in mixed deciduous forest, with more open habitats surviving above the tree line on hills, or on waterlogged or eroded areas. Since then people have had a major influence on habitats. They cleared the forest to grow crops for themselves and pasture for their animals, beginning where the trees were easier to cut down, on chalk land and sandy soils or where tree growth was checked by flooding. Analysis of **fossil pollen** records confirms that there was a decline in tree species in many areas and an increase in grasses, cereals and species adapted to more open habitats. These spread, over hundreds of years, either from the small British remnants of open habitat, or by wind or human dispersal from the continent. New tree species also arrived from the continent by similar means, including hornbeam, beech and ash.

Agriculture rapidly used up the available nutrients on the poorer soils that were the first to be cultivated and these areas often developed into chalk grassland or heathland. However, improvements in the quality of tools made it increasingly easy to clear the remaining large areas of woodland throughout the country. The Romans began the process of draining wetland areas such as the Fens of East Anglia, and also deliberately introduced new species, including the pheasant and sweet chestnut.

Land use changes

By the Norman conquest much of the original forest cover of England had been removed, while the great forests of Wales and Scotland were cleared in medieval times. A further influence on the habitats of the Scottish highlands has been the clearance of people from the land during the nineteenth century to make way for sheep farms, deer forests and grouse moors. The large scale commercial planting of trees, mainly conifers, that has taken place since the 1920s until the present day once again transformed the habitats of much of upland and some areas of lowland Britain. The comparable changes that took place on farmed land were described in Chapter 2.

As a result of these changes, some species have greatly increased in numbers, others have declined, and some have become extinct in this country. The following section explains the ecological processes that determine how different wildlife species will react to changes in their habitat.

3.3 Ecological processes

To manage wildlife habitats effectively, you will need to know the background to the present distribution of wildlife species and how your actions are likely to affect this. This section explains how plants and animals obtain their food, how they grow, reproduce and die, how they are dispersed in the environment and how they compete. These are the processes that determine which species are rare and which are common and how habitats will develop.

Nutrition and feeding

Plants are the only species that can grow and build up their tissues using only water, the minerals in the soil and the gases in the air. By the process of **photosynthesis** they use some of the energy contained in sunlight to manufacture sugars and other **carbohydrates** and then, indirectly, **proteins**. Some of the energy stored by plants in this way is passed on to animals when they eat the leaves of plants; some is then excreted in the animals' faeces or dung. When the leaves of a plant, or whole plants, die, they are broken up by worms and insects and decomposed by a range of bacteria and fungi. Some of the minerals contained in them will then be available for uptake by plants once again. The cycling of nitrogen in this way is illustrated in Figure 3.1.

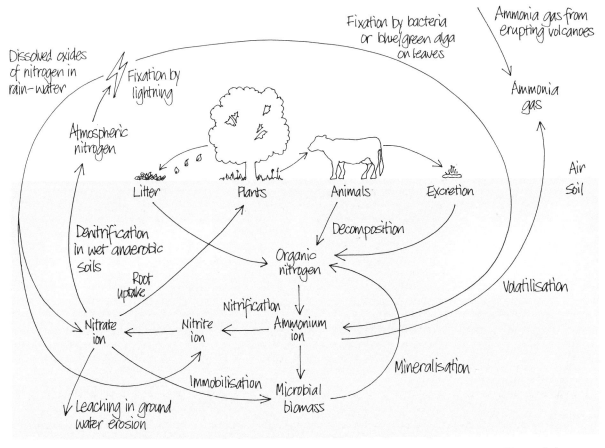

Figure 3.1
The nitrogen cycle

The rate at which minerals and nutrients pass through different stages of these cycles in any habitat will depend on the soil and climate, and the nature of the plants and animals that are present. Heavy rainfall, particularly on porous, sandy soils with little or no vegetation cover, will cause **leaching**, where the water percolates rapidly through the soil, washing out dissolved minerals. The decomposition of dead plant matter will be slowed down where there is a build-up of leaf litter on the floor of cool, temperate coniferous forests. In waterlogged situations, peat begins to form because the acid conditions are unfavourable to the organisms that normally break down dead plant materials.

Where land is cropped, for example by felling trees, harvesting wheat or mowing hay, the nutrients contained in the crop are removed from that habitat and cannot be recycled. In such cases, the land manager replaces the nutrients, mainly nitrogen, phosphorus and potassium, from an artificial source so that another crop can be grown on the same land.

Some plants can thrive on lower levels of nutrients than others, and the addition of artificial fertiliser to any soil will favour those that require high nutrient levels. Thus, unfertilised, **unimproved grassland** consists of a very wide range of plant species, adapted to living at low nutrient levels, including many different grasses and wild flowers. The addition of fertiliser creates **improved grassland**, where a few species of fast growing grasses take over the habitat, crowding out all the other species. Similarly, on heaths and moorland, the use of fertiliser will favour grass at the expense of heather and other heaths.

Because plants are able to build up their tissues using only the process of photosynthesis, they are known as **primary producers**. Everything else feeds on plants, either directly or indirectly: herbivores eat the leaves of plants, carnivores eat herbivores or other carnivores, and omnivores will eat plants and animals. The energy originally derived by the plant from sunlight flows along a **food chain**, for example:

> oak leaves → caterpillar → blue tit → sparrow hawk.

However, this is an over-simplification. The blue tit will eat more than one type of caterpillar and also the larvae and adults of other insects. The sparrow hawk will take other prey besides blue tits. In reality there is a network of interlocking food chains, known as a **food web**, as shown for a lake habitat in Figure 3.2.

Food preferences

The feeding preferences of animals have evolved over millions of years and insects are often particularly restricted in their diet. For this reason, species of plant that have been present in the country for a longer time, and are more widely distributed, will often provide food for a greater variety of insect life. Figure 3.3 shows that the willows and oaks, among the commonest tree

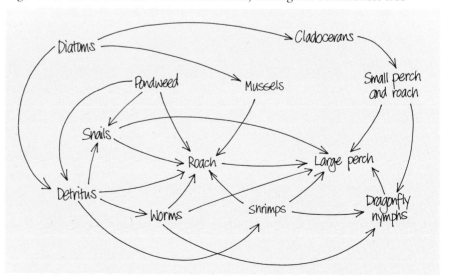

Figure 3.2 A food web for a small lake. Note: all species will contribute to the detritus food web

42

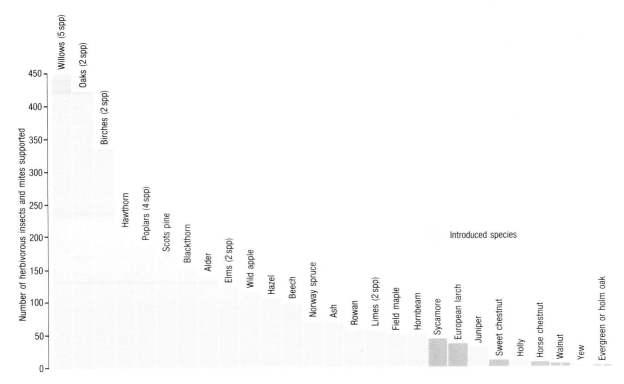

Figure 3.3 The number of herbivorous insects and mites associated with native and introduced trees

species, will support over 400 different insect species, while the sycamore, which is just as abundant but is a much more recent introduction to this country, will only support about 50 species. The evergreen holm oak, which was introduced around 400 years ago, supports less than ten insect species, in contrast to the related native oaks at the top of the scale. Although some native trees such as holly, juniper and yew support few other species, many of these species will be specialists not found elsewhere.

Food conversion

Each time one organism consumes another, some of the energy built up by the original plant tissues is lost, either as heat or through excretion. In general only about 10% of the energy stored at one level in a food chain is converted into the tissues of the organism at the next level and is therefore available as food for the subsequent level in the chain. This inefficiency of food or energy conversion has a major impact on the distribution of species in a habitat. Any predator will necessarily be a lot less common than its prey, and predators at the end of a food chain will be rarest of all. Another way of looking at this is to say that animals such as birds of prey or foxes will require a much larger territory than similar sized herbivores, and their numbers will always be regulated by the numbers of their prey. Among the most vulnerable animals to habitat changes will be large predators with a restricted range of prey species.

The implications for habitat management of nutrition and feeding are as follows (given comparable conditions of soil and climate):

▶   the greater the number of plant species in a habitat, the wider the range of herbivores and carnivores it will support;

43

- plant species that have been native to this country for a very long time, and are widely distributed, will support a wider variety of insect species than more recent introductions, and hence provide more food for predators further along the food chain;
- the larger the number of species overall, the less vulnerable any one species will be to temporary fluctuations in its food supply (except in the case of specialist feeders);
- the bigger the area of a habitat, the greater its likelihood of being able to support predators at the top of the food chain;
- the less human intervention there has been, particularly the addition of artificial fertiliser, the greater will be the total number of species present and also the greater the number of specialists rather than generalists;
- the efficient cycling of nutrients from decaying plants and animals by worms, insects and micro-organisms (the **detritus** food chain) is important for the long-term stability of most habitats.

Population dynamics

Many populations of plants and animals show fluctuations in numbers from time to time and from one generation to another. Some changes are due to natural processes and others are the result of human activities. Some species can recover much more rapidly than others after a drastic population crash.

Box 3.1 illustrates how natural interactions among **predators, parasites** and the available food supply affect the population of the winter moth. Box 3.2 (overleaf) shows how changes in agricultural systems have affected the population of the grey partridge.

The points illustrated in Boxes 3.1 and 3.2 can be applied in many situations. Serious population crashes are usually caused by removal of an organism's food supply or, even more drastically, by removal of its habitat. The populations of predators and parasites are usually *regulated by* the populations of their prey, rather than the other way round.

Reproductive strategy

The rate at which a species can recover after a population crash depends, among other things, on its reproductive strategy. Some species, including many insects, frogs and toads, produce very large numbers of young, only a few of which survive to adulthood. Given favourable conditions, they obviously have a greater potential to replace their numbers quickly after a bad breeding season than species that produce fewer young. Most predators, and many other birds and mammals, produce small numbers of young and so will take longer to recover their numbers if the adult population declines. (Predators are usually long-lived and, provided the adults survive to breed again, their population can recover quite quickly after a bad year.) Where a population decline is caused by a long-term change in the habitat of the species, often caused by human activities, the population may recover if the original habitat is restored, but this is by no means certain.

The population dynamics of a species thus have the following implications for its conservation:

- It is important to distinguish between short-term population fluctuations with natural causes and long-term changes, often due to human activities.
- Long-term changes will be most serious for species with a low reproductive capacity, often predators at the top of a food chain, and for specialist feeders.

Box 3.1 Population dynamics of the winter moth

Figure 3.4 shows the fluctuations that can occur from year to year in the population of the winter moth, a common insect whose caterpillars feed on the young leaves of oak trees. The two most important factors influencing population numbers are the effects of the available food supply and the effects of predators and parasites.

Each female lays about 200 eggs on the twigs of oak trees on a warm night in early winter and the timing of the egg hatch in spring is crucial to the survival of the caterpillars. If the eggs hatch too early, before the oak buds burst, the young caterpillars will starve. If they hatch too late, the young oak leaves will be too tough and will contain too high a level of tannin, which inhibits the growth of the caterpillars. Natural selection has obviously favoured winter moths that hatch just as the oak buds burst, but variations in the weather from year to year make it very difficult to synchronise this exactly. In a good year for the caterpillars, the oak trees may be almost completely defoliated (but life will be a great deal easier for the blue tits).

The caterpillars that do not starve or get eaten by a predator will lower themselves to the ground when fully grown, usually in May (about eleven will reach this stage out of the 200 eggs laid). Here they will

pupate, preparing to emerge as adults the following November or December (on average two adults will survive for every 200 eggs laid).

While they are in the soil, their main hazard arises from beetles and shrews. These eat a relatively greater number of **pupae** when the population is high, but predators cannot usually respond very rapidly to an increase in numbers of their prey by improving their own breeding success. An increase in the numbers of winter moth pupae in one year will tend to lead to an increase in predator numbers in the *following* year.

Thus, the main factor causing sharp fluctuations in winter moth populations from one year to another is the survival of **larvae** immediately after hatching. Predation on pupae while they are hidden in the soil will tend to even out these fluctuations, but it is not very effective.

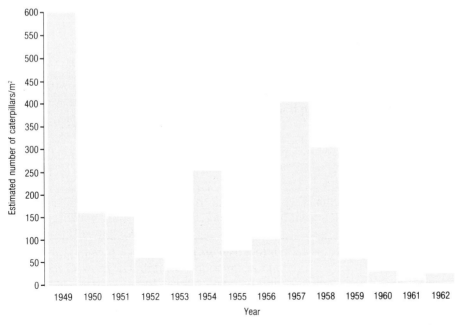

Figure 3.4 Population fluctuations for winter moth caterpillars on oak trees in Wytham Wood

45

Box 3.2 The decline of the grey partridge

As the grey partridge is a valuable game bird, long-term records of the numbers shot each year are available (see Figure 3.5), which allow biologists to estimate the total population numbers. Like the winter moth it seems that there are quite large fluctuations in population from year to year. However, beginning around 1952, there appears to be a general trend towards a serious, long-term decline. Situations like this are a warning of possible problems for the long-term viability of the species as a whole.

The Game Conservancy has done a long-term study of the niche occupied by the grey partridge. They found that, in their first few days, the young chicks need to feed on insects and other small invertebrates in the margins of cereal fields, particularly the larvae of sawflies and leaf and ground beetles. As they grow older they move on to eating weeds growing in the crop.

Since 1952 there has been a steady increase in the extent to which cereal crops are treated with herbicides, so that weed populations are kept low,

as are the insects that live on them. The situation has been made worse by the decline in the practice of undersowing cereal crops with grass and clover. This used to leave the soil undisturbed over the winter, encouraging a large increase in the numbers of sawfly larvae.

The Game Conservancy now recommends that spraying of cereal crops should be strictly limited on the strip of land immediately next to the field margin (**conservation headlands**) and this has resulted in increased chick survival and higher populations wherever it has been put into practice.

Other species that have been badly affected by changes in farming practices are the corncrake and the hare. However, farmers would need to adopt different strategies, with a serious effect on profit margins, to restore these species to their former numbers. The corncrake is now almost entirely restricted to the **crofting** areas of Scotland where traditional practices still exist.)

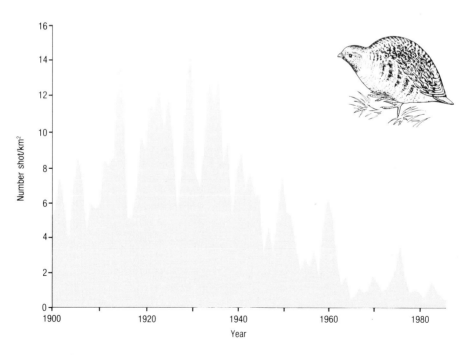

Figure 3.5 The number of grey partridge shot per square kilometre between 1900 and 1986 (Source: Potts, 1986)

46

As with populations, habitats are dynamic and ever changing, and any assessment of a habitat is a snapshot in time of a temporary community. Furthermore, no two patches of vegetation are ever exactly alike in the combinations and proportions of the different species present. However, patches of vegetation growing under similar environments with similar plant species are still recognisable as defined habitats. It is important to make the distinction between short-term fluctuations and the long-term process of succession. Fluctuations are generally reversible and few, if any, new species appear in the habitat as a result. They are caused by the same kinds of process that affect population dynamics, operating at the habitat level. Succession is a long-term, directional change, the inevitable result of ecological processes going on in the habitat, and often triggered by a series of fluctuations that fail to reverse themselves. It can take from a few years to several hundred years.

Figure 3.6 (overleaf) shows the succession of habitats to woodland from bare soil and from water. The succession of habitats on land (Figure 3.6a) was described in Section 3.2 and Figure 3.6b shows the succession of habitats from water to woodland under a similar set of conditions. Both figures represent generalisations: for example, if bare ground is not too lacking in nutrients it may be colonised by a **pioneer** tree species such as birch or oak, rather than herbaceous plants, missing out the other stages in the succession. The number and type of plant species at various stages of the succession will be heavily influenced by soil type and climate, and by the chance factor of which species happen to colonise the area first. These first colonists, the pioneers, will change the habitat, mainly by adding organic matter to the soil when they die, and create conditions suitable for the growth of a different set of species that will take over from them. During the early stages of a succession there will be bare ground between the plants, but in the later stages the vegetation cover becomes more and more closed, preventing any pioneer species from establishing themselves.

Successions that begin on virgin surfaces, such as volcanic ash or land recently exposed from beneath a glacier, are known as primary successions. Those that begin on disturbed ground, such as ploughed agricultural land, are known as secondary successions. The end result of the process of succession is a relatively stable state, known as a **climax community**, usually woodland in this country. Over a very long period the species present in the wood may change, but it will still remain woodland: for example, oak trees become established relatively easily in open disturbed ground, but the seedlings are not very tolerant of shade, and as a result in a mature forest they tend to be replaced by other species when they die.

The process of succession can be stopped at any stage by natural events such as recurring floods or fires, or by agricultural activities, creating what is known as arrested climaxes. One example is the maintenance of grassland or heathland through grazing by animals, preventing its progression to scrub and then woodland.

The implications of succession for habitat conservation are as follows:
▷ a climax community takes an extremely long time to develop and therefore ancient woodland is a very highly valued habitat, particularly now that it has become so rare;

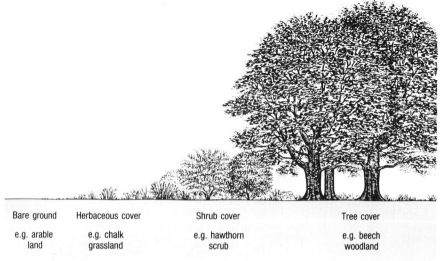

Bare ground
e.g. arable
land

Herbaceous cover
e.g. chalk
grassland

Shrub cover
e.g. hawthorn
scrub

Tree cover
e.g. beech
woodland

(a)

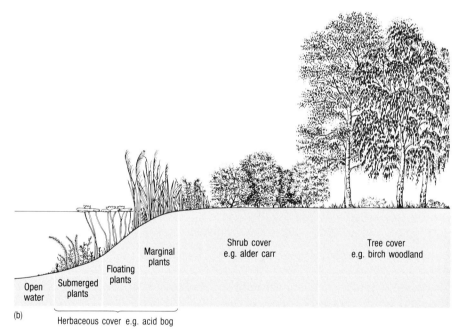

*Figure 3.6
(a) A generalised
terrestrial succession.
(b) A generalised aquatic
succession*

Shrub cover
e.g. alder carr

Tree cover
e.g. birch woodland

Marginal
plants

Floating
plants

Open
water

Submerged
plants

(b)

Herbaceous cover e.g. acid bog

▶ arrested climax habitats often need to be managed or they will gradually develop into climax communities;

▶ climax communities can become arrested, for example by excessive grazing that prevents replacement of dead trees by young saplings.

Distribution and dispersal

As with population dynamics, the dispersal ability of plant and animal species also affects their response to disturbances such as flooding, drought, forest clearance, farming and drainage of the land. Those that can disperse easily will be able to take advantage of new opportunities, to find and exploit niches as they arise, and will therefore have a wider distribution. Those with a poor dispersal ability will be confined to the generally smaller and more fragmented areas of natural and semi-natural habitat that remain in the countryside. A small population that is isolated in this way may become increasingly vulnerable to local extinction.

The dispersal ability of a species is related to some extent to the type of habitat in which it evolved. Small bodies of water have always been relatively short-lived features of the environment being gradually filled in by the process of succession. Species that live in water have therefore had to evolve as good dispersers in order to survive. When a new pond is created and stocked with plant species native to the area, it will quickly become colonised by some animals. However, specialists will take much longer to invade new territory than generalists, so if you already have an old pond, look after it.

Box 3.3 describes two butterflies with a poor dispersal ability that are becoming increasingly rare.

The dispersal ability of a species will have several implications for habitat management:

▶ newly created habitats will be poorer in species than older, well-established habitats;

▶ species with a good dispersal ability are likely to be more common and to colonise newly created habitats early;

▶ where the wildlife habitat in an area consists of many small sites, dispersal can be helped, for some species, by leaving wildlife 'corridors' such as hedgerows or ditch banks linking the sites.

3.4 Major habitat types

As implied by the definition in Section 3.1, habitats are often classified according to the nature of the dominant vegetation, as in broad-leaved woodland, or chalk grassland. However, there is unlikely to be a sharp dividing line between any two habitats: muddy shores grade into sandy ones; hedgerows, **copses** and woodland are a continuum; in the process of succession, scrub gradually becomes woodland, or a pond becomes marshland.

In this section, six major habitat types are described:

▶ woodlands;

▶ wetlands and fresh water (including running and standing waters);

▶ boundary habitats (including hedgerows, ditches, banks, road verges, railway cuttings);

▶ grasslands, heathlands and moorlands;

▶ coastal habitats;

▶ urban habitats.

Each category contains numerous subdivisions depending on the underlying soil type and the vegetation cover; identifying habitats at a very detailed level is a job for the expert. Boundary and urban habitats may seem to fit oddly into their classifications; hedgerows are equivalent to woodland edge, ditches to wetland edge, and urban habitats could be grassland, wetland, woodland

Box 3.3 Dispersal and distribution of butterflies

The black hairstreak butterfly

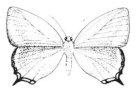

The woodland fritillary butterfly

Some butterflies find it relatively easy to disperse to new areas in search of a mate or their **host plant**. However, the black hairstreak, whose caterpillars feed on blackthorn in ancient woodland in the south Midlands, is one of many exceptions. In the past, ancient woodland used to be much more common and it was managed by coppicing which allowed sufficient light into the understorey of the woodland to enable the blackthorn to survive. Now, not only has the area of woodland declined, but what remains is rarely coppiced, with the result that the blackthorn dies from lack of light. As a result, the black hairstreak has disappeared from many of the woods where it used to be found.

Although blackthorn is a common shrub in the hedgerows of the south Midlands, the black hairstreak has not been able to exploit it. Apparently, it is a poor disperser and instinctively avoids flying across open country. As each area of woodland becomes smaller, there will be a greater chance that natural fluctuations in climate will reduce the local black hairstreak population to a level from which it cannot recover (see Box 3.1). In the long term, only the very few large areas of suitable woodland will be able to keep their black hairstreak butterflies. There is a brighter side to this story — conservationists have successfully introduced the black hairstreak to suitable areas of woodland, in some cases outside its original range.

Woodland fritillary butterflies have recently disappeared from most of south-east England. Their caterpillars feed on wild violets found in the ground flora of recently coppiced woodland. When coppicing was no longer carried out, the violets declined and the fritillary populations became too small to survive, in much the same way as the black hairstreak.

One wood originally contained the silver washed fritillary, the high brown fritillary, the pearl bordered fritillary and the small pearl bordered fritillary, all of which had disappeared by 1970. Since coppicing has been re-instated, the violets have returned, but only the silver washed fritillary has re-colonised the wood. There are very few fritillary populations within 100 km and the surrounding area is heavily treated with pesticides. Human intervention may be able to solve this problem, as with the black hairstreak, by actively re-introducing species to suitable habitats.

or scrub. They are treated separately because they exist largely as a result of human influence. Both are usually relatively small areas of land, bordering on much larger areas of very intensive human activity, with important implications for the way they are managed to encourage wildlife.

Woodlands

The long and varied history of woodland in Britain has produced a variety of types, each dominated by a limited group of species with characteristic associated plant communities. Most **semi-natural** woodland, particularly in the south, consists of deciduous, rather than coniferous, trees. Birch and pine tend to be dominant at higher altitudes and further north, while oak and chestnut are more widely spread, partly because they have been deliberately planted in many places. On more fertile, less disturbed sites, beech, elm, lime and hornbeam are more common.

Much of the forest planted in this century has been non-native conifers, such as Norway spruce, sitka spruce, European larch, Douglas fir and lodgepole pine. Plantation woodland like this is now by far the commonest type in the country (see Figure 1.1). **Primary woodland** occurs where there has been a continuous history of natural and semi-natural tree cover on the site for many centuries, perhaps in some cases back to the original primeval forest. Where woodland is planted on a site that has not grown trees for some time, it is known as **secondary woodland**. Whether natural or planted, secondary woods are rarely as rich in species as primary woodlands, for the reasons described in the previous section.

Many woods have a number of distinct layers in the vegetation. The tallest trees form the upper or **canopy layer**, which limits the light that can penetrate to the vegetation beneath the trees. In some beech woods very little light filters through and the ground is almost bare, but oak and ash cast less shade, allowing plants to grow beneath them.

Below the canopy are tall bushes and small trees, forming the **shrub layer**, sometimes referred to as the **understorey**. Growing beneath the shrub layer are the herbaceous plants that form the **herb layer**. Many of the latter blossom early in the year to make the most of the available light before the canopy layer comes into leaf. The lowest layer of all is the **ground layer** of mosses and other low plants that are green all year.

In a completely natural woodland that has matured to high forest there will be a wide range of different tree and shrub species of all ages and the layer structure will probably be obscured. Managing woodland as coppice with **standards** will favour the development of a layer structure.

Wetlands and fresh water

These habitats can be divided into two broad categories: wetlands where there is little open water, but much soil and vegetation (pond edges, river banks, fens and bogs); and areas where there is much open water, either running as in rivers and streams, or standing as in large ponds, lakes and reservoirs.

Fens and **bogs** are permanently wet habitats where the decomposition of dead plants is or has been greatly slowed down, leading to the accumulation of peat. Bogs usually develop where the ground water is poor in nutrients and acid, while fens develop where the ground water is rich in minerals and often alkaline. Where the peat surface is raised above the water table for at least part of the year, wet scrub and woodland or **carr** communities may develop.

Where rainfall is high, fen peat may become leached and more acidic, leading to colonisation by bog mosses. Raised bogs develop over fen deposits in lake basins and river flood plains, while blanket bogs (so-called because they smother everything in a blanket of peat) develop directly over mineral soils. In some cases, open water is colonised by vegetation from the water's edge, forming floating rafts on which peat can accumulate (basin bogs). Valley bogs occur beside streams on lowland heaths.

Similar types of vegetation to bog communities (dominated by rushes and sedges) are also found on **marshes** on mainly **inorganic** soils, often closely linked to grasslands and heaths (see also 'Coastal habitats').

An important feature of lakes, ponds and reservoirs is their nutrient content. When this is low (**oligotrophic**), few organisms can be supported; if it is too high (**eutrophic**), one or two species, for example some algae, may proliferate and dominate the habitat.

In deep lakes, the water is normally stratified — warm at the top and cold at the bottom. This prevents mixing of the nutrient-rich bottom layer with the top layer, affecting the ability of species to survive in the top layer. Also, the decomposition processes on the lake bottom will use up the available oxygen in the absence of mixing, affecting the wildlife in that layer.

Boundary habitats

Boundary habitats are the areas that divide the countryside and provide corridors linking other isolated habitats. They often mark changes in ownership or in land use and are particularly prone to disturbance. They include hedgerows, green lanes, footpaths, roadside verges, ditches, railway banks and walls.

The tree and shrub species present in a hedgerow will affect the other wildlife that is found there. Generally speaking, as with woodland, older hedges will have more plant species, and hence a greater diversity of animal life, than new hedges. Hedgerows are cut regularly, sometimes leaving occasional trees to grow to their full height and the style and timing of management will also affect their value as habitat. Thick, full hedges will provide more food and shelter than those that are small and closely cropped. If the hedge is cut in late autumn, the berries that would have provided winter feed for birds and small mammals will be lost. If it is cut in spring, nesting birds will be disturbed. Similarly, the style of management will affect the quality of the other boundary habitats.

The boundaries are even more likely than other habitats to be affected by activities on the adjoining land. Roadside verges will be affected by pollution, particularly from salt applied to the road in winter; hedgerows and ditches will be affected by fertiliser and pesticide drift, or damaged by straw-burning; green lanes, footpaths and hedgerows are prone to being used as rubbish dumps in heavily populated areas.

Grasslands, heathlands and moorlands

The grasslands of interest from a wildlife conservation point of view are unsown or 'rough' grasslands, rather than those that have been created by ploughing and re-seeding. As explained in Section 3.3, a soil that has not been fertilised will generally support a greater number of species or range of specialist species.

Chalk grasslands are found in chalk or limestone areas, mainly in the southern and eastern parts of the country, with alkaline soils containing high levels of calcium carbonate, conditions favoured by a highly specialised group of lime-loving plants.

Neutral grassland is found on soils that are neither acid nor alkaline, usually in lowland areas. Such land is usually in agricultural use and there are few neutral grasslands remaining as wildlife habitat. A great variety of management practices are used on unimproved neutral grassland, including cutting, grazing and manuring, and this, combined with variation in soil and climate, has led to a large range of grassland communities, each with their own local characteristics.

Acidic grassland is usually found in upland areas in the north and west of the country. The heavy rainfall in these areas helps to provide the acid conditions, with high concentrations of iron, aluminium and manganese in the soil. Acidic grasslands are the most extensive of our unsown grassland habitats and, although relatively poor in plant and animal species compared with the other types, they are often important nationally and internationally.

In some areas, usually on acid soils where grazing is not too intense, heaths can dominate, producing **heathland** and **moorland** habitats. Moorland is typical of the north and west of the country, on blanket peat, containing bilberry, crowberry and cotton grass as well as the dominant heather. Heathlands occur in lowland Britain on drier, usually sandy soils. Such soils are usually markedly acid, but under some circumstances chalk heaths are found where chalk soils are heavily leached.

Coastal habitats

Coastal habitats include rocky shores, sand and mud flats, saltmarsh, sand dunes and shingle beaches, depending on the type of rock, the rate of erosion and deposition and the effects of the prevailing winds and tides. The plant and animal communities found there have to be able to tolerate a lack of water and nutrients, the effects of salt spray and the instability of the soil.

Cliffs and rocky coasts are difficult habitats to colonise, but they do contain some of our most natural communities. The sea moderates the temperature and a wide range of species can survive in sheltered coves and gullies.

Sand and mudflats occur between the low and high water marks and so are exposed only for part of the day. The vegetation is mainly microscopic algae, with larger algae and eelgrass in some areas. The microscopic algae bind the sediments and eventually allow larger plants to establish themselves. As the sediment builds up above the high water mark, new plant species such as glasswort establish themselves, increasing the vegetation cover to produce saltmarsh. Saltmarsh may eventually develop by a process of succession into a variety of other habitats, depending on the conditions.

The formation of sand dunes from sand blown inshore is helped by plants such as marram grass that can grow on the shifting sand, throwing up new shoots if it becomes covered. Further inland the dunes become more fixed as the vegetation cover closes over, and the nature of the succession from then on will depend on the grazing pressure, the level of nutrients and the climate.

Shingle beaches, like cliffs, are difficult to colonise, being unstable and lacking in nutrients. The vegetation is therefore sparse and open. Sometimes in large shingle beach systems, a scrub of blackthorn, hawthorn and gorse may develop.

Urban habitats

Urban habitats include public parks, recreation grounds and playing fields, cemeteries, gardens, and derelict and abandoned industrial land. Where the land is managed, it often consists of heavily mown grass, a few broad-leaved tree species and beds of ornamental plants, and occasional areas of natural woodland or ponds. Such habitats are usually subject to heavy disturbance through amenity use, industrial activity or the dumping of rubbish. Many habitats are also only temporary features on building sites.

The soils of such sites are often poor in nutrients, but some are rich in minerals such as calcium or iron, depending on the previous use of the site, and can develop rich and varied plant communities. Recently, local authorities have begun to encourage the management of amenity areas and the reclamation of derelict sites for conservation purposes.

3.5 Criteria for assessing the wildlife value of a habitat

The key to the development of criteria for assessing the value of wildlife habitats lies in the ecological processes discussed in Section 3.3. A highly valued habitat is one that will encourage these natural ecological processes to continue unhindered, as shown in Table 3.1. Where the wildlife habitat is part of a land unit that is being managed primarily for some other purpose, there will sometimes be constraints on the extent to which this is possible. However, if this is the case, you should recognise that it is not an ideal situation from the wildlife point of view, and assess it honestly. Opportunities may then arise in future to improve things.

To assess the wildlife value of habitat on land used mainly for non-conservation purposes, the most useful criteria are naturalness, diversity, rarity and area.

Naturalness

'Natural' is a term applied to habitat that appears to be unmodified by human influence. For the reasons outlined earlier in this chapter most British habitats would be more accurately described as 'semi-natural'. This criterion is region-specific: what is natural to one region will not be natural to another. It also implies that old habitats should be more highly valued than newly created ones, because they are probably closer to the natural habitat for the area and have had a longer period of time for a wide range of specialist species to move in and become established. (A list of plant species typical of different habitats is given in Appendix III.) Newly created habitats will be more valuable if they have been designed eventually to conform with what is natural for that situation.

Representative species

Given the earlier description of the process of succession, you could claim that many grasslands, even if very rich in wildlife, are interrupted successions and therefore less 'natural' than woodland in their area. However, naturalness is only one criterion out of several, and it should not necessarily be allowed to over-ride factors such as diversity and rarity. A herb-rich grassland would be well worth preserving for these other reasons and should not be planted with trees, not even native species.

Diversity

Diversity usually refers to the variety of species within a particular habitat, but is sometimes related to the variety of habitats within an area. The simplest way of measuring diversity is to count the number of species found on the site (species richness), but care is necessary in interpreting the information. If you are to be able to compare measurements taken from the same site at different times, or taken from more than one site at the same time, then you must use a standard procedure. (The longer you spend

Table 3.1 Wildlife value of habitats

Outstanding value	*High value*	*Low value*
Woodland		
Old (shown on early maps) woodland of native species (usually deciduous), larger than 1 ha with uneven-age structure, old standing timber and dead wood	Small old woodlands, more recent woodland of native species, even-aged with few old trees or dead wood	Even-age plantations of introduced species with no old trees or dead wood
Hedges		
Dense, long-established hedges more than 2 m in width with occasional mature trees and more than one hedge-forming species	Close-cut but stockproof hedges with width 1−2 m usually only one hedge-forming species	Heavily cut, sparse or leggy hedges less than 1 m in width, no hedgerow trees
Grassland		
Unimproved natural grassland with numerous grass and herb species	Unimproved grassland with few species	Grasslands improved by re-seeding, herbicides and fertiliser
Peat bogs		
Large bogs with thriving community of mosses and other bog plants, little evidence of recent burning, over-grazing or drainage	Smaller areas, or areas where mosses have been damaged by burning, over-grazing or drainage causing some erosion of the peat	Small fragments, or areas where burning, over-grazing and drainage have destroyed mosses and caused large-scale erosion of the peat
Hill or rough grazing		
Large areas of unimproved land not intensively grazed or burned	Smaller areas of unimproved land or areas frequently grazed or burned	Areas with heavy grazing, frequent burning or improvements
Flowing open water		
Burns and rivers with pools, meadows, braided channels, long-established bankside vegetation	Burns and rivers with pools, meadows, braided channels cultivated to bankside	Burns and rivers which have been straightened and canalised without bankside vegetation
Standing open water		
Long-established, unpolluted ponds and ditches which have been cleared out a part at a time over a number of years, with well-established bankside vegetation	Newly established ponds and ditches cleared out in one operation with limited bankside vegetation	Ponds or ditches polluted with chemicals, slurry or silage effluent, regularly cleared out with heavy machinery, no bankside vegetation
Mosses and marshes		
Long-established large areas carrying semi-natural vegetation with water levels suitable for wildlife all year round	Smaller areas or areas where water level is suitable for wildlife only part of year	Fragments where water level is lowered to drain surrounding fields

(Source: Countryside Commission for Scotland, 1986. *Countryside Conservation: A Guide for Farmers*)

counting species or the greater the area you cover, the more you will find.) You should also take account of seasonal changes. Some species will migrate from an area at particular times of year, and others, many plants for example, will become dormant.

The maximum level of species richness will vary with the habitat, so always compare like with like. Chalk grassland, for example, will always have many more species than acidic grassland. Also, remember that the level of diversity will increase with increasing age of the habitat and a habitat that is not diverse at present may have considerable potential in the future, particularly if it is close to similar, older habitats.

Rarity

Four aspects of the **rarity** of a species need to be considered:

1 Is it rare on your land, in your region, or in the country as a whole? (Note that a species may be common on your land but rare regionally or nationally.)

2 Does it occur over a wide area or in a small locality?

3 Is it found in a wide range of habitats or only one?

4 Does it have large populations somewhere in its distribution range or are the numbers low wherever it occurs?

The first two aspects are also relevant to assessing the rarity of habitats.

A relatively common species with a wide distribution and large population, but usually restricted to one or two habitats, is wood anemone, found mainly in deciduous woods and hedgerows. The lady orchid is rare both nationally and regionally, being restricted to some woods on **calcareous** soils, mainly in Kent. Yellow horned poppy is widely but sparsely distributed, being restricted to shingle beach and bank habitats in England (see Figure 3.7).

Provided you can identify different species (see Box 3.4 overleaf), it is possible to discover whether a particular species on your land is nationally or locally rare. In some cases there are well documented local or national records of the distribution and status of species, as shown in Figure 3.7, and a good identification handbook will give an indication of rarity and distribution. If you are in doubt, seek professional advice about identification and rarity of a species or habitat.

Area or size

The larger the area of a habitat, the greater the number of species it will be able to support and the more likely that it will include species at the top of the food chain, as described in Section 3.3. Very small areas, on the other hand, will be in danger of losing some species, as described in Box 3.3.

Interpreting habitat assessment information

It will be obvious from this brief summary of the criteria for assessing the wildlife value of a habitat that they do not lead to absolute measures above which you can say that the habitat is very highly valued. For your purposes it is probably best to use the criteria in a relative way. Look at comparable habitats nearby, or on the rest of your own land, and decide whether yours is better or worse than they are in terms of naturalness, diversity, rarity and area.

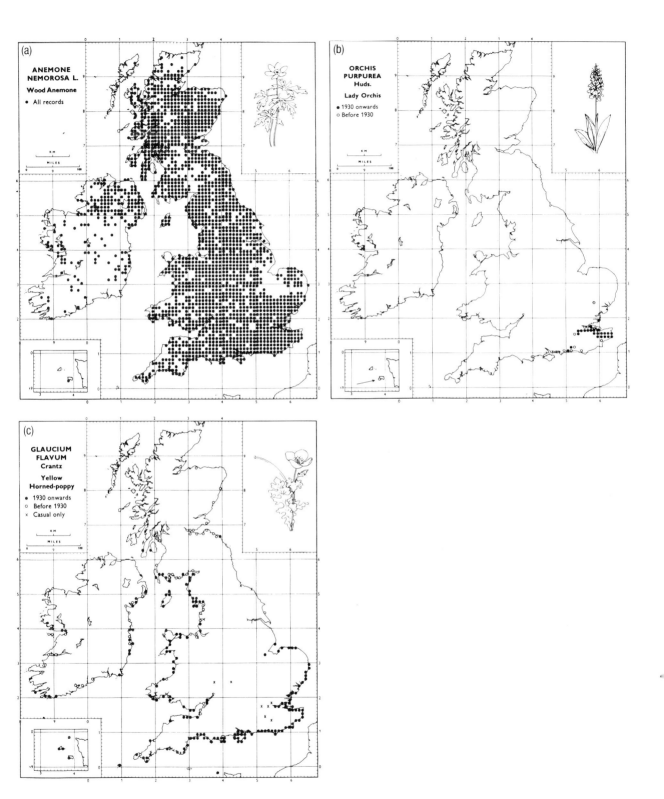

Figure 3.7 *Distribution maps for (a) wood anemone, (b) lady orchid and (c) yellow horned poppy (Source: Perring and Walters, 1962)*

Box 3.4 Identifying wildlife species

Plate 11 shows some of the birds found by a lake shore and Plate 12 shows wild plants found in a typical meadow. If you intend to take an interest in wildlife conservation, you will find it more rewarding if you learn to identify plants and animals accurately. There are many handbooks and field guides available, some of which are listed in Appendix I. Some groups will be more difficult than others to learn to identify: for example, there are at least 20 000 insect species in Britain.

When species are described in books they are given two names, the common name and the scientific name. For example, the two spot ladybird could also be referred to as *Adalia bipunctata*. The first part of the scientific name, which always begins with a capital letter, is the generic, or 'family' name. The second part of the scientific name, which always begins with a small letter, is the specific name and therefore describes the species. The scientific name is more accurate because it is universally recognised, whereas the

common name will vary from place to place. Common names have been used in this book but Appendix IV lists the scientific names of all the species mentioned.

When identifying species, do not collect them from the wild, because many plants and animals are protected. Either identify them in the field without disturbing them, take a photograph, or ask an expert to visit the site to help.

3.6 Wildlife and habitat assessment methods

As with landscape assessment, it is important to assess wildlife and habitats in a systematic way to provide yourself with a long-term record that you can update regularly and to help you to communicate information about your site to other people. Section 3.8 shows how the habitat assessment was done for the case study farm.

Drawing a habitat and wildlife assessment map

Visit your site with a blank map, as for landscape assessment, mark on it the wildlife habitat areas and make notes describing each area. Take photographs, in colour if possible, of any interesting features. If these are permanent, immobile features, mark on the map the spot where you took the photograph so that you can take a series of photographs at intervals to show seasonal or year-by-year changes.

Assessing individual habitats

Draw a sketch map of each major area of habitat on your site and mark any significant wildlife features. If you can visit the site regularly over a period, you could mark each season's features on the map with a different coloured pen.

Table 3.2 provides a checklist and space for a sketch map to record the value of each habitat on your land. This checklist will not necessarily cover every situation and you may need to add to it to suit your own circumstances.

Table 3.2 Habitat assessment profile

Land holding   Habitat type

A *Physical features*

1 Land use: Past uses   Present uses

2 Physical conditions:

Terrain	flat, sloping, undulating
Age	<5 years, 5–10 years, 10–50 years, >50 years
Area	<0.5 ha, 0.5–1 ha, 1–5 ha, >5 ha
Soil wetness	well drained, occasionally waterlogged, always waterlogged
Soil texture	silty, sandy, clayey
Soil chemistry	acidic, neutral, alkaline

B *Wildlife features*

1 Vegetation cover
     (∗ = present; ∗∗ = moderately common; ∗∗∗ = frequent)

Mosses	Grasses	Shrubs
Ferns	Herbs	Trees

2 Animals
     (∗ = present; ∗∗ = moderately common; ∗∗∗ = frequent)

Insects	Amphibians	Birds
Molluscs	Reptiles	Mammals

3 Habitat assessment criteria
     (∗ = low value; ∗∗ = moderate value; ∗∗∗ = high value)

Diversity	Naturalness
Rarity	Area

C *Land use features*
     (∗ = low value; ∗∗ = moderate value; ∗∗∗ = high value)

Wildlife	Education	Forestry
Recreation	Agriculture	Industry

D *Summary assessment*

I thought you said there were badgers in this area!

If you fill in a sheet like this for each habitat on your site, supplemented where possible with colour photographs and a list of species found at the time, you will have a long-term record to remind you, not only of the value you placed on the habitat, but also why. The species list can also be updated from time to time, noting any new species that have appeared, or any that seem to have disappeared. This list can be compared with the list of representative species shown in Appendix III.

Your assessment will be more accurate if you standardise the habitat survey by adopting a standard walk or **transect**. You should walk a regular path across the habitat and count all species or assess particular aspects within a standard distance of your route, say from one metre to ten metres on either side. Ideally your path should follow a straight line but this may not be possible; the important point is to avoid visiting *only* the richer or more appealing parts of the habitat.

If time is short, you could write a brief note, giving a description of the habitat and a value rating, as in the examples in Table 3.1.

3.7 Making your own habitat and wildlife assessment

When making a landscape and wildlife assessment, particularly on land you know well, avoid taking for granted its more familiar aspects. Think about how the wildlife will interact with the wider countryside round about. Try to think about the future of the land, not just what wildlife will be present next winter or spring, but what are the processes of ecological succession taking place within it. For example: is that damp patch you drained getting wet again already; are the young trees in your woodland a different species from the old ones; are domestic or wild animals preventing any regeneration in

60

your woods; are grass and bracken increasing at the expense of heather on your moorland; is the pond silting up or becoming choked by vegetation?

In assessing wildlife and habitats note any interesting species of plant or animal that you find, or that you remember seeing at another time of year (see Appendix III). Note also any areas that have a particularly wide variety of species, or large numbers of the same species, even if they are relatively common. Are there a lot of frogs in spring, or migrant birds in winter? Is that apparently lifeless stretch of grass covered in flowers in summer? Do you see bats flying at dusk? Do you remember seeing species in the past that have disappeared? If you find species that you cannot identify, use one of the reference books recommended in Appendix I.

You should now carry out a habitat assessment for your own site, based on what you have learned in this chapter.

You will need the same equipment as for landscape assessment.

As for landscape assessment, check whether the land management is subject to any restraints for wildlife reasons, for example designation as a **Site of Special Scientific Interest (SSSI)** (in this case the NCC will already have a complete description of its habitat value).

Walk round the site and mark on a blank map the areas of wildlife habitat value, adding a brief description of each if necessary.

Summarise the wildlife value of each habitat area, either using a map and checklists or summary notes.

3.8 Case study:
Wildlife and habitat assessment

This farm is much richer than most in wildlife habitat interest and it was chosen to give you a wide variety of examples so do not be surprised if your area is much less complex than this.

The three landscape areas described in Section 2.5 and Figure 2.6 contain a wide range of habitats:

▶ the area of heather moorland with a relatively low stocking rate and a fairly diverse plant community;

▶ the largely arable section on the lower slopes of the hill, with most of the wildlife interest in the field boundaries;

▶ the area of trees and parkland, relatively rich in wildlife habitats, in particular woodland and wetland.

The areas of wildlife habitat interest on the farm are shown on Figure 3.8 (p 64). Tables 3.3 and 3.4 (overleaf) show how the checklist in Table 3.2 was completed for two of the habitats, and summary descriptions of all the major habitats are given below.

Table 3.3 Habitat assessment profile   Habitat number 25

Land holding   *Case study farm*   Habitat type   *Moorland*   Date 14/7/87

A *Physical features*

1 Land use: Past uses   *Rough grazing*   Present uses   *Rough grazing*

2 Physical conditions:

Heather, bell heather, cross-leaved heath, blaeberry

Scattered larch

Scattered broad-leaved trees and Scots pine

Buzzard's nest

Rabbit warren

Ferns, heaths and heather

Rushes and marsh violet

Terrain	flat, (sloping,) undulating
Age	<5 years, 5–10 years, 10–50 years, (>50 years)
Area	<0.5 ha, 0.5–1 ha, 1–5 ha, (>5 ha)
Soil wetness	well drained, (occasionally waterlogged,) always waterlogged
Soil texture	silty, (sandy,) clayey
Soil chemistry	(acidic,) neutral, alkaline

B *Wildlife features*

1 Vegetation cover

(✳ = present; ✳✳ = moderately common; ✳✳✳ = frequent)

Mosses   ✳ ✳   Grasses ✳ ✳   Shrubs

Ferns   ✳ ✳   Herbs   ✳ ✳ ✳   Trees   ✳

2 Animals

(✳ = present; ✳✳ = moderately common; ✳✳✳ = frequent)

Insects   ✳ ✳   Amphibians   Birds   ✳ ✳ ✳

Molluscs   Reptiles   Mammals ✳ ✳

3 Habitat assessment criteria

(✳ = low value; ✳✳ = moderate value; ✳✳✳ = high value)

Diversity ✳ ✳ ✳   Naturalness ✳ ✳ ✳

Rarity   ✳ *(unusual association of ferns with heather)*   Area   ✳ ✳

C *Land use features*

(✳ = low value; ✳✳ = moderate value; ✳✳✳ = high value)

Wildlife ✳ ✳   Education   Forestry

Recreation ✳   Agriculture ✳   Industry

D *Summary assessment*   (see Section 3.8, number 25)

Table 3.4 Habitat assessment profile

Land holding   *Case study farm*   Habitat type   Wetland-ponds

Habitat number   I

Date   14/7/87

A *Physical features*

1 Land use: Past uses   Curling pond   Present uses   Duck/rearing/shooting

2 Physical conditions:

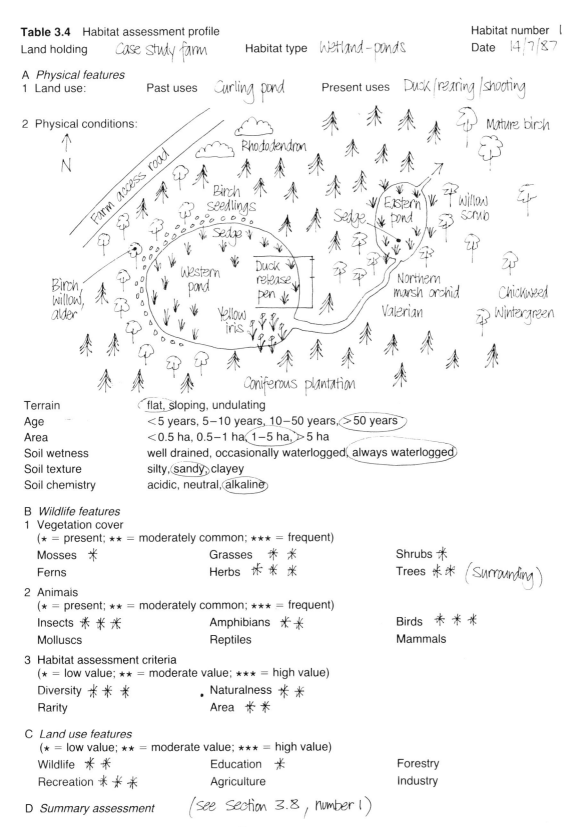

Terrain	flat, sloping, undulating
Age	<5 years, 5–10 years, 10–50 years, >50 years
Area	<0.5 ha, 0.5–1 ha, 1–5 ha, >5 ha
Soil wetness	well drained, occasionally waterlogged, always waterlogged
Soil texture	silty, sandy, clayey
Soil chemistry	acidic, neutral, alkaline

B *Wildlife features*

1 Vegetation cover
   (∗ = present; ∗∗ = moderately common; ∗∗∗ = frequent)

Mosses ∗   Grasses ∗ ∗   Shrubs ∗

Ferns   Herbs ∗ ∗ ∗   Trees ∗ ∗ (Surrounding)

2 Animals
   (∗ = present; ∗∗ = moderately common; ∗∗∗ = frequent)

Insects ∗ ∗ ∗   Amphibians ∗ ∗   Birds ∗ ∗ ∗

Molluscs   Reptiles   Mammals

3 Habitat assessment criteria
   (∗ = low value; ∗∗ = moderate value; ∗∗∗ = high value)

Diversity ∗ ∗ ∗   . Naturalness ∗ ∗

Rarity   Area ∗ ∗

C *Land use features*
   (∗ = low value; ∗∗ = moderate value; ∗∗∗ = high value)

Wildlife ∗ ∗   Education ∗   Forestry

Recreation ∗ ∗ ∗   Agriculture   Industry

D *Summary assessment*   (see Section 3.8, number I)

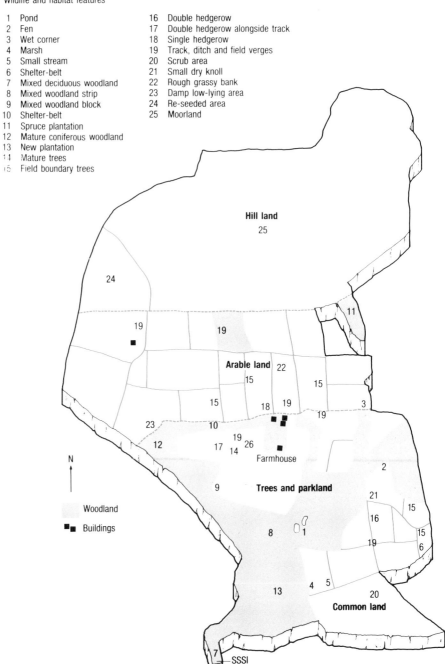

Wildlife and habitat features

1	Pond	16	Double hedgerow
2	Fen	17	Double hedgerow alongside track
3	Wet corner	18	Single hedgerow
4	Marsh	19	Track, ditch and field verges
5	Small stream	20	Scrub area
6	Shelter-belt	21	Small dry knoll
7	Mixed deciduous woodland	22	Rough grassy bank
8	Mixed woodland strip	23	Damp low-lying area
9	Mixed woodland block	24	Re-seeded area
10	Shelter-belt	25	Moorland
11	Spruce plantation		
12	Mature coniferous woodland		
13	New plantation		
14	Mature trees		
15	Field boundary trees		

Figure 3.8 Case study farm: location of wildlife habitat features

64

The assessment was carried out on one day in July, with the help of the farmer who has a very detailed knowledge of his land. There was not time to make a quantitative estimate of the species found. While this is not ideal, it is realistic — time will put a limit on the amount of detail in many wildlife and habitat assessments.

Wetlands and watercourses

1 *Two ponds*, 2 hectares and 1 hectare in area. The western pond is very attractive with large areas of open water and islands of vegetation. It is spring-fed, quiet and sheltered, surrounded by coniferous plantations with some birch, willow and alder at the edge. There are large numbers of birch seedlings, about two inches high, on the north and east sides. The main plant species in the pond are bottle sedge, iris and water horsetail, with self-heal, bugle and figwort in the narrow fringe at the edge. Birds seen included tufted duck, mallard, coot, moorhen and Canada goose, and the pond is also valuable for insects and amphibians. The shoot on this pond is let to a syndicate, which recently erected a small duck release pen and stocked it with over 200 ducklings, without first consulting the farmer. The large number of ducks, concentrated in one small section of the pond, could create excessively high levels of nutrients in the water. They are already damaging the vegetation on the bank by trampling it.

The eastern pond is largely invaded by willow scrub, with bottle sedge on the few remaining open areas. It is surrounded by woodland, mainly conifers with birch on the south and west and much birch regeneration beneath the trees. The ground vegetation includes valerian and northern marsh orchid in the more open marshy areas and chickweed wintergreen in drier areas beneath the trees. The thick cover of this pond is an attractive breeding ground for small birds.

Being surrounded by trees, neither pond is visible from a distance and both are relatively undisturbed for most of the time. The smaller pond has little remaining open water and, in the process of succession, it is gradually converting to woodland. This will continue unless the pond is cleared from time to time.

2 *Fen*, 0.4 hectares. This important small site lies at the bottom of a poorly drained, permanent pasture beside a coniferous plantation. There is a wide variety of plants including ragged robin, lesser spearwort, northern marsh orchid, marsh bedstraw, marsh marigold, meadowsweet, marsh violet, devil's bit scabious, marsh thistle, carnation sedge and the nationally rare lesser tussock sedge. There are several mature birch trees and a few willows and also some standing dead tree trunks that are valuable habitats, particularly for insects.

3 *Wet corner in arable field*, 0.2 hectares. Several unsuccessful attempts have been made to drain this area, and in recent years it has not been cultivated. There is not much plant interest at the moment but the area will be of some value to amphibians and invertebrates because of the lack of disturbance.

4 *Marsh*, 2 hectares. A small area of wet ground to the west of the right of way, fairly heavily grazed by sheep. Plants include ragged robin, valerian, violet, marsh bedstraw, lady's smock, sneezewort, meadowsweet, stitchwort, marsh cinquefoil and soft rush. Several white (unidentified) and small tortoiseshell butterflies and a frog were seen.

5 *Small stream*, 300 metres. As this is fenced off from stock, vegetation has flourished, including marsh and creeping thistle, birdsfoot trefoil, ladies and marsh bedstraw, angelica, wild raspberry, nettle, horsetail, brooklime, tormentil, sneezewort, broad-leaved dock, and common sorrel. There is a rapid flow of clear water and several white (unidentified) and small tortoiseshell butterflies and a hunting stoat were seen. In the absence of any management of the vegetation this area will eventually be invaded by bushes and trees.

Woodlands

Most of the woodland consists of non-native coniferous species, grown as a commercial crop and approaching maturity. Some areas, particularly in the parkland, have a variety of species, structure and wildlife.

6 *Shelter-belt*, 0.2 hectares. A stand of about 30 mature ash, sycamore, beech, larch and pine. These are significant in the landscape but of limited value for wildlife as there is no understorey.

7 *Mixed deciduous woodland*. The north end of this woodland is an SSSI, of which just under 1 hectare extends into the farm. It is an ancient woodland with a great diversity in structure and species. Originally, oak, ash and elm were dominant, but it is now being invaded by beech and sycamore, which are less desirable in wildlife conservation terms. Wild Solomon's seal is also found there.

8 *Mixed woodland strip*, approximately 15 hectares. This contains birch, rowan, elder, willow and some fine mature fir trees, including two monkey puzzles. Red-berried elder is found here, introduced from central Europe, rather than the native black-berried elder. The red species is common in the woods on estates in the area. The wood is fairly open so there is a wide variety of ground cover plants: in the damp areas meadowsweet, valerian, angelica, creeping thistle, and yellow flags; on the dry grassy **knolls** self heal and eyebright. There is some birch regeneration, patches of wild raspberry and ferns (unidentified). Rhododendron has become the dominant understorey species in much of this area and is disliked by the farmer.

9 *Mixed woodland block*, 2.5 hectares. This includes some fine old beech, Norway spruce and Scots pine trees, with areas of shrub growth, particularly birch and red-berried elder, increasing the conservation value.

10 *Shelter-belt* (1.5 hectares) including wild cherry, birch, sycamore, elder, willow, wych elm, oak, ash and beech, forming an attractive wood with a varied age structure. Rosebay willowherb is common in the open areas.

11 *Spruce plantation*, 3.5 hectares, nearing maturity at the north end, with a fringe of broad-leaved trees on the west side (birch, willow, rowan, beech and elder) to add diversity and improve the wildlife value. A separate compartment at the south end, dominated by sitka spruce, is under 10 years old with heavy natural invasion of bracken, broom, birch, elder and gorse.

12 *Mature coniferous woodland*, 7.5 hectares. A large block of Scots pine with spruce along the north side. The more open habit has encouraged the development of a limited understorey of elder, ferns, grass and chickweed wintergreen. Around the edge of this wood are several fine old beech, oak and lime trees.

13 *New plantation*, 2 hectares, three years old. Largely conifers with a patch of broad-leaved trees in tree shelters. There are many foxgloves here, with much re-growth from old sycamore and elder stumps.

Parkland and boundary habitats

14 *Mature trees*, isolated and in small groups, are scattered about many of the permanent pasture fields, mostly oak, beech, sycamore, ash, with occasional lime, rowan, alder, birch, Scots pine and larch. These trees provide shelter and food for birds. Due to heavy grazing, there is no understorey or regeneration, and the bark of some trees, particularly beech and ash, has been damaged by stock. (A pony, overwintered in one of the fields, passed this skill on to the farm rams.)

15 *Field boundary trees.* On the arable land, many field boundaries have mature hardwoods growing along their length, some over-mature and beginning to die back, particularly the elm, which is suffering from Dutch elm disease. Other species include beech, sycamore and ash and, as they are largely unprotected from stock, the bark has been damaged in some cases. These trees are of limited value for wildlife, but contribute greatly to the variety of the arable landscape.

16 *Double hedgerow* alongside a track, 440 metres, fenced from stock, including mainly hawthorn with some elm, elder, rowan, beech and dog-rose. It has not been trimmed for several years and is very thick in places. However, some sections are rather thin and there are gaps, particularly at the south end. This is now a very attractive and diverse habitat, but if not managed by regular cutting it will begin to lose wildlife value.

17 *Double hedgerow*, 250 metres, extremely tall and thick with good diversity of species, mainly hawthorn and beech, plus some ash, elder, rowan, elm, birch and willow. It has not been trimmed for several years and now gives excellent shelter and valuable habitat for breeding and wintering birds, among other wildlife, but again should not be left unmanaged for much longer. There are a few gaps.

18 *Single hedgerow*, 270 metres, mainly beech (suffering from fungal attack) with some sycamore, elder, and elm. It has not been trimmed for several years and is fairly thin in places at the base, becoming thicker at the top.

19 *Track, ditch and field verges.* On this farm, the narrow strips of grassland bordering tracks, ditches and fields are often ungrazed and also not contaminated with fertiliser or pesticides, thus increasing their potential value. The verge alongside the double hedgerow (17) includes meadow vetchling, bush and tufted vetch, harebell, hogweed, wild raspberry, cocksfoot, cow parsley, rosebay willowherb, ribwort plantain, knapweed, germander speedwell, ladies' mantle, birdsfoot trefoil, and also a great variety of insects including hover-flies and bumble-bees. On another field verge, marked by a derelict drystone wall, there was a family of wheatears, a stoat and many insects on the flowers. Another verge bordering a ditch is about three metres wide with occasional young ash, rowan, elder, and sycamore, a variety of wild flowers and some small tortoiseshell butterflies.

Scrub

20 *Scrub area* claimed as 'common land' by the local community, about 20 hectares of which belong to the farm. It is mainly covered with whin, which protects a large rabbit population, plus an occasional tree (larch, willow, rowan). The area provides shelter and breeding sites for small birds. The heavy grazing by sheep belonging to a neighbouring farmer will prevent the natural succession of this area to woodland. The following plants were found: foxglove, tormentil, eyebright, thyme, harebell, self-heal, yarrow, white clover, milkwort, heath bedstraw, violet and blaeberry (bilberry).

Pasture

The farm has only limited areas of meadow that have not had any previous application of lime or fertiliser and have a good diversity of plant species, compared with improved pasture (21 and 22).

21 *Small dry knoll*, 0.4 hectares, with tormentil, yarrow, harebell, eyebright, self-heal, lesser stitchwort. Meadow brown butterflies have been seen at this site.

22 *Rough grassy bank* between fields with reasonable diversity of plant species — yarrow, hop trefoil, germander speedwell, tufted vetch, cow parsley, dandelion, lesser stitchwort, meadow vetchling, pignut, cocksfoot.

23 *A damp, low-lying area* of about 2 hectares, taken out of cultivation recently due to poor drainage. The vegetation cover includes a tall growth of dock, nettle, timothy, rye-grass, white clover, creeping thistle, chickweed, and redshank in the wetter areas. The plant community is not of any particular conservation interest, but the area will be valuable to invertebrates and small mammals because of the lack of disturbance.

Upland

24 *Re-seeded area*, 10 hectares, treated 1972–1973, now forming a productive grass **sward** with nitrogen applied each spring. It is used by lapwings and curlews and probably has a diverse invertebrate population.

25 *Moorland*, 105 hectares. Most of the hill land is lightly grazed moorland with heather predominating. The plant life is relatively diverse due to the low stocking density of sheep and cattle and the fact that the heather has not been burned for several years. It includes male fern, hard fern, gorse, blaeberry, tormentil, petty whin, cowberry, bell heather, birdsfoot trefoil, cross-leaved heath and chickweed wintergreen. In some of the wetter areas soft rush, sharp flowered rush and marsh violet grow. This area is of considerable wildlife interest both for the flora and for the value of the habitat to birds and insects. Birds seen included buzzard (a nesting pair in a group of trees), lapwing, curlew, mistle thrush. On the south-west side of the hill there is a large rabbit warren that is hastening the erosion of the thin soil. The farmer has, on several occasions, tried to control the rabbit population, without success. Hen harriers and short-eared owls are sometimes seen in this area, and also young peregrines in August. The heather is now quite old and thick, which could make future management difficult.

Among the heather there are scattered coniferous and broad-leaved trees, remnants of a forest that covered much of the area in the last century. Areas of attractive mature pine and some young larch will be of wildlife value for birds but as the moorland is grazed there will be no further regeneration. At the eastern end of the hill land, there is a wider variety of species, including alder, birch, beech, willow, sycamore, oak, larch, pine and spruce. These trees will provide shelter and food for birds and insects.

Buildings

26 *The ice house*, noted in the landscape assessment section, was inspected for bats but none was found, perhaps because light was getting in through a hole in the roof.

Chapter 4
INTEGRATED ASSESSMENT

Summary

This chapter links landscape and wildlife aspects of site assessment and integrates both with the business assessment of the land, from the point of view of its primary (usually commercial) purpose. Landscape and wildlife can interact with one another in both beneficial and conflicting ways. Where the business use of the land is extensive, conservation can be a major interest over the whole land area, but where it is intensive conservation interest will be strongest in non-working areas. Business assessment requires consideration of management activities on the land, availability of money from outside sources such as grants or from the land manager's budget, and availability of labour and machinery. Integrated assessment considers the relative intensity of land use and profitability of each area, the attitudes and preferences of the manager and the influences of other people. The link with Stage 2 of the management planning cycle is made by considering the degree of control that the manager has over various factors that influence the land use.

4.1 Integrated assessment and land use management planning

Integrated assessment is the first stage of management planning, as shown in Figure 1.2. The landscape and habitat assessments are important components of this stage, and in practice they would not usually be kept separate. They have been treated separately so far to make it easier to understand the different approaches and methods used in each case.

In this chapter you will be considering how landscape and habitat aspects of your land area interact with one another and with business aspects such as farming, forestry, recreation, management of a water catchment or provision of a public service.

Attitudes and values

The attitudes and values of the land manager are an important part of integrated assessment, as are the attitudes and influence of other people who may be affected by the management of a site. If the business is a family one, as on many farms, then other members of the family will also have opinions, particularly for a topic such as conservation. Managers are subject to pressures and restrictions from the owners of a business and tenants from their landlords. An increasingly well-informed public regards the countryside as an important part of their environment and would like to have a say in how it is managed. In addition, a wide range of official and semi-official organisations has an influence on land management.

The integrated assessment stage thus has to take account of several aspects:
- ▶ the habitat/landscape;
- ▶ the business;
- ▶ the attitudes and values of the land manager;
- ▶ the views of other people with an influence on the land manager.

The following sections explain in more detail how landscape, wildlife and business assessments will interact, how to carry out a business assessment for conservation purposes and how to carry out an integrated assessment.

4.2 Linking landscape and wildlife assessment

Beneficial interactions

Landscape and wildlife can interact in a variety of ways and there are many occasions when what is good for one will also be good for the other. For example, on many coniferous forestry plantations, creating irregular boundaries for landscape reasons will increase the length of the boundaries, which are often the most diverse areas of wildlife habitat. At the same time, diversity of the woodland edge is being increased by planting native species or allowing natural regeneration to take place. Diversity is being further increased by planting a wider range of species in the forest itself. All will have beneficial effects for both wildlife and the landscape.

Working with nature

The landform, soil and climate will have an impact on the structures found in the landscape. The use of local stone, brick and roofing materials will be responsible for giving buildings their local character. Rich fertile soils are more likely to be cultivated for agriculture; less fertile areas will have more natural vegetation cover and wildlife habitats. If you do not understand ecological processes (nutrition and feeding, population dynamics, competition and succession, and distribution and dispersal), you will not be able to appreciate why the vegetation cover of the landscape has developed as it has, or to predict how it might change in future.

There is thus a very intimate relationship between the quality of the landscape and the quality of the habitats found there. Often, the plants most likely to look right in a particular situation are those that will grow there naturally, and these will provide an abundant source of food for the animals further along the food chain. Working with nature is usually cheaper and easier in the long run than working against it and the job of the manager is to make sure that the nature of the site, the plants, animals and human influences blend harmoniously together.

In some respects, our landscape preferences are changing to become more in tune with the need to create better wildlife habitats. For example, in assessing the value of urban or other derelict land, people are now much more likely to look at the range of species or habitats represented there, or to see it in archaeological terms rather than as a landscape to be despised because of its industrial past.

Potential conflicts between landscape and habitat value

There are a few cases where features that might be highly valued as landscape are not ideal from a habitat point of view and vice versa. For example, the idealised landscape picture of a pond often includes at least one tree, providing a vertical feature contrasting with the horizontal lines of the water. Some tall vegetation round a pond is good from a wildlife point of view, to provide shade and cover for frogs, toads and newts and nesting sites for

birds, but too much is bad. The pond needs light to allow aquatic plant life to flourish, and if it becomes choked with decaying leaves, the oxygen which supports much of the wildlife in the water will be used up. When considering the landscape value of trees beside ponds, you therefore need to think about their wildlife implications: trees on the north and east sides will cut out less light (because the sun is always angled towards the south) and deposit fewer leaves (because the prevailing winds are from the south-west). The same will be true of small streams that can become totally enclosed by trees, restricting the diversity of the wildlife that is found there.

The appreciation of trees for landscape reasons can sometimes be different from their wildlife value. For example, you may like the look of sycamores and they are often a very useful broad-leaved tree for exposed sites. They will also support very large numbers of aphids, providing food for birds and other insects. However, they also have some disadvantages. They will not support such a wide diversity of species as, for example, oak, birch or willow (see Figure 3.3). They can also create problems in mixed woodland because their seedlings are very vigorous and shade tolerant and, once established, sycamore will eventually dominate the area.

The kinds of tree present in a woodland will also affect the nature of the understorey and therefore its value for wildlife and the diversity of the landscape. Among the conifers, larch loses its needles in winter allowing light to penetrate to the ground, encouraging grass and other plants to grow to a greater extent than under evergreen conifers. Among broad-leaved trees, beech has an extensive root system close to the surface which dries out the soil and very little will grow underneath it, while oak allows a much more diverse understorey to develop.

These are not arguments for always planting oak trees, but you do need to be aware of such differences in the landscape and wildlife value of features on the land in order to assess and manage them properly.

Tidiness

The urge to 'tidy up' the landscape, mentioned in Chapter 2, often means that people want to remove dead and fallen trees. However, these are frequently very valuable for wildlife. The decaying timber provides food for a host of insects, some of which have become quite rare. These insects will in turn feed birds such as woodpeckers and the timber will provide them with nesting sites. Likewise, on farmed land the desire for a tidy landscape can mean removing rough areas of grassland or scrub, applying weed-killer to hedge bottoms, or otherwise simplifying the habitats unnecessarily. Such an attitude will make it difficult to practice good wildlife conservation and can also be a waste of time and money.

If you feel very strongly about tidiness, try to compromise and look at the land from the point of view of others. For example, local authorities gave up the practice of spraying roadside verges with herbicides in the 1970s, largely as a result of public pressure, mowing regularly instead. This encouraged a diverse roadside vegetation that supported a wide range of other animals further along the food chain. Given that the road network includes over 200 000 hectares of central reserves and roadside verges, this could have a very large impact on wildlife and landscapes in places that are seen by many people. However, recent economy measures have reduced the extent of mowing on verges and you can see the process of ecological succession beginning to take place, with the invasion of the grassland by shrubs.

4.3 Interaction between conservation and business interests

Hedgerow removal, simplification of waterways or filling drains and small streams are all examples of straightforward conflict between conservation and business interests. The extent to which habitats have already been removed or altered will have a major impact on the present conservation value of the land. However, one of the purposes of this book is to show how you can maintain or improve the land's conservation value without drastically affecting the business interests. (Here 'business interests' is taken to mean the primary non-conservation related land use, such as farming, forestry, recreation, roadside and waterway management.)

Intensive and extensive land uses

The way you assess the conservation value of land and the range of management options open to you as a result of your assessment will depend to some extent on whether the business management of the land is **intensive** or **extensive**.

On intensively farmed land, the wildlife habitat value of, for example, a field of oilseed rape will never be very great, although some people will appreciate its landscape value. We cannot expect the land manager to allow his or her business interests to suffer seriously for the sake of habitat or landscape conservation. The areas of conservation interest will mainly be those that are not directly involved in the business use of the land, such as field verges, hedgerows and small woods. In such places land managers can be expected to think first of the landscape and habitat value, to avoid any adverse impacts from the business use of the land and, provided the business can afford it, to invest in their improvement.

Box 3.2 showed how intensive, modern farming methods have affected populations of the partridge and what can be done to improve its survival rate in field margins at no great cost to the farmer. Box 4.1 (overleaf) shows how tree planting schemes in upland areas can be designed to minimise damage to lakes or lochs and rivers. On intensively managed land, there are many ways of ensuring that the business and conservation aspects can co-exist, without damaging one another and with only a small cost, or sometimes even a benefit, to the land manager.

Farming and forestry

The place of conservation is different on extensively worked land such as hill farms or in Less Favoured Areas. Here, the important wildlife habitats are likely to be on the same land that provides the manager with a living, for example the grass fields or moorland where the animals graze. Figure 4.2 (p 75) shows the unusually diverse range of habitats found on two hill farms in Northumberland — Ottercops and Raechester. An integrated assessment should identify which areas of the worked land are most valuable and most in need of protection or improvement, as well as looking at areas that are not managed primarily for business purposes. It would not be fair to expect someone who is struggling to survive on difficult land to give up some of their income for the sake of wildlife or the landscape, but there are often options for managing the land that will benefit wildlife and the landscape without affecting incomes. Where some costs are involved, there is an increasing number of financial incentives to encourage conservation on such land.

Box 4.1 Coniferous plantations and upland water pollution

Often when coniferous trees are planted in upland areas, it is necessary first to plough and drain the land to make it easier for trees to establish themselves. In the past ploughing was often brought as close to the edge of streams as possible with the drains feeding directly into the stream. Where trees have been planted close to the edges of small streams, the canopy often completely closes over so that heavy falls of needles and lack of light prevent other streamside vegetation and most wildlife from becoming established. The drainage pattern causes a much more variable flow of water than before, resulting in more severe scouring of the stream bed and also much heavier deposits of silt. This covers the ground of fish spawning beds and clogs fish gills and filter-feeding invertebrates so that the whole food chain becomes impoverished.

Another problem is caused by the increased interception of acid rain by the forest compared with the surrounding countryside. Where the drains are more efficient, this reaches the streams and lakes or lochs more quickly and the acidity of the water can become too high to support most aquatic life. This tends to happen where the soil does not contain minerals that can neutralise the acid in the water, as is the case in many areas of Wales and Scotland.

The suggested solution to this problem is to keep the ploughed and planted area well clear of the water's edge, as shown in Figure 4.1. The 'reserve strips' should be at least ten times the width of the stream overall, up to a maximum of 30 metres. This will solve the problems of silting and shading and will usually improve, but not cure, the acid run-off problem. Groups of broad-leaved trees, planted close to streams inside the reserve strip, will not cause problems and will in fact be a benefit to the stream. Up to 60% of fish food can come from leaves and animals falling into the stream, and the trees cast a lighter shade.

(Source: adapted from Forestry Commission, 1986. *Design of Streams and Watercourses*)

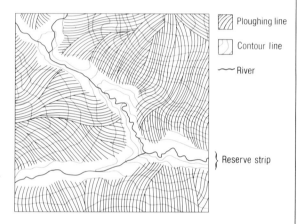

	Ploughing line
	Contour line
	River
	Reserve strip

Figure 4.1 Pattern of ploughing and planting to protect streams during coniferous forestry developments

Recreation

Intensive land use for recreation can create as many problems for wildlife habitats as intensive farming or forestry. Here, as before, it may be most important to think about ways of preventing the impact of the recreational use from spreading to surrounding areas that are valuable wildlife habitats, rather than trying to retain the wildlife interest in the intensively used area. Examples would be ski-ing developments, motorbike scrambling and the use of parks and recreation areas as playing fields. Some sports such as fishing, walking, pony-trekking or hunting can be much less damaging to habitats, provided too many people are not concentrated in one area. The integrated assessment should consider the extent to which human pressures are damaging habitats and landscapes and how the area could be managed better to avoid this.

Field sports

There is no doubt that much wildlife habitat has survived on farmed and wooded land because of people's desire to hunt some of the animals found there. The survival of heather moorland in many upland areas is due to grouse shooting. However, in the case of heather moorland, business and

[handwritten margin note: Recreation sure ... make are not ... people are not concentrated in one area. X]

74

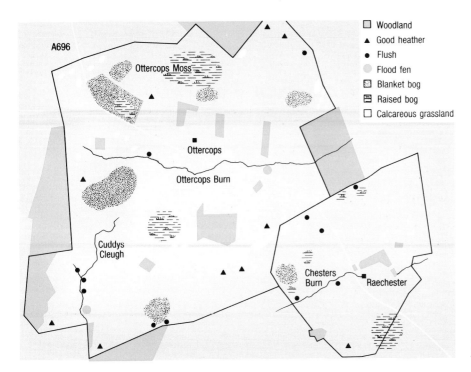

Figure 4.2 Areas of conservation value on extensively farmed land (Source: Countryside Commission, 1987. CCP 231)

conservation interests no longer coincide to the same extent as they have in the past. Box 4.2 (p 76) describes how a cycle of interactions between government policy, farming and sporting uses of the land is leading to the replacement of large areas of heather moorland by coniferous woodland.

Game shooting provides an example of the distinction between intensive and extensive recreational use of the land. The more intensive the exploitation of the sporting interest, the greater the danger of damage to wildlife species, habitats and the landscape. Where partridge, pheasant, duck, trout and other hunted species are attacked by predators, the land manager may want to control the predators. This will be particularly true where large numbers of birds or fish have been intensively reared in captivity and then released, becoming more like a crop than a wild animal. Some of their predators will be species widely regarded as vermin and not protected by law, such as foxes, crows, stoats. Other predators, such as buzzards and wild cats, are legally protected species. Remember what was said in Chapter 3, in the section on nutrition and feeding: in general, the numbers of predators are regulated by the numbers of their prey, and not the other way round. The number of predators is therefore most unlikely to get 'out of control'.

The artificial feeding of game species can cause other problems in wildlife habitats. If large numbers of ducks are kept on one pond, there will not be enough natural food to support them and they will have to be fed artificially. Any unused food and the droppings of so many animals in one place will excessively fertilise the water and it will become eutrophic, upsetting the balance of other wildlife species. The ducks will also damage the vegetation on the banks by trampling it with their feet. Similarly, artificially feeding pheasants in woodland will damage the vegetation in the areas where it takes place and it can introduce the weeds of arable crops into the woodland floor.

Predators

Box 4.2 Heather moorland, forestry and farming in the uplands

Heather moorland is one habitat that is now much less common, due to pressures from both farming and forestry. It is either an interrupted succession, having developed over the past 2500 years following large-scale burning and destruction of upland woodlands, or a regression from former woodland due to climatic changes. Light grazing by sheep and periodic burning of the heather prevent the re-establishment of woodland (see Chapters 2 and 3). *V, carefull managment*

Very careful management is needed to prevent heather moorland from degenerating to rough grassland. If the moor is over-stocked with sheep, then excessive grazing, uprooting of young shoots and trampling of the plants will eliminate heather over a period of a few years. Careful burning at intervals of about 6–10 years, depending on conditions, will rejuvenate heather but excessive burning will greatly speed up the problems caused by over-grazing. Also, if the heather is allowed to become too old before burning, the excessive heat generated will kill it and expose the underlying peat to erosion.

Heather moorland forms a habitat for a highly specialised range of species not found elsewhere. Among these, the red grouse is very valuable commercially, and a well run grouse moor can bring in a good commercial return. However, in recent years there has been a serious decline in the numbers of grouse on heather moorland throughout the country, due to a combination of suspected disease, over-grazing and poor management of the heather. As the profitability of grouse moors has declined, managers of the land have resorted to planting large areas of coniferous woodland or further over-stocking with sheep (encouraged by grants and tax incentives) in an attempt to make up the extra income.

Where conifers are planted, the forest areas may harbour foxes and carrion crows, the chief predators of grouse, causing a further decline in numbers on the moorland nearby. Heavy grazing will reduce the amount of heather available for the grouse. The resulting decline in grouse populations will increase the attractiveness of forestry in the uplands, and so on. These interacting vicious circles, representing a conflict between conservation and business interests on the land, are illustrated in Figure 4.3.

Good wildlife habitat is not incompatible with generating a healthy income, but it needs sensitive and understanding management. Once the habitat begins to deteriorate the pressures for a less conservation-friendly management regime can prove irresistible. These pressures can in turn create further pressures on nearby areas of high conservation value.

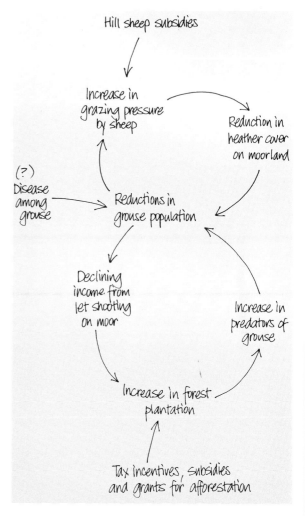

Figure 4.3 The vicious circles affecting heather moorland

4.4 Methods for business assessment

There is not space here to deal with business management planning in its own right. For conservation purposes you will need an assessment of the nature of the main business activities taking place:

- on a farm: which crops are grown, or what livestock are kept and where;
- on land managed by a water authority: the demands for ensuring a free flow of water, preventing flooding or avoiding pollution;
- on forested areas: the age classes of the timber, felling and re-planting patterns;
- on parkland: the levels of public use in various areas.

In each case you will also need to consider:

- the availability of labour and machinery;
- any special designations of the land that might affect the availability of grants, either for conservation or for intensification of the business land use; for example, as a Less Favoured Area or an Environmentally Sensitive Area;
- how the business use of the land is affecting the areas of landscape and conservation interest;
- your own attitudes and preferences, or other social pressures.

Detailed profit and loss accounting of the business aspects is very useful if you are going to plan an integrated programme of conservation work spanning a number of years, but it is beyond the scope of this book. At the very least, you should be aware of the overall financial position of the business to understand the nature of the pressures for land use changes and the scope for flexibility in introducing conservation options. If there is any income from game, fishing or other recreational activities, this should be noted here.

If you are not the land manager, perhaps acting as an adviser or conservation consultant, you may find that managers are reluctant to give you full financial details of the business. However, most managers will be prepared to give you enough information to do an integrated assessment adequately.

Box 4.3 (p 78) gives the basis for a business assessment of the Countryside Commission demonstration farm described in Figures 2.2 and 2.4.

As with habitat and landscape assessment, business assessment should be made partly by walking round the land area concerned and making observations on blank outline maps and notes. This would include drawing a map of **land use capability** and associated land uses. On complicated sites, it is better to keep maps and notes on the business assessment separate from your previous conservation assessments. However, on a fairly simple site they could all go on one map, provided it does not become too cluttered.

Make notes about the nature and state of the business in general. Keep your mind on the past and current states of the business and on how it might change if you fail to take remedial action — a business equivalent of ecological and landscape succession. (Future business plans are part of the next stage of management planning where you decide on your objectives.) Some aspects of business assessment can be done in the office where you will probably have fairly detailed records of the state of the business.

Business assessment maps and notes produced for the case study are shown in Section 4.6.

Box 4.3 Basis for a business assessment of Kingston Hill Farm

In 1968 Poul Christensen acquired the tenancy of 121 hectares of Kingston Hill Farm which was in a poor condition: 20 years of arable farming had left poor fertility and a heavy infestation of weeds. Intensive efforts have been made to remedy this situation and, with newly added land, the farm now totals 294 hectares.

The River Thames forms the northern boundary of the farm. Next to the river is land subject to flooding (Grade 5). The land gradually rises through sticky Oxford Clays (Grades 3 and 4) to a ridge of light sandy-loam soils; south of this ridge are good quality (Grade 2) loam soils.

The growth of the farming enterprise has been rapid, with the investment of considerable tenant's capital to establish a large livestock herd which is the cornerstone of the farm system. Currently dairy cows, young stock and beef cattle total between 750 and 800 with a high stocking rate of around 2.5 livestock units per hectare.

The development of the farm has been possible through greatly increased grassland productivity together with investment in many new fences, improved field water supplies, new concrete roads and an extensive range of modern buildings. Much of the work has been undertaken by farm staff.

Following the introduction of milk quotas farm policy has changed to one of producing a fixed

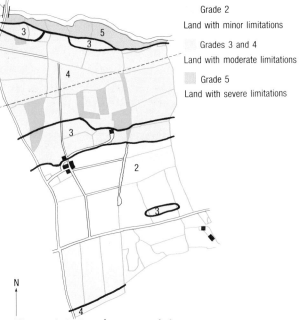

Grade 2
Land with minor limitations

Grades 3 and 4
Land with moderate limitations

Grade 5
Land with severe limitations

Figure 4.4 Land use capability

quantity of milk at the lowest price with no loss in profitability.

(Source: Countryside Commission, 1986. *Demonstration Farms Project. Kingston Hill Farm*)

Table 4.1 Farm profile

		1968/1969	1980/1981	1984/1985
	Total area (ha)	212	294	294
	Productive area (ha)	197	278	278
	Non-productive area (ha)	7	6.5	6.5
Cropping	Forage crops (ha)	137	146	146
	Arable crops (ha)	60	35	35
Average yields	Barley (tonnes/ha)	3.2	4.9	–
	Wheat (tonnes/ha)	–	7.4	7.5
Stocking	Dairy cows (no.)	156	320	400
	Followers (no.)	–	160	270
	Beef animals (no.)	–	276	150
	Average yield/per cow (galls)	800	1085	1085
	Livestock units per ha	1.1	2.5	2.5
Key statistics	No. men employed	3.5	6	6
	Total gross output (indexed and adjusted for inflation)	100	253	284
	Average field size (ha)	5.5	6.2	6.2

Now make a business assessment for your own land area case study:

▷ Draw a map showing the various land uses.

▷ Make brief notes about the nature and state of the business in general.

▷ Note what you like and dislike about the business aspects of the land use and why.

▷ Note any pressures from financial or technical advisers or landlords, neighbours or visitors, family or employees.

4.5 Methods for integrating conservation and business assessments

Two approaches to integrating conservation and business assessments are described here. The first involves a straightforward description of interactions taking place on your land, following the examples in Section 4.4. You should now identify similar interactions that apply to your land. Section 4.6 shows how integrated assessment was done for the case study farm.

> Note the interactions that seem to have an impact on the conservation value of your land area. Consider the intensity of land use on different areas of the land. Note where most profits are being made and where the contribution to business use of the land is marginal (the latter areas may have more potential for further conservation development).

The second approach described here takes the idea of integration more seriously and also helps to make the link to the second stage of management planning, deciding on your objectives and constraints, which should follow logically from this integrated assessment stage. The key to this link is the amount of control that you, or the land manager, have over the various factors affecting land use. In Stage 2, **objectives** will relate to aspects over which you already have control or could gain control if you took some appropriate action. **Constraints** will relate to aspects over which you have no prospect of gaining control, at least in the short term.

The factors you consider from this point of view will be those that arose from the landscape, habitat and business inputs to your integrated assessment. The following two exercises will help you to think about this constructively. They should be done by at least two people, including the land manager, an adviser or consultant, the manager's family, neighbours, or anyone else with an interest or involvement in the land area. It is sometimes difficult to envisage the benefits of this approach until you have done it for yourself. However, it is an excellent way of summarising all the information collected at the integrated assessment stage. It has the additional benefit of helping the manager to express attitudes and values related to conservation and business aspects of the land use that may not have been mentioned beforehand. As a result, it can be extremely effective at giving the land manager a new, integrated perspective of the land use system.

You can approach the first exercise in one of the two following ways:

1 Compile two lists, one of factors over which the land manager has or could gain control, and the other of factors over which he or she has no control.

2 Draw a large circle on a sheet of paper. Inside this circle place the factors over which the land manager has or could gain control, and outside it place the factors over which he or she has no control.

In both cases it is important to recognise that the situation is not static — with some factors there is likely to be a strong sense of either gaining or losing control.

Be prepared to make several rough attempts at this and, if you have time, to produce a tidy version summarising your diagram or table.

If you are not in a hurry, pin your diagrams or lists to a wall and look at them from time to time over a period of days, adding any new items as they occur to you.

The second integrated assessment exercise explains in more detail the interactions between landscape, habitat and business aspects of the land use. Among the various factors brought together on the list or diagram drawn up in the previous exercise, some will be more closely linked than others. You can show this by making several short lists, each including a set of linked components, representing one of the important conservation management *themes* for this area of land.

Draw up several such lists for your own case study area. Then summarise in your own words the conservation management theme that each illustrates. Each theme will probably contain a mixture of conservation and business-related issues and your summaries will describe the relationships among them.

Do not worry if you need more than one attempt at the last two exercises. Even experienced people usually work this out by a process of trial and error.

4.6 *Case study: Business assessment*

The business assessment map is shown in Figure 4.5.

Agriculture

The total farm area is 526 ha, of which 384 ha are in agricultural use and the remainder largely in forestry. It is all classified as a Less Favoured Area. On the agricultural land, there are 182 ha of rough hill grazing and the remaining 202 ha are down to crops and grass, including 20 ha barley, 8 ha swedes, 6 ha let to a contractor growing seed potatoes and 4 ha fodder rape. (The farmer does not like the high level of pesticide use on the seed potato fields, over which he has no control, given his policy of minimising the use of pesticide on the rest of the farm.) All the barley straw is used on the farm and no stubble burning takes place. The remaining area of agricultural land is either under permanent pasture, or the grass is used for hay or silage.

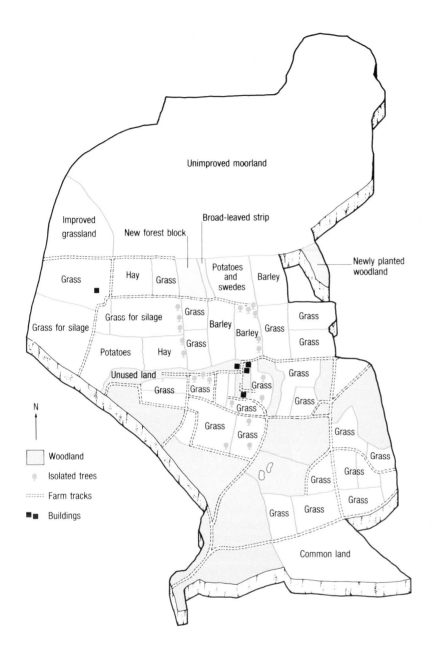

Figure 4.5 Case study farm: business assessment map

During the past two years the farmer has been experimenting with reduced pesticide application to the headlands of barley fields and has avoided using herbicides when possible on these areas. It is difficult to assess the relative costs and benefits of this as many field edges are subject to heavy rabbit damage. Rabbits are a very serious problem throughout the farm, and various suggestions for their control, such as gassing, have already been ruled out for practical reasons.

The farmer is worried about possible soil erosion problems on the fairly light land in the arable area. In October 1984, while ploughing, a worker struck a buried pipe that had previously remained below the reach of the plough.

81

The farm supports a flock of 600 black-face ewes, plus 500 lambs bought in and fattened, a suckler herd of 70 cows, plus 60 heifers.

Forestry

The woodland on the farm amounts to 121 ha, the majority of which is coniferous, grown as a commercial timber crop. There are blocks of Scots pine, spruce and larch, with compartments of varying ages that give added diversity to the landscape.

There are also about 20 ha of broad-leaved and mixed woodland, with a wide variety of species and some fine specimens, as described in Sections 2.5 and 3.8.

A block of 4.6 ha was planted with trees during the winter of 1986/1987 by the farmer's mother, who has a lease of the area in question, with the help of a Forestry Commission grant. The main crop is coniferous with broad-leaved trees interspersed throughout. Down the east side of this block is a strip entirely of broad-leaved trees in tree shelters. The whole area has been fenced against rabbits and there is an attractive growth of grasses and wild flowers. The farmer did not apply any herbicides as there were no particularly aggressive species present. However, a wet summer encouraged the grasses to grow very vigorously, threatening to kill a few of the trees. The forestry consultant for the farm advised that the cost of replacing a few trees would be less than the cost of applying weed-killer at this stage.

The farmer does not like the extent of unrelieved coniferous woodland on the farm and would like to see more diversity of species.

Game

Shooting on the farm is let to a syndicate which pays the shooting rates plus an additional £1100 per year. (In Scotland, on a small estate like this, the local authority will assume that the land is let for shooting purposes and will charge an additional rate. Stopping the shooting let would mean a loss of income to the farmer plus the additional cost of paying the shooting rate.) This year the syndicate that has the shooting on the pond (Figure 3.8, Table 3.4 and Plate 3) fenced off a small pen and released over 200 ducklings. They also release pheasants in the woods and feed them. They have one day's shooting a year for grouse on the moorland, and take pheasants, partridges and hares on the farm in general. There are also roe deer and occasional fallow deer in the woods.

Buildings

Six cottages on the farm are let to local tenants. (This helps to keep the local school open.)

Labour

1 Permanent farm hand.

1 Student on a Youth Training Scheme. (The previous student was a very mixed blessing, but the current one is good.)

There used to be a gamekeeper on the farm, but the farmer could not afford to keep him on. He still lives in the area and helps from time to time on the farm.

Cottage tenants also help with occasional labour, such as tree planting.

The agricultural part of the enterprise only just breaks even at the moment and most of the profit arises from the shooting let, the letting of farm cottages and the rental of land to grow seed potatoes.

On the forestry side, two small shelter-belts behind the house are ready for felling and should bring in a reasonable income. This will be done, one at a time over a period of years, to preserve some shelter. Income from the woods will mainly go to the Inland Revenue to pay a Capital Transfer Tax bill.

4.7 Case study: Integrating conservation and business assessment

(These notes on interactions between conservation and business aspects of land management should also be seen as an explanation of Figure 4.6 and Table 4.2. They are based on discussions between the farmer and a conservation adviser while the figure was being drawn.)

The farmer's concern with the financial viability of the business has implications for the conservation interest on the land. The most profitable activities at present are forestry (capitalising on past investments), the shooting let, the rental of land to grow potatoes, and the rental of farm

Table 4.2 Factors affecting land use and the extent to which they are under the control of the land manager

(The factors are ranged on a crude scale, from completely under the manager's control on the left to not under the manager's control on the right. The arrows indicate factors that seem to be changing, moving out of or into control.)

Under control	Not under control
Financial viability ⟶	Weather
Cash flows ⟵ Past burden of debt	
Game keeper ⟶	Shooting rate burden
Livestock	
Tree plantings	Poachers
Shooting syndicate ⟶	Predators
Public relations	Public access
SSSI	Rabbits
Soil erosion ⟶	Rhododendrons
Labour	Roe deer
Seed potato contract ⟶	Subsidies and grants
Inputs	Tax man
Drystone walls	EEC sheep regime
Hill land	Market forces
Rented cottages	Scrub area ('common land')
Crops and grass	
Unsprayed headlands	Local school
⟵ Land with drainage problems ⟶	
Wildlife habitats	
Ducks ⟶	
Coniferous woodland	
Parkland trees ⟶	
Archaeological sites	

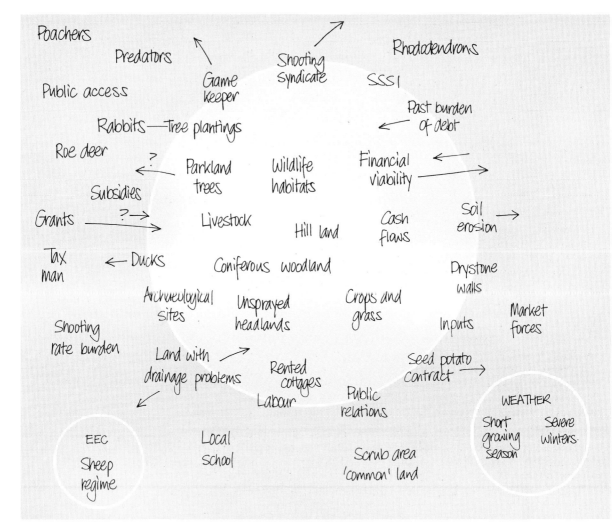

Figure 4.6 *Factors affecting land use and the extent to which they are under the control of the land manager. (Factors inside the large circle are those that are seen to be under the control of the land manager. Factors outside the circle are not under control. The arrows indicate those factors that seem to be changing, moving out of or into control.)*

cottages. The first three all have implications for conservation on the farm: the forestry creating the opportunity to plant more broad-leaved trees to improve wildlife and landscape conservation; the shooting let capitalising to some extent on the present high conservation value of the land; and the land rented out for growing potatoes being the only area of the farm heavily treated with pesticides.

The primary land use activity on the farm is rearing cattle and sheep but it only just breaks even financially at the moment. There is scope for expansion as the hill land could support more sheep if the grazing was improved and more winter feed could be grown if more intensive methods were adopted on the arable area. This would be damaging to some of the wildlife and landscape features on the farm. However, it would need some financial investment and may be risky in view of uncertainty about the future of the EEC sheep regime and the availability of various grants and subsidies.

The weather has recently caused a lot of problems for farming and forestry with the coldest winter, the driest summer and the wettest summer recorded for many years. No direct effects on wildlife have so far been noticed by the farmer.

The farmer is very keen to preserve and, if possible, enhance the various conservation features on his land, provided this can be done without affecting the financial situation. The SSSI is only partially in the farmer's control as he would need to prepare a **management agreement** jointly with the Nature Conservancy Council before undertaking any management on this land, but he is quite happy about this situation. He regards the rhododendrons, on the other hand, as being 'out of control' and would like to get rid of them. However, the shortage of labour on the farm has prevented him from tackling this so far.

There was little evidence of the current business land use having any direct adverse effects on conservation. However, the shortage of labour and money to invest in conservation has meant that some habitats and landscape features are now in need of management or they will begin to deteriorate (hedgerows, drystone walls and parkland trees). The smaller of the two ponds will soon be completely covered by vegetation and will continue the process of ecological succession to woodland if not managed to some extent.

The farmer has mixed feelings about a range of issues surrounding the shooting let, the problem of rabbits and the role of predators. He did not feel sufficiently in control of the activities of the game syndicate and was not consulted about their plans to release ducks on the pond. He is also unsure about their attitude to predators, particularly foxes, stoats, buzzards and wild cats.

He does not see the rabbits as a problem from the wildlife point of view. They are a major source of food for predators, and perhaps an alternative source to lambs in springtime. However, they eat grass and forage crops that would otherwise be available to livestock and are a major nuisance where the establishment of woods is concerned.

Although the area of scrub land perceived as common land is, for practical purposes, out of the farmer's control, he is happy for it to remain that way as a contribution to good public relations. The local people wanted to set up a committee to manage this land, but their efforts were blocked by the owner of the remainder of the land. There is public access to the farm, but this is not a source of many problems for farming or wildlife, although some poaching does go on. The farm is large and none of these activities has a major impact on the farm management or the farmer. He is happy with the present situation and would not want any additional public intrusion on his privacy.

Tables 4.3 to 4.6 (pp 86 and 87) outline the important conservation management themes for the case study farm. The brackets enclose sets of inter-related factors relevant to the particular theme and each set interacts with other sets in a variety of ways as indicated in the notes at the foot of the tables.

Table 4.3 Conservation management themes: (1) Shooting and wildlife

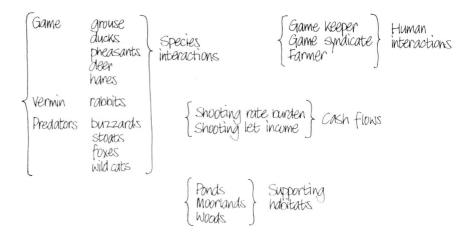

The farmer needs to bring in an income from the shooting let, but feels that the syndicate is not sufficiently under his control. The moorland and woodland areas provide habitat for game, but also for the rabbits, which are a serious pest. The predators that will help to keep down the rabbits will also prey on game and hence attract the attentions of the game keeper and game syndicate. Attempts to increase the numbers of game, through breeding, releasing and feeding ducks and pheasants, will degrade some of the wildlife habitats. Only small numbers of grouse are currently present, but they will only stay if the heather moorland remains stable.

Table 4.4 Conservation management themes: (2) Financial survival

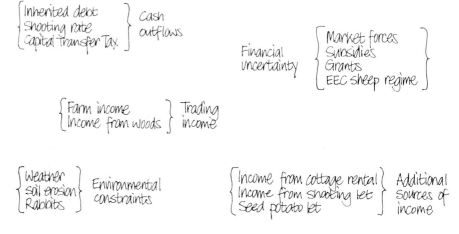

The farm is in a Less Favoured Area with severe winters and late springs and suspected soil erosion and rabbits are causing concern. These factors will add to the difficulties of coping with the heavy cash outflows. However, despite them, the inherited debt has been greatly reduced. The financial uncertainty over the future of income generation from agriculture and forestry makes it difficult to plan for the future. The most profitable and certain future sources of income all arise from peripheral activities such as cottage rental, the shooting let and the seed potato let. There is therefore little spare income to invest in improvements connected with conservation.

Table 4.5 Conservation management themes: (3) Management priorities for farming/forestry and wildlife/landscape

Commercial management paramount
{ Coniferous woodland
Improved hill land
Arable land
Seed potato let land
Improved pasture and grassland }

{ Newly planted woods
Field headlands
Herb-rich pasture
Heather moorland
Ponds
Parkland trees }
Commercial and conservation interests co-exist

{ Drystone walls
'Common land'
Track verges
Hedges
Broad-leaved woodland
Archaeological sites }
Landscape/wildlife interests paramount

On the most intensively used land commercial considerations had been paramount and would have to continue to be so. However, there were also many areas where the land use was less intensive and where commercial and conservation interests were co-existing, and in some cases reinforcing one another. On the boundary habitats of the intensively used land and also on the broad-leaved woodland areas, landscape and wildlife interests were seen to be paramount.

Table 4.6 Conservation management themes: (4) Public relations

Recreational activities
{ Farm paths used by public
'Common land' }

{ Cottage tenants
Farm labour
Local school }
Mutual benefit

{ Occasional poaching } Unacceptable activities

Local people use areas of the farm for recreation and other activities, and while this provides no benefit to the farmer, it does not particularly intrude on his privacy. Letting farm cottages to local tenants does bring in an income and incidentally helps to keep the local school open and provides an occasional source of farm labour. The occasional poaching that the farmer is aware of is unacceptable but very difficult to control in the absence of a full-time game keeper.

Chapter 5

IDENTIFYING OBJECTIVES
AND CONSTRAINTS

Summary

Objectives will relate to factors affecting the land use that are, or could be brought, under control; constraints relate to factors that cannot be controlled. From a conservation point of view, relevant objectives will be *to maintain*, *to improve*, or *to create* landscape features or habitats, depending on the outcome of the assessment. The important points to note are: objectives are related to one another at a series of different levels (strategic, management and tactical); the range of relevant constraints and how they operate on different types of objective; and the need to incorporate objectives and constraints that are personal to the land manager. Relevant objectives are described for a mixed farm in the south of England, for forest management and for the management of archaeological sites. The importance of a greater complexity of objectives in encouraging conservation is stressed.

5.1 *The link from integrated assessment*

An objective is the same thing as a goal. In our context it is an outcome that the land manager wants to achieve. Constraints are factors that limit or block the land manager's ability to achieve an objective. Objectives and constraints should arise naturally from the integrated assessment stage (Section 4.5). You can interpret the exercise of sorting relevant factors according to whether they are controllable by the manager (Figure 4.6 and Table 4.2) as follows.

In or out of control

Objectives are likely to be related to:

▶ those factors that are already under the control of the manager;

▶ factors at present outside the manager's control, where a valid objective would be to bring them under control;

▶ factors currently under control, but in danger of going out of control, where 'keeping them under control' would be a valid objective.

Constraints are related to factors that cannot be brought under the manager's control.

In Figure 4.6 and Table 4.2, the first type of objective is illustrated by coniferous woodland under the control of the farmer, who is not happy with its present condition; therefore, as he re-plants he has the objective of mixing conifers and broad-leaved species. The second type of objective is illustrated by the past burden of debt: the farmer could have chosen to treat it as a constraint, not capable of being brought under control, and presumably sold up and gone out of business as a result. However, he chose to treat its removal as an objective, now almost achieved. The problem of the shooting syndicate, where the farmer perceives them as tending to go out of his control, is an example of the third type of objective. The shooting rate burden, on the other hand, is a constraint — it has an impact on the land management, but there is nothing the manager can do about it.

Another link from site assessment to objectives will be the quality of the landscape and wildlife habitats that you find:

▶ If any of these are very high, your first objective will be *to maintain* them in their present state.

▶ If any are moderately good, you will be planning how to retain existing features and, if possible, *to improve* them (as was the situation on the case study farm).

▶ If the value is generally low, you will want *to create* new habitat and landscape features.

These three objectives — 'to maintain', 'to improve' and 'to create' — are the key to good landscape and habitat management, and choosing the right one for each situation is one of the most important skills of the manager. People who are new to management planning have a tendency to concentrate on creating new features, partly because such objectives are more clear cut and easier to identify, and also because it is easier to see progress. However, creating a new feature in an area of top quality wildlife habitat or landscape would not be good conservation. When it is justified to plan to create a new habitat area or landscape feature, remember that this still implies long-term *maintenance* if your efforts are not to be wasted, and this may place a heavy demand, for example, on labour resources.

Some people begin the process of land use management planning with 'identifying objectives and constraints' and then go on to do 'site assessment' — the reverse of what is suggested here. There are no right or wrong ways to do this and you should use whichever method gives the best results in your hands. However, the inputs from integrated assessment to the decisions on objectives and constraints, as described above, are very helpful and make this stage much easier, as well as adding richness and variety to the objectives you will identify. Beginning with objectives and constraints encourages you to make simplistic assumptions that do not reflect your own or the land manager's personal views and circumstances.

This chapter first deals with objectives and constraints in general terms, as they apply to a whole range of land uses, and then asks you to do this stage of management planning for your own site, following the example for the case study in Section 5.6.

5.2 The nature of objectives and constraints

Objectives

Having a clearly specified set of objectives gives stability without rigidity to the process of management planning. It will help you to target action and give a benchmark against which you can measure your progress. An important feature of objectives is that they are sequential — one thing leads to another, or more often, one thing leads to several others, forming what is called a hierarchy or 'tree'. An objectives tree is similar in structure to a family tree, but unlike a family tree objectives can be changed according to circumstances. However, this should only be done after carefully thinking through the implications of the changes for other related objectives and for the site in general.

An objectives tree can usually be divided into three distinct levels, as shown in Figure 5.1. Strategic objectives, at the top of the tree, tend to be very general, scene-setting, long-lasting and difficult to change. They are sometimes called 'overall objectives'. Examples of such objectives would be:

▶ to conserve and enhance the natural beauty and historic interest of the property (National Trust);

▶ to optimise yields from arable, forestry and sporting enterprises (country estate);

▶ to manage the unproductive land alongside the cultivated areas in ways which will also conserve wildlife and improve the landscape (farm or forest).

The management objectives, at the second level in the hierarchy, are more immediate and less general, related to the management activities needed to ensure that the overall objective(s) are satisfied. They are sometimes called policy objectives or policies.

At a lower level are the short-term tactical objectives, specifying how the management objectives will be put into practice. These are sometimes referred to as methods or prescriptions.

Figure 5.1 is an objectives tree for an upland estate managed by the National Trust. In some circumstances there can be conflicts between objectives, for example the second and third strategic objectives, about access and wildlife conservation. The Trust sees its management function as striking a balance between objectives, reconciling them as far as possible when they conflict. On any particular site, the relative weight given to different objectives will depend on the history, current state and importance of the site and the reasons for its acquisition, all factors that would already have been considered as part of the integrated assessment.

Conflict between lower level objectives therefore need not be a problem. It merely means that the manager has to make a conscious choice among the relevant objectives. Any conflict among strategic objectives is much more serious, and an organisation in this situation would soon find itself in trouble.

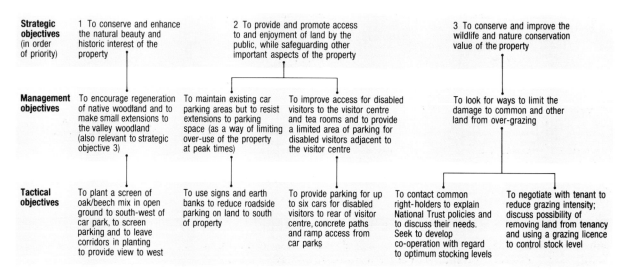

Figure 5.1 Objectives hierarchy for upland estate management (Source: Countryside Commission, 1986. Management Plans: A Guide to their Preparation and Use)

Figure 5.1 also illustrates the point that it is possible for a lower level objective to be relevant to more than one higher level objective. The management objective, 'to encourage regeneration of native woodland and to make small extensions to the valley woodland', and its associated tactical objective, are relevant to the first and third strategic objectives. When this happens, it reinforces the case for implementing such an objective.

Land managers will find themselves with varying degrees of flexibility in changing their objectives. If you work for a large organisation, objectives at the strategic level, and perhaps also at the management level, will be set for you by the organisation, and trying to change them would involve you in some long-term negotiations. If you are a farmer and own the land, you will have a large amount of flexibility at all levels of your objectives tree and have the freedom to change them without consulting anybody. Large organisations such as water authorities or the Forestry Commission, on the other hand, may have the resources to choose objectives that are not open to the small landowner who must make a steady living from the land.

Tenants often have very limited freedom of action, where tenancy agreements demand that the land should be kept 'tidy' and 'productive' in ways that would prevent the introduction of conservation objectives. On the farm described in Figures 2.2 and 2.4 a restrictive tenancy of this sort has been renegotiated with the landlord to allow the tenant to integrate conservation objectives with the business aspects described in Box 4.3.

There are two possible types of linkage between lower and upper levels in an objectives tree:

1 In some cases, several of the lower level objectives will have to be put into practice to achieve the higher level objective (both/and type).

2 In other cases, lower level objectives will be alternative ways of achieving the higher level objective (either/or type).

If you are dealing with 'either/or' objectives, you only need to select one of them to carry on to the next stage (exploring options), whereas if you are dealing with the 'both/and' type you need to carry them all on to the next stage. The objectives hierarchy for the case study gives some examples to illustrate this point.

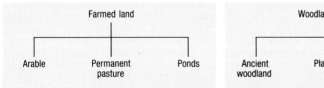

*Figure 5.2 **Not** an objectives hierarchy*

Note that objectives are about *doing* something: *to encourage* regeneration; *to improve* access; *to plant* trees. When people are learning management planning they sometimes make the mistake of producing hierarchies like those in Figure 5.2 which do not imply any action.

Constraints

Constraints are forces that block or limit your ability to achieve an objective. Financial and legal constraints often come most immediately to mind in relation to conservation. While it is possible to do a lot for conservation without it costing a great deal and there are many grants available to help, finance will sometimes be a constraint on your freedom of action.

Financial and legal constraints

There are a great many laws and regulations relevant to wildlife and landscape conservation, but the manager need not always think of them as constraints. The farmer in the case study example has a Site of Special Scientific Interest on his land and associated with this there is a recorded list of **Potentially Damaging Operations** (PDOs) about which he must consult the NCC. However, psychologically, this is not a constraint because he is quite happy with the situation. Sometimes, the existence of a protected area or species will provide opportunities for grants towards conservation and thus open up objectives that would otherwise be blocked by a financial constraint.

An important regulatory constraint for woodland management is the need, on most occasions, to have a felling licence from the Forestry Commission before you can fell trees. A licence is needed if you want to fell more than 5 cubic metres of timber in any quarter of a year, of which more than 2 cubic metres is to be sold (5 cubic metres is approximately equivalent to five fairly large trees).

Where an objectives tree, or list of objectives and constraints, is to be used to communicate a management plan to others, for example to a succession of managers, or to keep records on a long term basis, it is essential to include all legal and regulatory constraints, regardless of how the present manager may feel about them.

Personal constraints

Apart from financial and legal constraints there are also other types which are much more informal, and often much more personal to the manager. They can play havoc with the implementation of a management plan, so it is vitally important that they are included in the list of constraints.

We won't get away with it until old Jones dies!

Constraints can be written into the objectives tree as shown later in Figure 5.5. General constraints are at the same level as strategic or overall objectives, and they should be listed in a corner of the diagram. Other constraints will be much more specific, blocking off particular branches of the tree. Among such specific constraints will possibly be some factors arising from your integrated assessment. For example: unless the subsoil is impermeable or permanently wet, it will be difficult and expensive to maintain a pond on a particular site; or the existence of a particularly diverse area of grassland could place constraints on your grazing regime.

Plate 1 Case study farm: Part of the scene from viewpoint 3 (Figure 2.5)

Plate 2 Case study farm: Part of the scene from viewpoint 4 (Figure 2.5)

Plate 3 Case study farm: Eastern pond (site 1 on Figure 3.8)

Plate 4 Case study farm: View from the hill land, showing diverse heather moorland in the foreground (site 25 on Figure 3.8)

CONVERSION
SCALE
Metres Feet

Plate 5 Part of a Soil
Survey map showing
different soil types
(Source: Soil Survey of
England and Wales.
Crown Copyright)

Plate 6 Aerial
photograph: Buried
archaeological remains
under the arable land
show up as darker green
outlines

Plate 7 The rolling patchwork landscape of the Brecon Beacons

Plate 8 Over-mature hedgerow where sheep have removed bark from the bushes and eroded the underlying soil

Plate 9 Strategic landscape: Patterns of felling and re-planting on the Atholl Estate near Dunkeld

Plate 10 Strategic landscape: Mature forest owned by the Forestry Commission near Dunkeld

Plate 11 One of a series
of habitat posters
produced by the Natural
History Museum

Plate 12 An illustration
showing birds near a
wetland habitat (Royal
Society for the
Protection of Birds)

Plate 13 A tracked excavator working on a river bank

Plate 14 Laying an over-mature hedge

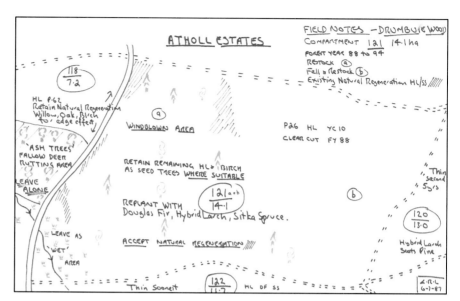

Plate 15 Part of the forest management plan for the hillside shown in Plate 9

Plate 16 A map from an estate management plan produced by the Ministry of Agriculture, Fisheries and Food

There is sometimes a temptation, if you know that a certain objective is blocked by a constraint, to leave both the objective and the constraint out of the tree diagram altogether. However, your diagram is a useful long-term planning aid, and the opportunity to remove a constraint may arise in future, even though it is insurmountable at present. (Old Jones will eventually die!) This argues for keeping the objectives tree as complete as possible, and incorporating constraints in the diagram. (This could, however, be embarrassing if old Jones is likely to see the plan.)

5.3 Conservation objectives for a range of land uses

This section gives some examples of relevant conservation objectives for a range of land uses, taken from publications by the Countryside Commissions, the National Trust and English Heritage (listed in Appendix I).

Note the lack of a personal flavour in most of these examples. They have obviously been 'sanitised' for publication and there is little impression of a living, breathing land manager, with likes, dislikes and prejudices behind them. When you are deciding on objectives and constraints for your own land area, remember to keep this human element in the picture, as in the case study in Section 5.6. (As implied above, if the organisation is large or if the management plan will be used by a series of managers, then it will have to be more impersonal.)

Objectives for farmland

The farm used as an example is in the south of England. It is largely arable with some pasture and includes a substantial area of woodland. The farmer plans his management around three themes: the farmed land, the farm infrastructure and the woodland estate. On the farmed land he considers individually the arable enterprise, the permanent pasture, the hedgerows, streams and ponds, and also shooting and recreation. 'Infrastructure' is divided into access, roads and tracks, and buildings. The woodland estate includes ancient woodland, plantations and amenity spinneys.

The *strategic objectives* for the farmed land are:

▷ to optimise the productivity of the existing arable acreage, while retaining valuable hedgerows and allowing for expansion of the shoot;

▷ to maintain flexibility in the farming system and experience of a range of crops and stock.

The following *management objectives* are seen as arising from them:

On arable land

▷ to complete the field rationalisation programme to give an average field size of 12 hectares (30 acres), **culverting** ditches and removing the least valuable hedgerows;

▷ to cut back shrubs and overhanging branches at woodland margins in co-ordination with a hedge maintenance programme;

On permanent pasture

▶ to retain most of the existing permanent pasture;

▶ to maintain the existing low intensity regime at an important archaeological site;

For hedgerows

▶ to establish regular rotational management of hedgerows by coppicing or trimming for thick bottoms according to their historical value, location and function in the farm system;

▶ to sell timber trees as markets become available, while ensuring continuity of standards;

For streams and ponds

▶ to improve cover on the banks by a programme of planting and scrub management without obstructing light or maintenance operations;

▶ to extend wet habitats where there is no loss of farm productivity by increasing pond size and establishing new ponds;

For shooting

▶ to enhance shooting beats by the establishment of patches of game crops where there is minimal loss of arable productivity;

▶ to keep fertiliser and chemical sprays away from ditches, hedge bottoms and field headlands to benefit game and wildlife;

For recreation

▶ to extend and improve facilities for public enjoyment of the estate by waymarking, path clearance, better provision of stiles and rustic seating and the establishment of a farm trail;

▶ to mitigate the effects of horse riding on footpaths by restricting access in wet weather.

Objectives for forest management

The National Trust believes that it is possible to produce well grown trees to yield a valuable and sustainable income when harvested and at the same time to favour conservation. The Trust has, therefore, in addition to the objectives in Figure 5.1, the *strategic objectives* to combine preservation, gradual replacement and prudent harvesting of a useful natural resource and to maintain the status quo in terms of broad landscape patterns.

Arising from their strategic objectives are a series of *management objectives* (referred to by the Trust as management principles) which will apply in varying degrees, depending on the site:

▷ to maintain any ancient monuments scheduled under the 1979 Ancient Monuments Act (which it has a statutory duty to do) and to preserve other lesser archaeological features, including ancient boundary banks, which its woodlands often contain;

▷ to convert broad-leaved woods gradually from their present over-mature, even-aged condition into a more irregular, uneven-aged form capable of being maintained in perpetuity, with the minimum of interference with their overall appearance in the landscape;

▷ to retain lowland coppiced woodland as a particularly valuable wildlife habitat wherever possible (there is a constraint here in that the resumption of coppice rotations on any scale will depend on the development of viable markets);

▷ (in the special case of coppiced oak wood) to single and to restore to high forest;

▷ to replace conifers with conifers and broad-leaved trees with broad-leaved trees and not seek to enrich the broad-leaved woodlands with conifers, or to replace conifers with broad-leaved trees as a mere cosmetic exercise when there is little prospect of genuine landscape or habitat improvement;

▷ to plant broad-leaf–conifer mixtures in the uplands where exposure is significant and in less sensitive lowland areas (on lowland sites the proportion of broad-leaved trees will frequently be higher than the 25% planted hitherto);

▷ to avoid deliberate afforestation on upland farms, except for shelter-belts (this policy may need to be reviewed if the current interest in transferring surplus farmland to forestry really develops);

▷ to develop wide forest **rides** both for nature conservation and for public enjoyment;

▷ to improve the timber quality in broad-leaved woodlands (while recognising the ecological importance of dead and dying wood, growing high quality timber is regarded as entirely compatible with its other overall and policy objectives).

As noted above, a woodland manager working for the National Trust would be expected to take these strategic and management objectives into consideration, to select tactical objectives for the woods and to ensure that they are implemented.

Objectives for the management of ancient monuments

Over 95% of the country's archaeological heritage is in the hands of private landowners and managers, some of whom are not even aware of their presence. There is no suggestion that the existence of an archaeological site on a piece of land should stop all development of that land — nobody wants to see a fossilised landscape. However, very often the management of land for other conservation objectives is perfectly compatible with the management of archaeological resources and the two will even complement one another.

The *strategic objectives* of archaeological resource management are:

▶ to retain the rich diversity of archaeological remains known to exist in the landscape;

▶ to make the archaeological heritage satisfy the demands made upon it by society as a whole;

▶ to reconcile conflict and competition for the use of land containing ancient monuments.

At the next level down in the objectives tree, there is no universal set of management objectives that can be applied to all archaeological sites. Each should be managed within the context of its own landscape, taking account of ownership, other land uses and land potential. As noted above, there is often common ground with other conservation objectives, for example the conservation of old pasture or the maintenance of wetlands on archaeological sites, for their wildlife habitat and landscape value. In other cases there is an overlap with the development of sporting, amenity, leisure and recreational facilities as business ventures.

The *management objectives* for archaeological sites fall into three groups:

1 Curatorial management

The main objective here is to stop the natural and human-induced processes of decay affecting a site and to prolong its life. Arising from this are two *tactical objectives* of the *either/or* type:

▶ to conserve the site by planning day-to-day activities to avoid damaging it, and to take urgent remedial action only if it inadvertently becomes damaged, for example by grazing livestock;

▶ or to preserve the site by anticipating a range of specific threats and taking action to avoid them.

2 Exploitation

The main objective here is to permit the site to be used for public enjoyment or for academic interest, both of which will invariably alter its character and may contribute to its decay. Several *tactical objectives* of the *both/and* type arise from this:

▶ to clear the site to make it visible;

▶ to improve access;

▶ to provide displays and visitor facilities;

▶ in exceptional cases to excavate interesting or significant details;

▶ to undertake the necessary strengthening and repair work to ensure public safety.

3 Rescue excavation

Rescue excavation has the objective of excavating and recording as much as possible of a site, to record its structure and form and, in effect, preserve it on paper. This is usually undertaken when the archaeological value of a site is outweighed by some other purpose, such as the building of a road, in which case it will be destroyed.

The above is just a small sample of the possible conservation objectives for the range of land uses likely to be found in this country. It is intended to show you what is expected at this stage, but should not be treated as a set of examples to be slavishly copied. Your own circumstances will always be unique in some ways and this should be reflected in your management plans.

These examples should also make it clear that the three categories of strategic, management and tactical objectives overlap to some extent.

5.4 Complexity and land use diversification

As a general rule, if you are very concerned to simplify your management objectives for the land and to cut complexity out of your life, it will be more difficult to find room for conservation. As the examples below will show, the more complexity or diversity you are prepared to tolerate in your organisation and its objectives, the greater can be the opportunities for conservation. However, diversification of the business aspects of the land use can take place without any benefits to conservation and can actually cause damage. Given the current economic pressures on agriculture, farmers are being encouraged to diversify the basis of their business so that it will be more flexible when subjected to changing economic circumstances and hence more viable in the long run. Unless conservation is specifically included in the strategic objectives of the business, this will not necessarily be beneficial, as shown by the following example.

To diversify or not to diversify

Large-scale forestry

When the Forestry Commission was first set up it was given the very straightforward strategic objective of maximising the production of marketable timber. Figure 5.3 shows the objectives tree that resulted. The public response to this outcome has been generally adverse and the Forestry Commission has changed its approach in recent years, but as trees are such a long-lived crop, the effects of the old policy will be with us for many years to come.

Since the early 1970s the Forestry Commission has been gradually increasing the proportion of its financial resources set aside for conservation. However, the passing of the Wildlife and Countryside (Amendment) Act, 1985, gave the Commission a statutory duty to seek a reasonable balance between timber production and wildlife conservation and thus officially included this aspect

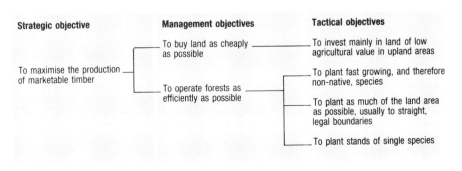

Figure 5.3 A simple strategic objective for large-scale forestry

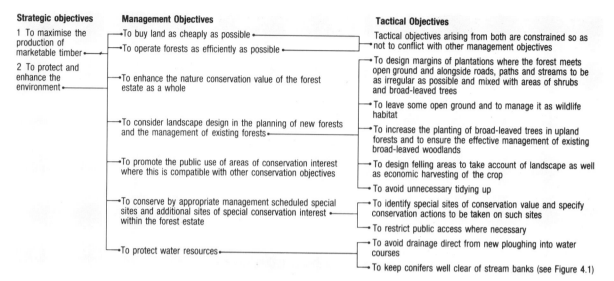

Strategic objectives	Management Objectives	Tactical Objectives
1 To maximise the production of marketable timber	To buy land as cheaply as possible	Tactical objectives arising from both are constrained so as not to conflict with other management objectives
2 To protect and enhance the environment	To operate forests as efficiently as possible	
	To enhance the nature conservation value of the forest estate as a whole	To design margins of plantations where the forest meets open ground and alongside roads, paths and streams to be as irregular as possible and mixed with areas of shrubs and broad-leaved trees
		To leave some open ground and to manage it as wildlife habitat
	To consider landscape design in the planning of new forests and the management of existing forests	To increase the planting of broad-leaved trees in upland forests and to ensure the effective management of existing broad-leaved woodlands
	To promote the public use of areas of conservation interest where this is compatible with other conservation objectives	To design felling areas to take account of landscape as well as economic harvesting of the crop
		To avoid unnecessary tidying up
	To conserve by appropriate management scheduled special sites and additional sites of special conservation interest within the forest estate	To identify special sites of conservation value and specify conservation actions to be taken on such sites
		To restrict public access where necessary
	To protect water resources	To avoid drainage direct from new ploughing into water courses
		To keep conifers well clear of stream banks (see Figure 4.1)

Figure 5.4 Mixed strategic objectives for large-scale forestry

objectives

among its strategic objectives. Figure 5.4 shows the difference this has made to the objectives tree. The commercial management objectives have now been considerably modified to accommodate the new strategic objective of protecting and enhancing the environment. All this involves some loss of potential income to the Forestry Commission and hence to the public purse. However, it is being done for an obvious public benefit.

Suppose the complexity of the objectives tree was further increased and an additional strategic objective was added to the two given in Figure 5.4 — 'To obtain an income from hunting deer and other game'. What effect do you think this would have on the management and tactical objectives? It might make the landowner less inclined to encourage public access and more inclined to control predators, but most of the land management options proposed to benefit wildlife and the landscape would be equally beneficial to game species. In addition, the fact that hunting was contributing to the income from the land would make it possible for the manager to take up these options on a greater scale and would increase his or her enthusiasm for maintaining them in the long term.

Farmed land

In most cases, on farmed land diversification and conservation will support one another, so that the existence of conservation objectives eases the process of diversification, and an increase in the diversity of management objectives will strengthen the commitment to conservation. However, whether diversification is beneficial to conservation will depend on the type of land that is diverted to new crops, the intensity of their management and the pattern of distribution of chemical inputs.

For example, the destruction of ancient semi-natural habitat that has not in the past been treated with chemicals in order to grow organic crops would be a conservation disaster. An intensively managed cereal crop with wide, unsprayed margins and tall hedges with trees *may* have a greater conservation value than an organic field with no margins where the crop is kept clean using mechanical cultivations.

For lowland farms some **agroforestry** developments are being proposed, such as the planting of rapidly maturing poplars, widely spaced so that cereal production or the grazing of animals can continue during the early years of growth when no income is being generated. This increase in cropping diversity will have little advantage for wildlife unless conservation is also adopted as a strategic land use objective when, for example, a tactical objective could be to encourage the growth of wild flowers on the grass strips between the trees.

The proposed addition of woodland management to the policy objectives of many lowland farms, with the help of incentives such as the Farm Woodlands Scheme, is largely an attempt to make these woods economically productive so that they can supplement the farmer's income. Those who support more intensive management of farm woods sometimes claim that there will also be conservation benefits and this may be true. For example, keeping animals out of heavily over-grazed woodland to allow the growth of the understorey and some natural regeneration will provide a benefit. However, clear felling an area of old oak woodland to re-plant with a mixture of broad-leaved trees and conifers would be very unfortunate for the landscape and wildlife.

Having the right objectives for wildlife and landscape conservation is therefore only half the battle. Choosing appropriate options to put them into practice is just as important. Stage 3 of land use management planning, described in Chapter 6, deals with this aspect. It takes you from the objectives tree to thinking about how you might be able to achieve your objectives. However, first you need to construct the objectives tree for your own area of land as outlined in the next section and in the case study.

5.5 *Constructing your own objectives tree*

Some people prefer to tackle this stage by beginning with the strategic objectives and building the tree down from there. Others are more comfortable with lists of objectives, and write down all the objectives that seem appropriate before trying to order them in a hierarchical fashion. The first is more logical, but the second will link more easily with the integrated assessment stage.

Section 5.6 shows a list of objectives for the case study farm, derived from Section 4.7, supplemented by discussions with the farm manager. The objectives tree in Figure 5.5 was based on this list. Do not expect your tree to look as tidy as this at the first attempt. They are difficult to arrange neatly, so use a large sheet of paper and be prepared to throw away at least the first one you draw. Section 5.6 also includes some notes on the objectives tree and the constraints. This is useful to refresh your own memory when you come back to it at a later date, and it will be essential if you want to communicate it to someone else.

Go back to your own case study and draw an objectives tree, first making lists of objectives and constraints if you prefer to work like that. Remember to:

▶ use a large sheet of paper;

▶ make it personal to the land manager;

▶ incorporate general constraints as a list at the bottom of the page;

▶ add any specific constraints that would block certain paths in the tree;

▶ note any sets of objectives that are of 'both/and' or 'either/or' type.

5.6 Case study:
Identifying objectives and constraints

The following lists of objectives and constraints and the objectives tree in Figure 5.5 were based partly on the integrated assessment for the case study, particularly Section 4.7, and partly on discussions with the land manager. The strategic objectives will emerge from the discussions, rather than from the integrated assessment. Because the objectives and constraints are personal to the manager, they cannot be right or wrong, although they could, in another case, have been bad for conservation.

If the objectives tree is to be used as a long-term benchmark against which to measure progress, then some of the lower level objectives here will need to be firmed up and made more quantitative. For example, 'extend areas of unsprayed headlands' would need to say how much they were to be extended and where. However, it is not necessary, and could be a waste of time, to do this before Stage 3, 'Exploring and choosing the management options'.

Objectives

Maintain financial viability (overall, strategic objective)

Grow less barley

Encourage wildlife diversity

Encourage predators

Maintain interesting diversity of habitats on moorland

Have good relations with local people

Abandon letting the land for shooting on the farm

Control shooting syndicate better

Improve diversity in commercial woodland

Have as little impact on landscape and wildlife as possible and improve them where practicable (overall, strategic objective)

Plant more broad-leaved trees

Check scheduled archaeological sites

Encourage greater diversity of herbs in meadow areas

Minimise chemical inputs where possible

Avoid damage to rare sedge habitat

100

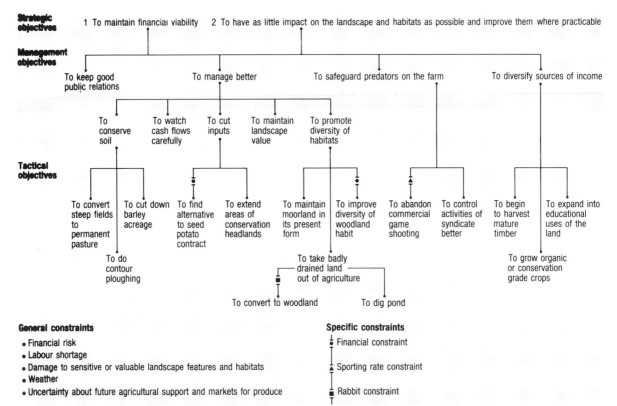

Strategic objectives

1 To maintain financial viability   2 To have as little impact on the landscape and habitats as possible and improve them where practicable

Management objectives

To keep good public relations

To manage better

To safeguard predators on the farm

To diversify sources of income

Tactical objectives

To conserve soil

To watch cash flows carefully

To cut inputs

To maintain landscape value

To promote diversity of habitats

To convert steep fields to permanent pasture

To cut down barley acreage

To find alternative to seed potato contract

To extend areas of conservation headlands

To maintain moorland in its present form

To improve diversity of woodland habit

To abandon commercial game shooting

To control activities of syndicate better

To begin to harvest mature timber

To expand into educational uses of the land

To do contour ploughing

To take badly drained land out of agriculture

To grow organic or conservation grade crops

To convert to woodland

To dig pond

General constraints

- Financial risk
- Labour shortage
- Damage to sensitive or valuable landscape features and habitats
- Weather
- Uncertainty about future agricultural support and markets for produce

Specific constraints

Financial constraint

Sporting rate constraint

Rabbit constraint

Protect parkland trees
Manage the land better
Enjoy farming the land
Allow damp areas with drainage problems to come out of agricultural use

Constraints

Uncertainty about EEC sheep regime
Uncertainty about EEC cereals regime
Lack of spare labour
Rabbit problem
Tax
Sporting rates
Lack of money for unprofitable projects
Weather and short growing season
Market forces

Figure 5.5 Objectives hierarchy for the case study farm

Notes on objectives tree and constraints (Figure 5.5)

The overall objective 'maintain financial viability' is intended to imply that this farmer will be happy with a satisfactory income and does not necessarily want to maximise his profits. The second overall objective is subordinate to the first but reflects a very strongly-felt attitude to his environment.

The objective to manage the farm better is the primary management objective and has an impact on all the others. Looking at the branching set of objectives that arises from it, the personal nature of the hierarchy is again in evidence. For this farmer, cutting inputs and promoting diversity of habitats were seen as possible routes to better management, which would not necessarily be the case on all farms.

The reference to 'contour ploughing' means ploughing across the slope of the hill, rather than up and down.

General constraints are factors that affect a wide range of objectives at all levels of the hierarchy. The impact of the general financial constraint on two of the branches in the hierarchy is also illustrated. One specific constraint is also illustrated — the fact that the existence of sporting rates on this farm makes it impossible, for the moment, to abandon letting the land for shooting and therefore 'chops off' this branch of the hierarchy. This list of constraints is as important to bear in mind for the next stage as are the objectives — some of the most imaginative options could be ways of getting round constraints just as much as ways of achieving objectives.

Chapter 6

EXPLORING AND CHOOSING YOUR OPTIONS

Summary

Two aspects of exploring and choosing options are considered: knowledge of
the various options available to achieve landscape and habitat objectives, and
an imaginative approach to the business, landscape and habitat possibilities.
Options are summarised for the conservation management of: grassland;
heathland and moorland; lowland wetlands and marshland; open water;
hedgerows, field margins and roadside verges; broad-leaved woodland;
coniferous woodland; scrub; structures. Techniques for stimulating an
imaginative approach to options are illustrated and guidelines for the choice
of options suggested.

6.1 The link between objectives and options

The word '**options**' implies choice; in this case it involves exploring a wide
range of possible means of achieving the objectives decided on in Stage 2. The
more imaginative and knowledgeable you are, the more likely that you will
find the best possible answer to your land use requirements. This chapter
deals with both these aspects — knowledge (summarising, in Section 6.2,
some of the many options available to achieve landscape and habitat
objectives) and imagination (describing, in Section 6.3, techniques for
stimulating your own ideas).

In Figure 5.1, the management objective 'to encourage regeneration of native
woodland and to make small extensions to the valley woodland' led to the
tactical objectives 'to plant a screen of oak/beech mix in open ground to the
south-west of the car park to screen the parking area' and 'to leave corridors
in the planting to provide a view to the west'.

The land manager could legitimately go straight from there to Stage 4 of
management planning, draft a formal plan of action and implement the two
objectives. However, these are only two of a whole range of tactical
objectives that could contribute to achieving the management objective.
There may be some better options available if the manager had the time and
took the trouble to think about it more carefully, or, if necessary, called in a
specialist adviser. Options are therefore at the same level as tactical
objectives, but they imply a more imaginative approach, suggesting a wide
range of possibilities from which the manager then chooses.

The options finally chosen are then incorporated into the formal plan of
action as management prescriptions.

6.2 Landscape and habitat management options

This section summarises very briefly the main options for the management of habitat and landscape features, with their associated benefits, constraints and conflicts. Only a very superficial treatment can be given here, but more information is given in some of the publications listed in Appendix I. The more you know and understand about this, the more enjoyment you will get out of the conservation side of managing the land.

Conserving habitats and landscapes

Most of this book is about conservation in relation to whole habitats and landscapes. However, you may have found a rare species when doing your habitat assessment, and will therefore want to provide the best environment for it, or you may want to encourage a particular species or group of species onto the land. Factors such as these will affect the way you decide between various habitat or landscape options.

Encouraging particular species

If you want to encourage birds then you may want to encourage scrub to develop on an area of grassland, but if you want to have grassland rich in wild flowers and the butterflies that accompany them, you will be looking for ways to prevent the encroachment of scrub. The summaries given here refer briefly to some of these differences and the reasons for them, to help you to make better informed decisions about your own options.

If you are interested in the preservation or introduction of a particular species of bird or butterfly, for example, you will need to provide exactly the right habitat, and even then, as described in Section 3.3, this is not a guarantee that the species will be present. Many societies have been set up with the aim of encouraging individual species such as barn owls, badgers or otters and they will give advice on their habitat requirements.

Non-intervention

If you have very valuable habitat or landscape areas on your land, the appropriate management objective will be to maintain it in its present condition, and the best option may be to avoid making any changes in the current land management. A few hours or days of over-hasty action can destroy something that will take tens or hundreds of years to replace if it can be done at all. It is therefore important, but often difficult, to persuade managers about the value of doing nothing under some circumstances. If you are not sure how to devise the best options for the management of a highly valued habitat area, ask for expert advice.

Grassland

Fertiliser and pesticide avoidance

As explained in Chapter 3, applying fertiliser or slurry to grassland stimulates the growth of agriculturally useful grasses at the expense of the more diverse natural vegetation. It will also encourage the growth of invasive 'weeds' such as nettle and creeping thistle. If you stop applying fertiliser, the grassland will very slowly become more species-rich and these weeds may gradually become less troublesome. In most areas of herb-rich grassland, occasional patches of nettles or thistles can be tolerated, particularly if they are not spreading. Thistles will attract bees and butterflies to feed on their flowers and nettles are a host plant for the caterpillars of some common butterflies including the small tortoiseshell. If you need to control 'weeds' on herb-rich grassland, cutting them regularly before they flower can be as effective as herbicides in the long run, or alternatively use spot treatments of herbicide or a 'wick' applicator. It is also very important to avoid drift of pesticide and fertiliser from nearby fields.

In most parts of the country, by the process of ecological succession, grassland will gradually become scrub and then woodland if it is not managed, for example, by grazing. Even in the short term, if grazing is stopped, tall grasses will compete more effectively for light and nutrients, displacing some of the more attractive wild plants. On the other hand, excessive grazing will prevent most plants from flowering and seeding and can also lead to **poaching** and soil erosion. The access of animals may therefore need to be restricted, particularly in winter when the soil is wet. The placing of animal feeds in winter, including hay and straw, should either be restricted to an area as small as possible and kept away from any particularly valuable patches of habitat, or spread as widely as possible to minimise the overall damage. As a general rule, light to moderate levels of grazing, with animals excluded during the flowering and seeding period, is ideal to encourage herb-rich grassland. Note also that different animals have different grazing habits: horses are very selective grazers and produce an uneven sward, sheep will nibble the vegetation very close to the ground and cattle tear up rather than bite off the grass. But while sheep produce the shortest sward, cattle and horses deal much better with coarse tussocky grasses and small scrub plants.

encourage herb rich grassland

Controlled burning can be a useful alternative to grazing to remove rank grass growth that would prevent the establishment of a more diverse range of species. It should only be done at the beginning of a long-term management regime to bring more diversity into an area of grassland. The dead grass is best burned off on a dry day in very early spring, taking care to leave a firebreak and to burn only part of the area in any one year.

If carried out after the main flowering period, mowing is an alternative to grazing to maintain a herb-rich sward. If a heavy growth of mown grass is allowed to lie on the surface of the ground it will deprive the plants underneath of light and so kill them. Removing the mown grass helps to deplete the underlying soil of nutrients and will gradually improve the species diversity of the grassland.

Sowing, planting and turf laying are expensive ways to create herb-rich grassland on a large scale. If you have a patch of good species-rich grassland and you would like to encourage it to spread to adjoining areas, then extending the area under favourable management will probably do the trick, with the occasional transplanted turf or strip seeding helping to speed up the process. This is acceptable for the creation of new areas of species-rich grassland, but remember there will be constraints on the introduction of new species into existing good semi-natural habitats.

If grassland has been left unmanaged for long enough to allow scrub to grow, and provided that you want to remove the scrub for wildlife or landscape reasons, cutting bushes down to the stumps and treating the stumps with herbicide or pulling bushes up are the usual, somewhat expensive options. If scrub growth is not too dense and there are not too many thorn-bearing species present, re-introduction of grazing in summer can stop it spreading.

Bracken is not a particularly valuable wildlife habitat and is also poisonous to grazing animals, so clearance is usually seen as a desirable option. However, it does provide nesting sites for some birds and can promote the early growth of grass under the shelter of its dead leaves in spring. It can be cleared by mowing several times a year for three years but this is expensive. It can also be treated by herbicide, either from the air or from a hand-held sprayer. Such treatment must be followed up by a carefully balanced grazing regime otherwise bracken will re-invade the area.

Archaeological features

Grassland maintained by sheep grazing, or a combination of sheep and cattle, is often the best means of preserving archaeological remains, but where sites are near the surface, even minor disturbances to the grass sward can cause serious damage (for example, cattle can cause serious erosion on the steep banks of hill forts). Where the surface has become poached, either by grazing pressure from animals or through visitor pressure, areas can be fenced off and re-seeded until they recover (provided the area is not covered by a management agreement that forbids this). If a herb-rich mixture is used for re-seeding, there will also be corresponding benefits to wildlife. Chain **harrowing** and rolling to prevent matting and to flatten any molehills will not damage the remains if they are done when the ground is dry and you may need to control the activities of rabbits and moles. (However, there are obvious conflicts here between the archaeological and the wildlife interests.) Features that cause animals to congregate, such as water troughs, feeding points or scratching posts, should be sited away from archaeological features.

Arable land

On arable land, it is impractical to ask the manager to refrain from cultivating large areas of land, but where a small site is involved it could be left as a grassy, uncultivated island, with a buffer zone to protect it from encroachment. Anything that increases the depth of cultivation can cause damage, for example sub-soiling or even soil erosion which leads inadvertently to the plough penetrating into deeper soil strata.

Heathland and moorland

The aim of management on most heathland and moorland is to maintain healthy young growth of heather and other heaths and to prevent their replacement by grasses, bracken or scrub. When artificially managed, there should be a mosaic of heather stands of varying ages, with stands of up to two hectares in size being ideal for sheep, but stands of a much smaller minimum diameter, about 50 metres, for grouse. If the grazing pressure is low, you could consider letting bushes die naturally; they will then be replaced by new bushes, resulting in natural uneven-aged stands. This is good for the **lichens** that colonise old heather bushes.

Controlled grazing

Heather moorland is very vulnerable to changes in grazing intensity. Moderate grazing pressure, with about 40% of the weight of each year's production of heather being removed, will not cause any damage. Over-grazing, particularly in autumn and winter, will lead to rapid loss of heather plants. Young heather plants, about 4–8 years old, are preferred by sheep and are more resistant to grazing pressure than old heather. Any factor that concentrates animals at a particular site, for example the distribution of winter feed, will cause extensive damage to heather in the surrounding area by trampling. On peaty soils, over-grazing can lead to erosion, which can spread at an alarming rate, preventing the re-establishment of any vegetation.

Controlled burning

Moderate burning, ideally every 7–10 years, will encourage the regeneration of new, young heather growth, either from seed or from the base of the old stems. The older and taller the heather is allowed to become before burning, the greater the danger that fierce heat from the fire will kill it altogether, so failing to burn at the proper time can be costly. (Under these circumstances, the solution may be to burn under non-ideal weather conditions when the ground and the vegetation are slightly damp, but even then stock may have to be excluded from the area for two years afterwards to allow the heather to grow back.) On wetter, blanket bogs the heather is less vigorous, less likely to need regular burning, and may even be damaged by it. However, burning only small areas at a time is likely to concentrate too many animals on the new growth. The dates when heather can be burned are controlled by law, and some tenancy agreements will place additional restrictions on the tenant. Burning should be done early in the year, before the end of March and well before the time when nesting birds begin to claim their territories. It can sometimes be done in autumn, but the winter cold then has an adverse effect on the rate of regeneration. It is thus very important to achieve a balance between burning to give a carefully controlled age structure of the heather plants and the distribution and extent of grazing pressure on them.

Cutting

Cutting instead of burning heather can be useful close to trees, or where the plants have become very old and woody. However, the new growth sometimes takes place more slowly, at least in the short term, and stock may have to be excluded for a while.

Bracken control

Bracken invasion is a serious problem on moorland, particularly newly burned areas. It can be discouraged to some extent by leaving a broad strip of unburned heather around any patches of bracken. Methods for bracken clearance are described above under 'Grassland'.

Scrub clearance

Scrub can be a useful wildlife habitat and should not automatically be regarded as undesirable. However, it can make life difficult for shepherds, and the habitat it is invading may be more valuable still. Serious problems are created in some areas by the invasion of rhododendron, which can have a spectacular contribution to the landscape but is of little value for wildlife. The usual method of scrub control is to cut stumps close to the ground, burn the cut wood and treat the stumps with herbicide.

Re-seeding

Where heather has been killed off by excessive grazing or around areas where winter feed is put out, rotavating and laying heather litter on the surface, or re-seeding with heather will probably be necessary.

Archaeological sites

Archaeological remains found in lowland heaths are usually very fragile and vulnerable and many areas of lowland heath have already been lost to other land uses. The best management option is to maintain the vegetation cover intact. On upland sites, minimising disturbance is also the key to their preservation, and because the soil cover is often thin they can be very vulnerable. Stone clearance or the use of ancient **cairns** as a source of stone for other buildings should be strictly avoided. Avoid burning heather where there is a danger of disturbing archaeological remains.

Lowland wetlands and marshland

In lowland situations, if your objective is to retain or improve an area of wetland or marshland, it will sometimes need to be protected from incursion by scrub and also from the effects of other land uses on surrounding areas.

Water level control

If you have attempted unsuccessfully to drain an area in the past and have now decided to allow it to remain as wetland, you may need to block off old drainage ditches before it will develop its full potential as marshland.

Grazing control

Some grazing is beneficial to most marshy areas. For example, the fen violet was thought to be extinct on Woodwalton Fen National Nature Reserve until cattle grazing was re-introduced. However, excessive grazing can reduce the diversity of plant life and animals will break up the vegetation cover with their hooves (poaching). This can be particularly serious where animals collect regularly to drink and sensitive areas may need to be fenced off. On the other hand, poached areas will provide feeding sites for some birds. Restricting grazing to late summer, autumn and, to a lesser extent, winter is the best option. If grazing is prevented altogether scrub will probably encroach rapidly.

Scrub clearance

A few trees, such as willow and alder, can be interesting landscape features and, in moderation, they will probably improve the habitat value of marshland. However, unless you actually want to create woodland in the area in question, some of the invading scrub will need to be cleared manually by cutting and treating stumps with herbicide.

Pollution prevention

STOP fertilisation

Contamination with fertiliser can be just as damaging to wetlands as to grassland, causing a rapid reduction in species diversity. You should try to ensure that valuable conservation wetlands are not contaminated by run-off from fields treated with fertiliser and pesticides. In some areas you may also need to guard against contamination by sheep dips and silage effluent. Where contamination with fertiliser is inevitable, it may be better to plant an area with trees, rather than attempt to diversify the wetland interest. If an area has been fertilised in the past but this has now stopped, diversity will gradually increase and can be speeded up by cutting and removing the vegetation in autumn (a somewhat labour intensive exercise).

Archaeological sites

Wetland sites are particularly important for the preservation of archaeological remains, but these are very vulnerable to drying out or drainage of the area. Small areas of wetland are particularly important where drainage can be controlled by the landowner and where peat cutting has not penetrated medieval and earlier deposits. Traditional grazing practices and reed harvesting will preserve sealed remains. Trees should not normally be encouraged as they will tend to dry out the land and their roots will penetrate and disturb buried deposits. The edges of wetland areas are likely to contain some of the best archaeological evidence but will also be most at risk of drying out. It is often impossible to know what lies buried under peat and chance finds often lead to major discoveries.

Open water

Creating and maintaining areas of open water is usually closely linked with the management of marshy and wetland areas. You should only attempt to create new ponds in areas likely to retain water throughout the year and where the water is not contaminated with slurry, fertiliser, pesticide residues, or other pollutants. If you have a good clean water supply on soil that will not retain water, you can use special waterproof lining material.

Excavation

Ponds should have a varying depth (with at least 50% being 1.5–2 metres deep to avoid invasion by aggressive marsh vegetation and to prevent ice from forming right to the bottom in winter) and an irregular outline, with an island if possible. There should also be several areas where the banks slope gradually into the water to allow easy access for birds and small animals. A fairly shallow pond is fine for most wildlife purposes but if you want to keep trout in it, it should be at least 3.5 metres deep. Soil dug out of the pond should be spread far enough away to allow easy access to the banks. Take care to avoid dumping spoil on any species rich areas. If the pond is stream-fed, it is useful to have a sluice gate to control the inflow of water and a silt trap to prevent the pond from silting up. All ponds will eventually fill up with debris and require dredging from time to time (Plate 13), preferably on a rotational basis, covering only part of the pond area in any one season. If you have a pond that is a poor shape for encouraging wildlife and game, you can take the opportunity to change this when it is being cleaned out.

The requirements for the prevention of water pollution are similar to those of wetland and marshy areas.

Pollution prevention

Some trees around a pond are useful to provide shade, particularly if the pond is very shallow. However, as explained in Section 4.2, too much shade will prevent plant life, the basis of the food chain, from growing in the water, and too many decaying leaves will remove oxygen from the water. It is therefore better to place most of the trees on the north and east sides of the pond.

Clearing surrounding vegetation

If a few plant species native to the region are introduced to a new pond, they will quickly colonise it and attract insects, birds and other species. If you are cleaning out a pond, set aside some of the vegetation for re-planting afterwards.

Plant introduction

Ditches, drains and rivers

Like all linear habitats, these features are particularly useful as wildlife corridors, linking other areas of habitat. However, they have a major function in draining land and are often intensively managed in ways that are not very considerate of wildlife or the landscape. On farmed land, they are often affected by agricultural activity nearby. As with several of the other habitats dealt with above, there are three threats to the wildlife and landscape value of these features — over-zealousness, under-zealousness and pollution. Excessive zeal in keeping everything neat and tidy will retard the development of a diverse and interesting habitat; lack of management effort may allow a restricted number of species to dominate the area, reducing its diversity. Figure 6.1 (overleaf) is a plan for the management of a river by a water authority, showing how a range of options were put into practice.

For drainage ditches, it is necessary to keep the level of water below that of the field drains running into them, but within this constraint the ditch should be as shallow as possible. Drains will probably need to be cleared out once every 4–6 years and it is better to do short stretches in rotation than to do a long stretch all at once. The soil taken from a ditch bed is often rich in nitrogen and, if possible, would be better spread on adjoining agricultural land rather than on the ditch banks, which have the potential to support a diverse selection of wild plants. If there is water present all the year round in a ditch, there will be a greater diversity of water plants and animals. Emptying the water out of drains in winter is particularly bad for wildlife conservation. Even natural streams and rivers are often heavily managed, with the path of the stream being straightened out and obstacles to the flow of water removed. However, Figure 6.1 shows that this is not necessary for efficient river management.

Controlling the water level and flow

The use of herbicides and mechanical methods for the management of vegetation will have advantages and disadvantages for plant diversity. Clearing the banks in rotation, in a 3-year cycle, preferably in autumn, ensures that there is always some useful habitat available to act as a refuge for animals and insects. The same principles apply to river bank management but here the pressures for regular maintenance are not usually so great.

Bank management

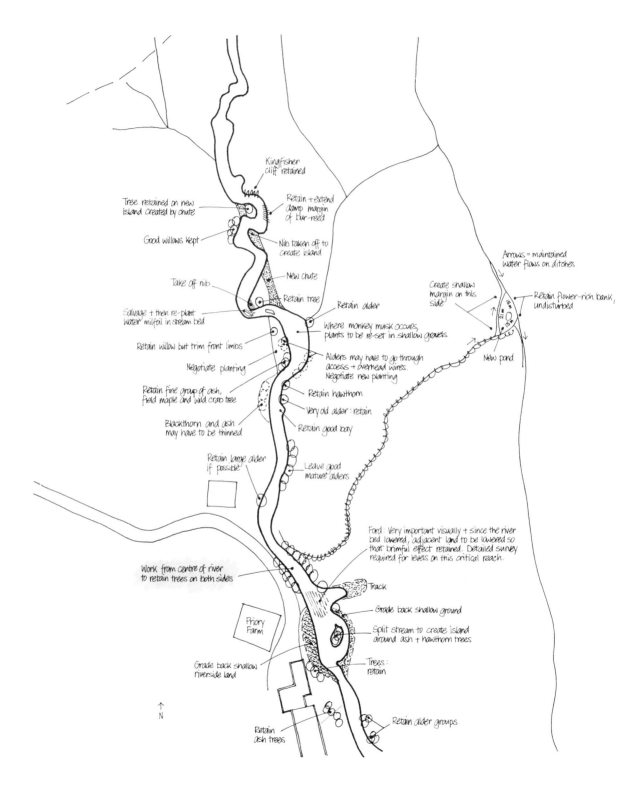

Figure 6.1 River and bank management: landscape and habitat options
(Source: Severn Trent Water Authority)

Drainage ditches on farms are particularly prone to contamination by pesticides, fertilisers, silage effluent and slurry. It is very important to avoid excessive applications of chemicals, to be careful not to spray under windy conditions, not to allow spray booms to contaminate the ditch bank and to keep a careful watch on effluents. Deliberate contamination with chemicals, for example by tank washings, is illegal. Because of their low profile in the landscape, ditches tend to be favoured dumping grounds for all sorts of rubbish and this should particularly be avoided for chemical containers, plastic sacks, oil drums and other farm wastes. *Pollution prevention*

The regular use of a river for drinking by grazing animals will quickly break down the banks. This can be controlled, if necessary, by using fencing to limit the animals' access to the river. However, up to a point, the opening up of river banks by animals in this way can be useful for wildlife, creating open, sunny banks for ducks and feeding areas for small waders. *Grazing control*

On deep narrow ditches and streams, leave an occasional branch or plank across the water to help small animals to cross and to provide perches for birds. *Providing crossing points and perches*

If a bank has been badly managed in the past, either by contamination with herbicide or by lack of cutting, it can be **scarified** and re seeded with a wild plant mixture appropriate to the local soil and conditions. *Re-seeding*

Rivers and streams can stand a greater amount of shading by trees than ponds, up to 60% shade being acceptable. Turbulence in the water will help to mix in oxygen and fallen leaves are less of a problem as the detritus food chain is very important here. Trees beside a river or ditch will restrict access for tractors and machinery. If the stream or ditch is not too wide, access to both banks can be gained from one side only without disturbing trees and bushes. Larger streams and ditches can be tree-lined on both banks with tractor access from the watercourse itself (Figure 6.1) provided it is not too deep and has a solid bottom, although this will damage the stream bed to some extent. Large tree roots and shrubs that may provide otter holts and hiding places should be protected. *Planting or removing trees and shrubs*

To protect archaeological sites in rivers, dredging and clearance work should not cut deeper into the river bed than the previous channel, and banks should be stabilised to prevent erosion. Weirs and other river features can be very old and care should be taken when repairing them. **Levees** and artificial banks often preserve interesting features, and maintaining pasture and minimising activity when the ground is flooded will continue to protect them. Where there are sedimentary deposits, the plough depth should be kept above the base level of the deposit and areas with surface earthworks should be kept under pasture. *Archaeological sites*

Hedgerows, field margins and roadside verges

These three habitats are often closely associated and the management options for one will often affect the others. Conservation headlands on arable fields have been developed as a way of minimising the impact of intensive agriculture on wildlife in the field boundaries, and these are also included under this heading. (See also Box 3.2.)

Large bushy hedges are better for wildlife and are also more prominent landscape features than small, neatly clipped ones. However, they do need to be managed carefully, by 'laying' the hedge (cutting part-way through the stems and weaving them together horizontally, as shown in Plate 14) every *Shape and regeneration of the hedge*

management of hedgerows

15–20 years and trimming, usually with a mechanical flail, at shorter intervals. If cutting is done in autumn on a rotational basis, every 3 years, it will allow some berries to remain on the bushes to feed birds in winter, avoid disturbing nesting birds in spring, and probably fit most conveniently with other business activities on the land. Different shapes of hedge will benefit wildlife in different ways and will have different landscape impacts. Unless there are reasons for having one shape of hedge on your land, it is probably better to have a variety. A tall 'A' shape encourages a thick hedge bottom and provides good cover for game. A hedge with straight sides and a rounded top will allow a greater diversity of plants to flourish in the hedge bottom. The advantages and disadvantages of various hedge management options are summarised in Table 6.1.

Hedge removal

Hedges are still being removed occasionally, for example to enlarge fields to make cultivations easier. If you are removing hedges for such reasons, take care to concentrate on the least diverse and least valuable from a landscape point of view, and try to re-plant an equivalent area elsewhere. On an arable farm, you may also want to consider the shade cast by the hedge on the crop (hedges running north–south create fewer problems of shading than those running east–west). However, if you are rearing animals, the shade will be a valuable asset.

Table 6.1 Hedge management options

	Advantages	Disadvantages	Frequency	Approx. cost
Laying	Creates stock-proof barrier Forms thick, dense shelter Young re-growth can be flail trimmed	Labour intensive Unsuitable for very overgrown woody or gappy hedges	Every 8–20 years	Contract labour £4 per metre at 15 metres per day; volunteer labour 50p–£1 per metre at 5 metres per day
Coppicing	Brings overgrown hedges back into management Encourages bushy growth and rejuvenates hedge bottom Provides firewood	Not stock-proof Susceptible to browsing Labour-intensive if done manually	Every 6–12 years	Contract labour £10–£15 per hour; volunteer labour £1–£2 per metre
Flail cutting	Quick, cheap method of regular trimming Keeps hedge thick and compact	Splinters older, woody growth Fertilises hedge bottom Repetition weakens hedge and loses 'bottom' Encourages cleavers and climbing plants	Every 2–3 years	Contract labour £10–£15 per hour at 3 miles per day, i.e. 2–3 pence per linear metre
Blade trimming	Tackles 2–5 year old growth Clean cut, less damaging to hedge than flailing No fertiliser effect to hedge bottom	Will not encourage bottom growth in very 'leggy' hedges Removal of cuttings time consuming Difficult to retain hedgerow trees	Every 2–3 years	As flail cutting

If hedges are trimmed to an 'A' shape, it is easy to mark strong young saplings to be avoided by the hedge trimmer and allowed to grow into hedgerow trees. Alternatively, trees, preferably native species, can be specially planted and marked to remind tractor drivers not to cut them. The usual marker used is a piece of durable plastic ribbon tied to a main branch.

Encouraging hedgerow trees

Hedges, like ditches, are particularly vulnerable to damage by fire during straw burning, or to contamination by fertiliser and pesticides as a result of spray drift. The same precautions should be taken as described for ditches.

Pollution and fire prevention

Where hedges have been allowed to become too tall with little growth at the base, they can be coppiced. Hazel, ash, hawthorn and blackthorn will respond particularly well to this treatment. The new growth will need to be protected from grazing animals and also from rabbits and hares (see Table 6.1).

Hedge rejuvenation

Where new hedges are being planted, or old ones re planted, a mixture of native species should be used. Where grazing stock have access to the hedge, it will have to be fenced off, on both sides if necessary and it may also need protection from rabbits and hares. If an old hedge is to be stock-proof, any gaps will need to be re-planted and also protected while young. However, if the hedge does not need to be stock-proof, a few gaps here and there may not be worth bothering about. They will let passers-by see through to a view that would otherwise be blocked by a tall hedge.

Planting and re-planting

The grass verge at the bottom of a hedge can be just as important for wildlife as the hedge itself. The management options, whether or not they are associated with hedges or ditches, are much the same as for other grassland areas. However, verges, being boundary features, are much more vulnerable to disturbance from the other activities going on around them. Roadside verges can become heavily contaminated by salt in winter and field margins are vulnerable to contamination by pesticides and fertiliser. Verges should be managed, if possible, by cutting and removing the vegetation, rather than using herbicides.

Managing grass verges

The suggestion to reduce chemical sprays on crop headlands at critical times of the year was first proposed by the Game Conservancy (see Box 3.2) and can also be applied to fertiliser spreading on grassland. Figure 6.2 illustrates the principles underlying this idea, which is to avoid spraying a 6 metre wide strip close to the hedgerow. Originally only herbicides were avoided, thus allowing annual plants to grow and provide food for game birds. But

Conservation headlands

Hedgerow

Sterile strip

← 6 m →
Unsprayed margin containing

Weeds	Insects
Knotgrass	Leaf beetles
Fat hen	Weevils
Mayweed	Plant bugs
Chickweed	Sawfly larvae
Annual meadow-grass	Caterpillars

Figure 6.2 Conservation headlands in cereal crops (Source: Potts, 1986)

113

increasingly insecticides and fungicides are also avoided, with little yield penalty from this reduced control. To prevent the invasion of the crop from the hedgerow by serious 'weeds', a sterile strip, either sprayed or cultivated, may be required. A sterile strip is less essential on grassland.

Broad-leaved woodland

The ideal options for landscape conservation and for wildlife in broad-leaved woodland often coincide but this is not always the case. For example, sycamores are less valuable than some other species as wildlife habitat but they may be a desirable option for landscape reasons and they are a valuable timber tree. In more exposed parts of the country sycamore may be one of the few large broad-leaved trees that will grow at all. The introduction of game-related objectives has, in the past, meant that many non-native shrub species were used in the understorey. However, yew and holly are just as useful as, for example, snowberry (an introduced shrub) in providing cover for game.

Planting

In the absence of other constraints, it is usually desirable to plant a mixed stand of broad-leaved species with compatible growth rates that are suitable for the soil and climatic conditions. Sometimes, a nurse crop of conifers will be helpful in establishing a broad-leaved stand. Table 6.2 gives a brief summary of the properties and requirements of common native trees. Your choice of species will depend partly on the extent to which you also want to make an income from the wood, either from game or from timber. You will often need to protect young trees from livestock, rabbits, hares or deer, and protection is usually compulsory for grant-aided schemes.

Coppicing

Many lowland broad-leaved woods were coppiced in the past: species such as hazel, ash and chestnut were cut on a 5 to 25 year rotation, with a scattering of standard trees, often oak, allowed to grow to maturity. Coppicing benefits many wildlife species, allowing light to get to the woodland floor and greatly increasing the diversity of the understorey, before the new growth eventually cuts out the light again. However, the process is labour intensive and in many areas there are few markets for the timber, although there are signs in the south-east of England of a revival in the market for firewood, coppiced chestnut and broad-leaved wood pulp. Sometimes volunteer labour can be found to do coppicing or, as it is a winter activity, there may be spare labour available to the land manager. Coppicing should not be chosen as an automatic option for broad-leaved woodland — it is only useful in woods that have the right ground vegetation to benefit from it.

Natural regeneration

Where woodland or patches of woodland have been felled, and where there is a plentiful source of seed, woodland will regenerate naturally. The species mix will be more uncertain but probably more natural for the area than a planted stand, and it may grow more quickly. Most people involved in woodland management can point to areas where trees have been planted at considerable expense, only to be overtaken rapidly by natural regeneration. Where good natural regeneration is taking place it may be worth using tree guards to protect saplings.

Ride and glade maintenance

The creation and maintenance of broad rides and glades in woodland has similar advantages for wildlife to those provided by coppicing. The edges of the **glade** or ride should be tiered, with close-cut grass in the centre, surrounded by longer vegetation cut every 2 years, and a coppiced area at the edge of the woodland.

From the business point of view, it is often useful to allow animals to graze in woodland or to shelter there in winter. As long as you do this on a rotational basis and take care not to allow the animals to debark the trees, this will do no long-term harm to the wildlife or landscape. If it is done to excess, the understorey will disappear, making the woods less valuable for shelter and there will be no natural regeneration. If the wood is large enough, excluding grazing animals on a 20 year rotation will allow natural regeneration to continue.

Grazing control

Standing and fallen dead wood is useful to many insects and birds, and leaving some in a woodland will have no adverse effects, even for commercial management. Excessive amounts can be cleared away. In amenity woodland, leaving some fallen trees can, for example, distract children from climbing standing trees, but it is important to make sure that such trees are safe.

Clearing dead wood

Where ancient woodlands are becoming invaded by unwanted species, such as sycamore or rhododendron, they should be removed and the stumps treated with herbicide. Large specimens of sycamore may have a commercial value as timber, but when such trees are removed there is likely to be a very rapid growth of young seedlings in the cleared area, and action will need to be taken to control them, either by cutting or spot treatment with herbicide. In secondary woodland, it is probably not worthwhile attempting to manage the species mix in this way, except when the wood is being re-planted.

Removing undesirable species

The kind of shrub and ground level vegetation in a wood is very important in determining its habitat value. Some trees, such as beech or sycamore, cast a dense shade and extract most of the water from the soil surface, making it very difficult to establish other plants beneath them. Native species that have berries, for example elder, hawthorn and bramble, will provide food for birds, but the roots of elder secrete a toxin that inhibits the growth of other plants. Many of the shrubs recommended for game **coverts** in woodland are not native species, but if they have edible berries they will provide food for other wildlife and also shelter in winter. Where there is a choice, native species will encourage a greater diversity of wildlife than non-native species.

Managing the understorey

The edge is the most important part of woodland habitat for many species of wildlife and game but it can be particularly vulnerable to interference from other activities on the land. In this respect it should be treated as hedgerow. It will also get more light than the rest of the wood and so develop a more prolific understorey. This can often be managed to create a fairly impenetrable boundary to the wood, controlling public access and giving greater shelter within the wood.

Managing the woodland edge

Ancient woodland is itself a feature of archaeological interest, and sites that have been wooded for hundreds of years will probably have ancient boundaries and evidence of various forms of woodland management such as coppicing, pasturing, or charcoal burning. Many areas of more recent woodland will conceal archaeological features that originated when the site was not wooded. Trees have in the past been deliberately planted on prominent features because no other productive use could be found for the land, or to enhance its visibility in the landscape. However, this is not recommended practice, as the roots of trees can cause serious disturbance to the underlying layers. Nevertheless, woodland has in some cases preserved ancient sites from cultivation and hence destruction. Ideally monuments should be preserved in clearings and glades within the woodland.

Archaeological features

Table 6.2 Native British shrubs and trees and their natural range

E	Box *(Buxus sempervirens)*	Only native on limestone in Kent, Surrey, Bucks. and Glos., but widely planted in gardens and churchyards.
	Bird cherry *(Prunus padus)*	Common on wetter sites, especially in valleys, in northern England, Wales and Scotland.
	Crab apple *(Malus sylvestris)*	Found throughout Britain, except in northern Scotland. Avoids dense woodland. Rarely exceeds 8 m in height.
	Hawthorn *(Crataegus monogyna)*	Widespread. Also known as may, quickthorn and whitethorn. Common in hedges; often planted.
	Midland hawthorn *(Crataegus oxyacanthoides)*	Also known as woodland hawthorn. Mainly in ancient woodland in south and east England, especially on heavy clay soils.
CF	Hazel *(Corylus avellana)*	Common throughout Britain except on very acid soils. Usually less than 10 m in height.
E	Common juniper *(Juniperus communis)*	On limestone soils especially of southern England. Also on acidic mountain soils in the north. Rarely exceeds 6 m in height.
	Bay willow *(Salix pentandra)*	Uncommon. On wet sites in N. Wales, northern England and Scotland.
CF	Goat willow *(Salix caprea)*	Widespread. Will grow on drier soils than any other willow species in Britain.

CT	Common alder *(Alnus glutinosa)*	Widespread, mainly where the water table is constantly high.
	Aspen *(Populus tremula)*	Widespread, except on soils with a high lime content and in dense woodland. Also avoids very dry soils.
CFT	Downy birch *(Betula pubescens)*	Widespread, but more common in the north and west. Grows on wetter and higher sites than its relative, silver birch, and chiefly on acid soils.
E	Holly *(Ilex aquifolium)*	Widespread and tolerant of a wide range of soil types. Often grows in the understorey of woodland.
C	Rowan or mountain ash *(Sorbus aucuparia)*	Widespread except in south-east England. In Scotland it grows at a higher altitude than any other tree. Avoids clay soils.
	Wild service tree *(Sorbus torminalis)*	With a few exceptions found only to the south of the Mersey/Humber. In woods, especially on clay soils. Most common in the south-east. Usually thought to be an indicator of ancient woodland.
	Whitebeam *(Sorbus aria)*	Mainly in woodland and scrub on limestone in southern England, with a scattered distribution elsewhere.
	Crack willow *(Salix fragilis)*	Widespread except in northern Scotland. Prefers wet, deep, but not too acidic soils. More tolerant of poor soil than white willow.
FT	White willow *(Salix alba)*	Widespread except in Scotland. Avoids acid and waterlogged soils, but mainly found in valleys and alongside rivers and streams.
ET	Yew *(Taxus baccata)*	Mainly on limestone in England and Wales in woods and scrub. Also widely planted, requiring a well drained soil.

CFT	Silver birch *(Betula pendula)*	Widespread, mainly on acid soils, and on drier soils than downy birch.
CFT	Wild cherry or gean *(Prunus avium)*	Widespread in Britain except in the extreme north. Frequent in woods and occasionally found in hedgerows, except on less fertile soils.
CF	Field maple *(Acer campestre)*	Can exceed 25 m (75 ft) in height on good sites. Confined to England and Wales. Frequent in woodland and hedgerows, especially on lime-rich soils in south and east England.
CF	Hornbeam *(Carpinus betulus)*	Native only in south-east England, especially on damp clays, but much planted elsewhere.

FT	Large-leaved lime (*Tilia platyphyllous*)	Native only on limestone soils in the Wye Valley and parts of the Pennines.
CFT	Small-leaved lime (*Tilia cordata*)	Found mainly in woods, particularly on deep, fertile and less acid soils. Confined to England and Wales. Now thought to have been much more abundant formerly, but poor reproduction by seed has caused its decline and confined it mainly to ancient woodland.
CFT	Sessile oak (*Quercus petraea*)	Widespread on acid soils and tolerant of a wide range of conditions, including both freely drained and frequently waterlogged soils.
ET	Scots pine (*Pinus sylvestris*)	Truly native only in northern Scotland, but occurs naturally elsewhere, particularly on heathland. Prefers acid soils, but is tolerant of both drought and some waterlogging.
	Black poplar (*Populus nigra* var. *betulifolia*)	This variety is the only native British black poplar. Confined to alluvial soils in England and Wales and now declining. Distinguished by its arching branches with their upswept tips.

Mature height range 36–45 m (118–147.5 ft)

CFT	Ash (*Fraxinus excelsior*)	Widespread and common. Tolerant of a wide range of soil conditions. One of the easiest species to establish successfully.
FT	Beech (*Fagus sylvatica*)	Native in southern England and Wales, but widely planted. Tolerant of all but poorly drained sites and sensitive to late spring frost.
CFT	Wych elm (*Ulmus glabra*)	Native throughout Britain but now much affected by Dutch elm disease. For this reason planting is not recommended at present.
CFT	Common oak (*Quercus robur*)	Widespread except in the extreme north and especially common on deep clays and loams. Less tolerant of dry, shallow soils and also waterlogging than sessile oak.

Native shrubs of Britain commonly associated with woodland

Blackthorn or sloe (*Prunus spinosa*) Up to 4 m (13′)	Widespread and common except in northern Scotland. On all except very acid or peaty soils. Intolerant of dense shade.
Alder buckthorn (*Frangula alnus*) Up to 5 m (16.5′)	Mainly on moist, acidic soils in lowland England and Wales, but also on lime-rich fenland peat. Cannot tolerate permanent waterlogging.
Purging buckthorn (*Rhamnus catharticus*) Up to 6 m (19.5′) rarely to 10 m (33′)	Confined to lime-rich soils, on limestone and in fens, in England and Wales.
Dogwood (*Cornus sanguinea*) Up to 5 m (16.5′)	Widespread in England and Wales, especially on lime-rich soils. Avoids dense woodland.
Elder (*Sambucus nigra*) Up to 10 m (33′)	Widespread except in northern Scotland. Frequently found on lime-rich soils, on disturbed land and on land rich in nitrogen.
Guelder rose (*Viburnum opulus*) Up to 4 m (13′)	Widespread, but rare in northern Scotland. Avoids very acid and very dry sites and dense woodland. Thrives on moist soils.
Privet (*Ligustrum vulgare*) Up to 5 m (16.5′)	Widespread in England and Wales, especially in light woodland on thin, dry lime-rich soils. Cannot tolerate waterlogging.
Spindle (*Euonymous europaeus*) Up to 6 m (19.5′)	In England, Wales and southern Scotland. Common in woods and scrub on lime-rich soils.
Wayfaring tree (*Viburnum lantana*) Up to 6 m (19.5′)	Confined to the south of England and Wales, nearly always on dry lime-rich soils. Cannot grow on waterlogged soils or in dense shade.
Grey willow (*Salix cinerea*) Usually to 5 m (16.5′) rarely to 10 m (33′)	Very similar to *Salix caprea*, but classed as a shrub due to its size. Widespread. More tolerant of acid soils than *S. caprea*, but less tolerant of dry soils, thriving in moist conditions.

Code: E: Evergreen   C: Coppices well   F: Suitable for firewood   T: Suitable for timber production

(Source: Hamilton, 1985)

As described already in Boxes 2.3 and 4.1, the objectives and options being adopted today for many commercial coniferous forests are very different from those of 20 years ago. Figure 6.3 illustrates some of the planting, maintenance, thinning and felling options now recommended by the Forestry Commission for encouraging wildlife and landscape conservation in commercial coniferous woods, as outlined below.

Planting

The Scots pine is the only native conifer and it has considerable wildlife value when planted in the highlands of Scotland. Some of the remaining patches of old Caledonian pine forest that used to cover large areas of Scotland are now preserved as nature reserves. Further south, the interesting shape of the trees can be an attractive landscape feature, but they have less wildlife value. The Scots pine is also a commercially valuable tree, although it is less useful for wildlife when planted at commercial densities. Most new commercial coniferous plantations will consist largely of non-native trees, usually a mixture of species to add variety to the landscape. Wildlife and habitat interest, and further landscape value, are added by encouraging or specially planting broad-leaved trees at the edges of commercial plantations and along roadsides and river banks.

Glade management

Glades in coniferous woods are essential for the efficient management of deer populations and they also help to increase the area of edge habitats that are more valuable for wildlife. Good fodder is needed to attract the deer and so glades are often sited along the banks of streams where conifers should not be planted (see Box 4.1). Also, when a new forest is being planted any areas of high quality grassland habitat can be left as glades, when natural grazing by deer will help to maintain their species diversity.

The design of roads, stream banks, fence-lines, firebreaks and felling patterns

As mentioned in Chapter 2, roads and firebreaks and felling coupes should not be cut in straight lines, but following the line of natural features to blend in with the landscape and within the constraints of the landowner's boundaries and economic considerations. Felling and planting patterns should be in sympathy with the landform and scale of the area. In hilly areas, as shown by the ploughing patterns in Figure 4.1, the forest edge should come further down the hill where the landform is convex, and retreat further up the hill where it is concave. Figure 6.4 (overleaf) shows how additional diversity of landscape and habitat can be introduced by planting irregularly shaped groups of broad-leaved trees. The most economical route for a boundary fence is as straight a line as possible, but this need not be an intrusive feature of the landscape if the forest edge inside the fence follows the landform. The best way to plan the design of these features is to begin with an enlarged photograph, drawing the features onto a sheet of tracing paper placed over it, or to project a transparency onto a large sheet of drawing paper. The final design should then be transferred to an aerial photograph or large-scale map, prior to marking areas out on the ground. Plate 15 shows a section of a working forest felling and re-planting plan prepared in this way for the hillside shown in Plate 9.

Archaeological sites

Modern ploughing machinery, often used to prepare upland sites for afforestation, should be kept well clear of any archaeological sites. Ideally, monuments should be preserved in clearings and glades within the woodland.

Figure 6.3 Options for improving upland forests for birds (Source: Forestry Commission, April 1982)

Planting

A *Planting is kept well back from the sides of streams, gullies, roads, large old trees, hedgerows, buildings and rock outcrops*

B *Natural broad-leaved trees are retained, allowing natural regeneration to colonise open spaces*

C *Small bogs and wet hollows are left undrained*

D *Existing natural features are used to create compartments or boundaries for varying species*

Maintenance

E *Retain all natural vegetation that does not threaten the planted crop*

F *Woody growth on road verges should be cut instead of using herbicides*

Thinning and felling

G *Avoid felling any broad-leaved trees on plantation edges including roadsides and riversides*

H *Keep clear of streams, hedgerows, clumps of broad-leaved trees when positioning rackways for timber extraction*

I *Brash should be kept back from banks to avoid choking streams*

J *Retain large dead trees and trees used for nesting*

K *Do not fell trees that would be uneconomic to extract from screes, crags or islands*

L *Avoid felling in sites identified as having special conservation value and do not extract timber through them*

M *By retaining small groups of mature trees, the diversity of the forest is increased*

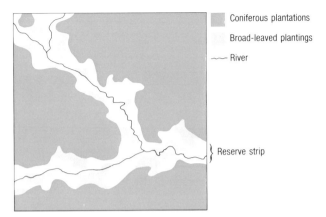

Legend:
- Coniferous plantations
- Broad-leaved plantings
- River
- Reserve strip

Figure 6.4 Introducing diversity in commercial coniferous forestry

Scrub

Scrub is often seen as undesirable habitat, something to be removed or converted to an earlier or later stage in the succession. However, it can provide very diverse wildlife habitat in its own right, because of the variety in vertical structure and numbers of species. It has usually developed on grassland that has been under-grazed and, if the right conditions exist, will be part of a long-term ecological succession to broad-leaved woodland. Areas of scrub with sufficient diversity to form good wildlife habitat have usually arisen as an accidental by-product of an unmonitored management regime, and it can be very difficult to reproduce the same conditions to order on a different site, or even to keep a good area in its present condition.

Mowing, cutting and grazing

If feasible, mowing can be introduced to create rides and glades and help to keep the open structure of the scrub. Where bushes have become too old and dense and formed a canopy they can be coppiced. The fresh young growth that results will be valuable for wildlife. As scrub is usually the product of a grazing regime, continued light grazing can be the best way of maintaining it. However, animals can be very difficult to control on such areas and if the land is to be used for pasture there will be a strong temptation to remove the scrub altogether.

Structures

Buildings and other structures such as walls, gateposts and stiles will have a major impact on the quality of the landscape and can also affect wildlife. Buildings may, for example, provide nesting sites for birds and roosting sites for bats. Old structures should be preserved where possible and new structures should be in sympathy with the existing local style. These points should be taken up with the architect or planner when new buildings are being designed or old ones renovated. Footpaths and rights of way should also be maintained regularly, in keeping with the surrounding landscape.

6.3 An imaginative approach to the business as a whole

Section 6.2 attempted to supply some of the background knowledge needed to choose the best options for your own land management objectives. This section helps you to provide the other key ingredient — imagination. It introduces techniques for stimulating creative ideas about new options for incorporating conservation alongside other land uses. Some people do this kind of thing naturally while others find it very difficult. Children are often particularly good at it so make use of any whose services you can call on.

1 *Being stimulated by your environment*. Try to think about your objectives in a completely unrelated context, such as what you see from the window on a train journey or an article in a newspaper or magazine. Keep a small notebook handy and write down any ideas as they occur to you — do not rely on your memory.

2 *Being provoked by your friends and colleagues (brainstorming)*. This is best done in a relaxed atmosphere where you will not be interrupted and can be as noisy as you like. The local pub would be a good place provided you have a sympathetic bar tender and a pencil and some paper to hand. Four to six people is a good number, not necessarily conservationists, but preferably people who have a detached view of your problem and have not been involved in the earlier stages of management planning. Each should suggest ideas as they occur to them, no matter how ridiculous they seem at the time, with a ban on criticism from the others. One person has the job of writing down all the ideas on a large sheet of paper. Every now and then, when the flow of ideas begins to dry up, the group should stop and review what has come up and see if any of the ideas suggest ways of making real progress.

3 *Inviting criticism*. Seek out people with different views from your own. Even if they seem ill-informed, or extremist, try to get them to tell you what they think, and listen to what they say. You may get some ideas you would never think of alone.

4 *Looking for new angles*. What fantasies can you spin around the ideas of your objectives and constraints? Write down the words or images that come to mind when you think about your objectives.

These techniques can be applied to your objectives and can help you to find ways around any conflicts, contradictions or constraints that may be embedded in them. The ideas you come up with should therefore be integrative. Figure 6.5 in Section 6.7 shows the result of a brainstorming session with the farmer, a conservation adviser and an outsider, based on the objectives tree in Figure 5.5. As you can see, most of the ideas that emerged were related to diversifying the farm business in ways that are 'friendly' towards conservation, i.e. ways of resolving the potential conflict between the two strategic objectives in the farmer's objectives tree.

Any of these techniques is likely to come up with more options than you could ever expect to put into practice, some of them fairly silly if you have been using the techniques properly. Before drafting a formal management plan, you will need to choose a final working set of options, as explained in Section 6.5.

6.4 Building on the experience of others

As more and more people try to integrate conservation objectives into their overall management plans, a body of good ideas and experience is building up for others to draw upon. Almost any issue of a trade journal or magazine you care to look at will have at least one article about wildlife or landscape conservation. You can also find out more about this by attending local meetings and talks or asking a farm adviser or consultant. The following examples illustrate some typical experiences in choosing options that will incorporate conservation alongside other land uses.

Pony trekking in Wales

A farm business in Wales had used government grants in the past to improve its pastures. Most of the enclosed fields on the farm were re-seeded and treated with fertiliser, greatly increasing the stocking capacity of the farm.

However, making use of this increased stocking capacity presented a few problems. The farmer did not want to increase his sheep flock. Some years ago, cattle would have been a logical alternative, but this would have required a building to house them, and the farmer did not want to take on such a large investment at that time. Having access to an attractive and extensive range of hills, the family decided on the option of diversifying into pony trekking and building up the recreational uses of the land.

This is now a major part of the family business with over 200 horses (housed away from the farm during winter), a new, large, well-planned hostel to accommodate school parties and an extensive network of trails through woodland, fields and onto the hilltops. The people who come on pony trekking holidays want to see an attractive countryside with diverse habitats, providing an incentive for this farmer to conserve wildlife and the landscape, as well as considerably supplementing the family's income.

This is an example where new commercial land uses are favourable to landscapes and wildlife, given that the diversification is of a 'conservation-friendly' type, and the people involved have conservation as one of their overall objectives.

A farming co-operative in Suffolk

A large farming co-operative in Suffolk has hired its own adviser to develop farm plans as a framework for making conservation practical and economic. The conservation syndicate now includes at least 54 farmers, covering 10 926 hectares (27 000 acres). The following are among the options being developed or considered that involve an element of conservation:

1 A pond on the farm is used as a breeding ground for fish that can be sold to pet shops and also provides a habitat for wild flowers and animals.

2 Cowslips and primroses provide eye-catching features in the landscape, and farmers are also collecting and selling the seed to companies specialising in wild flowers.

3 Special contacts are being developed with merchants to achieve higher prices for some of the timber from farm woods. Some of these have become derelict and will be restored by conservation-sensitive re-planting, using the Forestry Commission's 5 year broad-leaved woodland management scheme. Some trees are being pruned to produce better quality timber.

4 The achievements of the project have spawned successful residential weekends where people come to learn about wildlife gardening, woodland management or pond restoration.

5 Future plans include the establishment of a long-distance footpath that stops at members' farms, providing temporary stabling for visiting pony-trekkers, and providing homes and workshops for people engaged in local crafts (possibly using products from the syndicate's farms). One farm has also been identified as having an ideal traditional farm hall for the entertainment of visitors and the makings of a good rough shoot.

6.5 Selecting your options (management prescriptions)

As described in Section 6.1, before drafting a formal management plan you need to choose the options to take forward to this next stage. After you have done the exercises in the next section, you should have:

▷ a range of potential landscape and habitat options, relevant to your wildlife and landscape assessment, based on Section 6.2;

▷ some imaginative ideas related to incorporating conservation into the business as a whole, based on your own creative ideas and the experience of other people (Sections 6.3 and 6.4).

The criteria you use to make your choice of options should be directly related to your objectives and constraints from Stage 2, as illustrated in Section 6.7 and Table 6.3. Remember that some of these criteria should be related to your own personal likes and dislikes. If you find that you are not very comfortable with the options that seem to be favoured by the criteria you are using, this is a sign that you should go back and think again about your objectives and constraints, and revise them if necessary, until you feel happy with the outcome of both Stages 2 and 3 together. *Selection criteria*

The number of options you choose to incorporate in your final management plan in Stage 4 will depend on the size and complexity of the site and also on the resources available. In the case study example, the site is quite large and complex but resources are limited. There are therefore a large number of landscape and wildlife conservation options, many of which will have to be set aside at least temporarily on grounds of cost (a constraint). There are also quite a few options related to ways of increasing income which may in the long run enable some of the other conservation options to be included in the plan.

Table 6.3 shows how you can put your choice on a more formal basis, making you think about each option in relation to a set of selection criteria based on your objectives and constraints. The selection criteria should be ranged in order of priority to make it easier to read the table once it is completed. Include in your table all the options you would like to be able to proceed with, give them a star-rating against your chosen criteria, and use this table to narrow your choice further. Be particularly on the alert for combinations of options that will complement one another in a synergistic way, and try to avoid combinations that will obviously work against one another.

The final choice of options becomes the set of management **prescriptions** that are incorporated in your formal plan. However, do not discard your notes from Stage 3 — you may want to come back to them in future and reconsider some of your ideas. The options you choose to take forward to Stage 4 will become the management prescriptions in a formal plan that is actively evolving over time. Some may prove not to be feasible and their place may be taken by new options; some may be implemented but give rise to unexpected problems; others will have unexpected benefits.

6.6 Exploring and choosing options for your own example

Landscape and habitat options

Check through the options described in Section 6.2 for any that apply to your own case study and use them as examples. If you find this difficult, look around the neighbouring countryside, observe which plants or trees seem to be growing best on areas like those on your land, and see if you can pick up any ideas.

Supplement the brief summaries given here with additional information from specialist books and magazines if you have time. (You should be able to find them in your local library.)

Section 6.7 shows the options recommended for the case study example. Remember this is a very diverse site so the number of options is much greater than in many other cases.

Stimulating your imagination and building on the experience of others

Apply any or all of the techniques described in Section 6.3 to stimulate your imagination and suggest options arising from your earlier objectives and constraints. Section 6.7 gives a brainstorming example for the case study farm.

Find out what you can from local people. If there is an agricultural college nearby, they may hold meetings about conservation and business diversification periodically. Contact your local Farming (Forestry) and Wildlife Adviser.

Study the trade journals and note down any ideas that seem relevant to your case study.

Look at your objectives tree and notes on constraints to make sure you relate your ideas to the earlier stages of the development of your management plan.

Following the example in Section 6.7:

Draw up a table with your selection criteria (based on your objectives) ranged along the tops of the columns (see Table 6.3).

Add the options you would like to proceed with to the left-hand column.

Give each option a star-rating ***; ** or * for each criterion. (In some cases these ratings may have to be provisional, for example until you have done more detailed costings at the next stage.)

Choose the options that get the highest overall ratings on the most important selection criteria to be taken forward to the next stage, 'Drafting a formal plan of action'.

6.7 Case study: Exploring and choosing options

Habitat and landscape options

When it comes to drafting the management plan, a choice can be made from the following options for the management of habitat and landscape.

1 *Ponds.* The large western pond could be maintained as it is. Any invading willow scrub could be cleared from the water, but the encouragement of native tree species, e.g. willow, birch, alder, round a portion of the edge (up to 40%) would be advantageous. When the surrounding conifers are thinned, the first few rows of trees adjacent to the pond could be removed, to allow room for native trees and herbaceous plants to establish naturally.

Wetlands and water courses

The developing willow carr on the eastern pond could be maintained, while creating two clearings to increase the structural diversity. The development of birch woodland on the edge of the pond could be encouraged as it is good wildlife habitat and the open nature of birch woodland encourages a diverse ground flora. Some coppicing of birch in future years may be necessary to ensure structural diversity.

2 *Fen.* The present light grazing is a suitable management option. Light winter grazing by cattle helps to control scrub and to remove vegetation accumulated over the growing season. Fertiliser application within the catchment area should be kept to a minimum compatible with the grazing regime.

3 *Wet corner in arable field.* The farmer could fence off and plant small clumps of alder and willow (grey and goat). In open areas, meadow vegetation could be encouraged. This could be hastened by transplanting turfs with desirable species from other areas on the farm, e.g. meadowsweet, marsh marigold. (Only a small number of turfs from any one site should be taken, and rare or uncommon plants should not be dug up.)

4 *Marsh.* Maintain as it is. A slight decrease in grazing pressure in spring and summer would give the plant community a chance to flower more successfully. In future soft rush and tussock grass may have to be checked. If herbicides are used, a weed wiper bar is recommended to avoid harm to desirable species.

5 *Small stream.* This is an attractive habitat. Maintain stock-proof fencing and protect water supply from chemical inputs.

The tactical objective to maintain and improve the diversity of woodland habitat will enhance the landscape and conservation interest of the farm. In recent plantations there has been a strong broad-leaved element.

6 *Shelter-belt.* The trees here are mature and ready for felling in the next few years. It should be fenced and re-stocked using a broad-leaved mix in tree shelters, e.g. oak, ash, gean (wild cherry). Establishment of understorey and species such as rowan, blackthorn, hawthorn and bird cherry would increase its habitat value, although this may be difficult without rabbit fencing. A few evergreen conifers could be included to provide winter shelter.

7 *Mixed deciduous woodland.* Any management involving the SSSI must be in consultation with the NCC and should have the objective of enhancing the quality of the woodland, primarily for conservation.

8 *Mixed woodland strip.* This could be maintained as an open, mixed woodland. The introduction of a small number of oak, hazel and conifers throughout the area would ensure its diversity in years to come. The rhododendrons at the north end could be cleared by cutting stumps at ground level and painting with herbicide. This would give native species a chance to become established.

9 *Mixed woodland block.* Most of the canopy trees are mature and, for maximum wildlife value, felling and re-planting could be tackled in small blocks of 0.25 hectare spread over approximately 20 years to ensure woodland of uneven age structure. However, clear felling and re-planting in one block would be the best commercial option. Oak could be planted as the main timber species, with some evergreen conifers and holly for winter shelter. Birch, rowan, gean, hawthorn, blackthorn and hazel could be planted in small clumps to add to the diversity of the understorey.

10 *Shelter-belt.* Dead elm could be coppiced to encourage new growth from the roots and any gaps planted with oak, ash and gean in tree shelters.

11 *Spruce plantation.* Trees at the north end of this block should be felled within the next 10 years but the fringe of broad-leaved trees could be retained and, when re-planting, the banks of the adjoining ditch could be left open for five metres on either side.

12 *Mature coniferous woodland.* When this wood is harvested the mature broad-leaved trees around the edge should be retained if possible, and the area could be re-planted with a mixture of broad-leaved trees and conifers.

13 *New plantation.* There has been no weed control, increasing the amenity and conservation value. This could continue as long as no harm occurs to the commercial timber crop.

14 *Mature trees, isolated and in small groups.* The maintenance of these trees is strongly recommended because of their landscape value. Small areas could be tackled at a time to spread the cost of planting and the work load. Existing groups of trees could be fenced off and broad-leaved trees planted in tree shelters in gaps. Species such as oak, ash, beech, Scots pine and sycamore could be used with occasional lime, rowan, birch, larch, spruce and gean to add diversity. Once the trees are well established stock could graze beneath if necessary, although any damage to bark should be checked.

15 *Field boundary trees*. Maintenance of these is strongly recommended again for landscape reasons. Some of the dead wych elms could be felled and replaced with oak and ash in tree shelters. Other tree lines could be tackled gradually beginning with the most senile. Stock fencing will be necessary, if cattle are in the fields. If fencing is erected, some hawthorn and blackthorn could be planted to give ground cover and greater diversity.

16, 17 and 18 *Hedgerows*. These could be given an occasional light trim (e.g. late winter every third year) to prevent them from becoming too tall and sparse. Some of the gaps could be filled by planting hawthorn, blackthorn or holly. Every 10 or 20 metres a strong, straight stem of oak, ash, beech or birch could be left to develop into hedgerow trees.

19 *Track, ditch and field verges*. Where field verges are not grazed, the grass could be cut and removed in late summer or autumn once the main flowering period is past. This may be difficult due to the labour constraint. The reduced pesticide application on field headlands should be continued so long as it does not affect yields.

20 *Scrub*. At present this has a diverse age structure which is valuable for wildlife. Given the frequent use by the public and the difficulty of controlling activities on this area, it is probably best left alone.

21 and 22 *Knoll and grassy bank*. Current management should be maintained. It is important to avoid fertiliser application and to graze in winter to remove any accumulated vegetation after a season's growth.

Pasture

23 *Damp, low-lying area*. This area could be planted with a predominantly broad-leaved mix using species such as oak and ash for the main timber crop. Other species such as gean, holly, bird cherry, rowan, hawthorn and blackthorn in small quantities would add diversity and landscape interest. A small pond could be created in the wettest area, with an irregular outline and willow and alder planted nearby, to the north and east, coppiced regularly to keep them low and bushy.

24 *Re-seeded area*. Continue current management.

25 *The heather moorland* has not been burned for several years. Although sporting considerations are important, the number of grouse does not justify managing the moor under a systematic programme of burning, particularly as this is labour-intensive. The presence of scattered trees would make this more difficult, and burning may encourage the invasion of bracken, which is so far absent. The light grazing regime could be continued and hopefully the diversity of plant species will be maintained.

The trees on this area should be retained for their landscape and conservation value. Encouraging the establishment of seedlings would be expensive as rabbit netting would be necessary. Small areas including mature trees could be fenced off and the ground surface scarified. If no seedlings are established, bought-in plants of local origin, or seedlings grown in the garden from collected seed, could be planted out. The addition of birch and juniper would increase the diversity and the birch may encourage game.

The above, largely habitat-related, options would also have beneficial effects on the landscape, particularly the protection and re-planting of the parkland and boundary trees. The heather moorland is an attractive landscape feature from a distance and its retention would also be valuable. Maintenance of the hedges as a landscape feature would ensure long-term continuity of the links between the parkland and the arable land (Figure 2.6). The various

Landscape features

archaeological features discussed in Section 2.5 should be retained in their present condition.

Several of the drystone dykes (walls) within the arable section of the farm could be repaired, with those that will have an agricultural value being given priority. As repair work to walls is expensive a section could be tackled each year to spread the financial and labour input.

Stimulating imagination and building on the experience of others

Figure 6.5 is a tidy version of the output from a brainstorming session with the farmer, a conservation adviser and an outsider. As noted in Section 6.3, most of the ideas that emerged were related to diversifying the farm business in ways that are friendly towards conservation.

Several ideas, gleaned from the pages of farming magazines and from talking to farming and forestry advisers in the area, could be useful options for improving the financial viability of the farm but some of these have potential impacts on wildlife and landscape conservation that may not be obvious at first sight. Before taking up any of these options, it would be essential to negotiate a market outlet for the product.

Organic farming

A good premium can be obtained for organic produce and the market so far appears to be expanding. This farmer would be well-placed to take up this option, given his past experience in minimising fertiliser and pesticide inputs. Organically grown grain currently commands a premium of 25–40% which can compensate for the lower yields. The premium for organic vegetables can be 50–100%. Growing organic potatoes might be an interesting alternative option to the seed potato contract.

A less demanding alternative option is the growing of 'conservation grade' crops. The Guild of Conservation Food Producers has laid down standards permitting controlled use of selected fertilisers, herbicides and fungicides, which are considered least harmful to the soil, and continue to produce high yields. Skilled management is an important input to growing conservation grade crops, as with organic farming, but the risks and the premium are lower.

'Organic' animal husbandry, if it involved complete prohibition of antibiotics, the use of only organic feedstuffs, and the animals being born on an organic farm, is largely impractical. However, there is a flourishing market for 'additive-free' meat, where growth stimulants are not allowed, antibiotics are restricted to combating disease, and the content of purchased feed is regulated. Here, the optimum use of grassland, managed to organic or conservation standard, would be important.

Provided none of the high quality grassland that has not previously received chemical inputs is ploughed up, all these organic farming options would be beneficial to wildlife, and would create no change in the landscape. However, there may be a financial constraint in that organic growing is not recommended for farmers who are financially insecure.

Alternative livestock

A variety of exotic animals are now finding their way onto British farms. Deer were considered as an option and rejected, partly because of the uncertain marketing situation, but mainly because of the high cost of fencing enclosures.

Figure 6.5
Brainstorming exercise

Non-intensive carp farming was considered. These fish can be grown in farm ponds with a minimum flow of water, as is the case for the western pond on this farm, which is spring fed. Natural ponds with a good source of food can produce 14–22 kg/hectare of carp per annum. There is a limited, but growing demand for carp for human consumption, but the main market is to angling clubs and for decorative purposes. Any plan to implement an *intensive* fish farming operation, with artificial feeding of the fish, would be very detrimental to the conservation value of the pond because of the resulting pollution.

Goat production for fibre is suggested as a way of diversifying sources of farm income. Angora goats for the production of mohair are delicate creatures and are unlikely to survive the rigours of a hill farm but cashmere production could be viable.

Sheep production on the farm could be diversified in several interesting ways. An expansion into traditional coloured breeds could produce wool for the specialist craft market, meat from the lambs and attractively coloured lambskins for curing and sale, and the animals would still benefit from the provisions of the EEC sheep meat regime.

Expansion into milking breeds of sheep could enable the farmer to set up a sheep dairying business. Adding value by processing into yoghurt or cheese would probably be needed to make such an enterprise profitable and the very high solid content of the milk makes it ideal for these purposes.

The above three options for goats and sheep would have no particular impact on landscape or habitat conservation, but could put the farmer's finances on a more secure footing by increasing the income per hectare from the farm, and thus make more money available for other conservation options.

Forestry products

Growing exotic Christmas trees was considered as an option. Norway spruce is the usual species planted for the Christmas tree market but the noble fir, with its longer, thicker covering of blue-green needles is a much more attractive tree, rapid growing and suitable for exposed sites. There is also a fast-growing market for Scots pine Christmas trees, which do not drop their needles when cut and brought indoors. The farmer could develop a special market for such trees, hopefully commanding a price premium. If broad-leaved trees are being planted on any scale as a long-term investment, noble fir or Scots pine, for Christmas trees, could be incorporated as a cash crop to provide an income in the short term. There are constraints on this option: the presence of conifers in the planting mix would probably disqualify the area concerned from a Forestry Commission Broadleaved Woodland Grant, and Christmas trees are not a particularly easy cash crop to grow.

Specialist markets could be sought for some of the broad-leaved trees now reaching maturity on the farm, particularly sycamore and wild cherry. A craft industry producing small wood items could also be set up, based in some of the redundant outbuildings on the farm.

Selecting options

Based on the brainstorming session and the experience of other people, as described above, Table 6.3 was drawn up in consultation with the land manager. The selection criteria were placed, from left to right, in order of priority so that asterisks on the left-hand side of the table carry more weight than those on the right. The options chosen to be included in the table were those that seemed most attractive at first sight and seemed to have fewer constraints.

The farmer was not enthusiastic about any new business developments that would lead to large numbers of people using the farm, as he valued his peace and tranquillity. None of the recreational options from Figure 6.5 that would involve bringing large numbers of people onto the land was therefore included (for example, pony trekking, skiing and setting up a field centre). (Note that, for a brainstorming session to work well, it is important to avoid making judgements about ideas while they are being suggested; all the ideas that come up should be written down at the time and they should be looked at critically later, as was done here.)

Table 6.3 Choosing options

Options	Income diversification	Promoting habitat diversity	Avoiding financial risk	Maintaining landscape value	Soil conservation	Keeping good public relations	Avoiding labour constraint	Input reduction	Safeguarding predators
Carp farming	★★(?)	★	(?)	—	—	★	★	★★	★
Sheep dairying	★★	★	—	★	★★	★★	—	★	—
Free-range pigs	★★	★	★	—	—	—	—	★	—
Letting fields for horse pasture	★★★	★	★★	★	—	★	★★	★	—
Rough shooting ('organic shooting')	★	★★★	★★	★★★	—	★	★★	★★	★★
Pick-your-own firewood	★★★	★★	★	★★	—	★★	★★	—	★
Organic potatoes	★★	★★	★	—	★★	★	—	★★★	★★
Exotic Christmas trees	★★★	★★	★	★★	★★	★★	★	★	—

Some of the suggestions based on other people's experience reinforced options such as sheep dairying that had already come up in the brainstorming session, and encouraged the farmer to want to see them included in the shortlist. Other ideas gleaned from other people's experience were included if the farmer found them attractive and they seemed feasible.

Carp farming did not attract a particularly high rating, partly due to lack of information. The farmer decided to try to find out more about it in the medium term, but not to give it a high priority.

Rough shooting ('organic shooting') gained high ratings on quite a few criteria but the farmer did not think it likely that there would be a big enough demand locally to compensate for loss of income from the syndicate. The farmer decided to drop this option and to discuss with the syndicate the question of gaining a better control over their activities.

Of the animal husbandry options in Table 6.3, letting fields for horse pasture would be a very easy and cheap option to implement, so that was kept in the picture at this stage. Sheep dairying was also seen as quite attractive (there were some disused buildings available that could be developed as a milking shed and dairy).

Pick-your-own firewood and exotic Christmas trees both offered the chance to make more money out of the woodlands in the fairly short term and were also compatible with the gradual extension of the area of broad-leaved trees, thus promoting the landscape and wildlife diversity of the farm.

Are you sure these are organic peas?

Growing organic potatoes was also marked for further investigation as it offered an opportunity to move out of the only crop on the farm that had high levels of input. The labour constraint would prevent the farmer growing potatoes without outside help but he could, for example, hire another contractor to grow the potatoes organically, hire labour on a short-term basis, or sell the crop on a 'pick-your-own' basis.

Management prescriptions

In interpreting Table 6.3 remember that the selection criteria are ranged from left to right in order of priority, so that asterisks at the left-hand side of the table carry more weight than those at the right.

Many of the habitat and landscape options, suggested above, would be a direct drain on the farm's finances, particularly re-instating parkland and boundary trees, rebuilding drystone walls, filling gaps in hedgerows, rhododendron control, small areas of tree planting, and pond management. Others would have an opportunity cost (that is they would require the farmer *not* to take up certain opportunities to intensify his land management in order to increase his income). The point of the brainstorming exercise and looking at other people's experience was to see whether there were alternative opportunities for 'conservation-friendly' income-generating options that were in tune with the farmer's attitudes.

Several of the business options proposed seemed to fit this description and the farmer chose the following for more detailed consideration:

1 For the woodlands: a pick-your-own firewood enterprise, with wood sawn into transportable lengths for collection by customers (this could make an income from the larger branches not normally used when mature trees are

felled for timber); this option could be linked, at re-planting, to the growing of noble fir and/or Scots pine Christmas trees among the predominantly broad-leaved woodland.

2 On pastures: letting fields for grazing by horses and setting up a sheep dairying unit.

3 On arable land: the possibility of growing organic, or perhaps 'conservation grade' potatoes.

These, along with the landscape and habitat options proposed above will form the *management prescriptions* for Stage 4 of management planning.

Chapter 7

DRAFTING A FORMAL PLAN OF ACTION

Summary

This chapter describes how to cost the options chosen at the end of Stage 3 so that priorities can be assigned to them and they can be incorporated into a work plan, probably spanning a period of years. An example is given of the cost of creating a small pond surrounded by trees, shrubs and wild plants. Priorities should be assigned from an integrated conservation and business point of view, including financial and conservation factors and personal preferences. The management prescriptions incorporated in the final plan should be worded explicitly to make it easy to check whether they have been implemented. The importance of keeping records is stressed and guidelines are given for drafting a formal plan of action.

The previous stages of management planning were designed to make sure that the options you choose to put into the final plan are the best possible, both from a conservation point of view and from the manager's personal point of view. This chapter describes how to set out this plan, with examples to illustrate different styles. The options chosen at Stage 3 are costed in terms of time, money and other resources. Priorities are then given to the chosen management prescriptions and they are incorporated into a formal plan of action that specifies how and when they should be put into practice.

7.1 *Costs and benefits of options*

By Stage 4 most of the work of management planning has been done. All that remains is to work out the costs of your chosen options in terms of money, labour and/or opportunities foregone, so that you can compare one with another and with any financial benefits. Conservation-related benefits should also be considered but they are unlikely to be measurable in terms of money. Deciding the balance among these factors will be a fairly crude calculation, and the outcome will depend on your own personal attitudes and other influences, but this is an inevitable aspect of all decision-making, in conservation, agriculture, industry and elsewhere.

Costing landscape and habitat options

The factors that you need to take into account in costing landscape and habitat options are:

▶ the cost of materials bought in;

▶ the cost of any labour employed;

▶ the availability of grants from sources such as the Countryside Commissions, Ministry of Agriculture, Fisheries and Food, the Nature Conservancy Council, the Forestry Commission, local authorities or National Park authorities;

▶ any loss of income from opportunities not taken up (opportunity cost). (This should only be included in the costings if the manager feels it is important.)

In the following example, the option of digging a pond and encouraging wildlife diversity in its surroundings is costed for a farm in the south of England.

The landscape and habitat assessments for this farm had already shown that the area was of no particular value at present and the option was suggested as a means of creating a new, valuable feature and getting rid of an unwanted one, as most of the soil from the pond excavation could be used to fill in an unsightly rubbish tip.

Previously, trial pits had been dug to find out what the subsoil was like. As it contained a high percentage of clay, the conservation adviser decided that it would not need lining to hold water and could simply be 'puddled' using a tracked excavator. The excavated soil not used to fill in the rubbish tip would be banked up around the pond in a section not more than 1 metre high and 2–4 metres wide. The water level would be controlled by a piped outflow to an existing ditch and the inflow would also be piped from an unpolluted drainage ditch. A small island would be created, and a marshy area in one corner of the pond banks. Some bushes and trees were also planned for the site, with flowers and grasses around the edges, as illustrated in Figure 7.1.

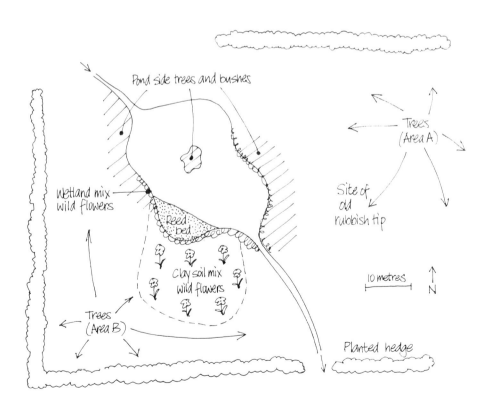

Figure 7.1 Excavation and planting scheme for pond and surrounding area

135

The estimated requirements were as follows:

Hire of excavator plus labour: 4 days (32 hours)

(Note: It is very expensive to hire equipment specifically for a conservation purpose. It is better to wait till the equipment is on the site for another purpose and to have the conservation work done for very little additional money.)

Hedge planting (200 metres)

900 hawthorn, 100 field maple, 50 blackthorn, 50 hazel (all at 45−60 cm size); 20 ash, 20 oak, 15 field maple for standards (at 60−90 cm size)

Tip site planting (Area A, Figure 7.1)

75 gorse, 75 goat willow, 75 silver birch, 20 rowan (to be planted in blocks: gorse + goat willow, 20 per group; silver birch + rowan, 5 per group; at 1−2 metre centres)

Pond surround planting (Area B, Figure 7.1)

35 ash, 35 oak, 20 birch, 25 alder (all at 60−90 cm size); 20 hawthorn, 25 hazel (at 45−60 cm size) (to be group planted, 5−10 per group, with 1−2 metre centres with hazel and alder individually planted at random to act as nurses)

Pondside trees and bushes

20 alder, 15 common sallow (both at 60−90 cm size), (planted at 1−2 metre centres);

Flower and grass seeding

Tip site and banking to be planted with a grass mix to prevent excess drying and to add humus to the subsoil
Wild flower meadow to the south of the pond, 300 square metres
Wetland wild flower mixture for the pond banks

You don't really need a BTCV work party Mr Archer try a drop of water!

Estimated costs were as follows:

Excavator plus labour (outside contractor)	£400.00

55 Ash @ 30p	£ 16.50
55 Oak @ 35p	£ 19.25
920 Hawthorn @ 17p	£156.40
100 Field maple (46–60 cm) @ 22p	£ 22.00
15 Field maple (60–90 cm) @ 25p	£ 3.75
50 Blackthorn @ 20p	£ 10.00
75 Hazel @ 36p	£ 27.00
75 Gorse @ 85p	£ 63.75
75 Goat willow @ 24p	£ 18.00
15 Common sallow @ 24p	£ 3.60
45 Alder @ 24p	£ 10.80
60 Silver birch @ 24p	£ 14.40
20 Rowan @ 23p	£ 4.60
	£370.05
Collection and cash (− 7%)	£ 25.90
	£344.15
VAT (+ 15%)	£ 51.62
	£395.77
160 60 cm tree guards + VAT	£ 40.48
1 15 kg bag Alginure soil improver + VAT	£ 17.76
Sub-total for trees	£454.01

Labour for tree planting were supplied through a government sponsored scheme. Trees to be pre-dipped in Alginure root dip and planted in November.

1 kg meadow wild flower mixture for clay soils (to cover 300 sq m)	£ 32.40
300 g cornfield mixture (to give first year colour and quick ground cover)	£ 21.00
500 g wetland wild flower mixture for banks and marshy areas	£ 28.50
	£ 81.90
VAT (+ 15%)	£ 12.29
Sub-total for flower seeds	£ 94.19

The flower seeds to be sown in autumn. The pond to be stocked using material collected locally under supervision to make sure that valuable habitats are not damaged.

GRAND TOTAL	£948.20

Table 7.1 The cost of conservation options

Option/proposal	Costs		Grants available
Restore a double row of trees and shrubs by double fencing and thinning existing trees by one third. Plant individual new trees (beech, ash, oak) in gaps	300 m sheep fencing 25 trees	£900 £ 37.50	Up to 50% grant may be available from CCs
Promote hedgerow trees by selecting individual shrubs to continue to grow	Nil		
Encourage development of scrub plus trees by fencing to protect from stock, plus some planting	140 m fencing 10 trees	£420 £ 15	Up to 50% grant may be available from CCs
Conserve wet area and allow more light to penetrate by impeding drainage and felling trees	Volunteer labour: overheads and transport, max. £60		
Increase wildlife diversity of grassland by harrowing pasture and overseeding with a wild flower mix	Seed £35 per kg Sowing rate 30 kg/ha		
Creation of a small copse, planted with oak, ash, beech	Plants	£700	FC grant at £700 for broad-leaved planting
Create a major area of woodland, with a coniferous core of sitka spruce and a broad-leaved edge including rowan, wild cherry and birch	800 m fencing £2400 22 ha planting £15 400 (Total £17 800)		FC grant at £5000
Deepen a pond to retain water all year	Extraction cost approx. $£2/m^3$		
Conserve damp flushes and herb-rich grassland by avoiding chemicals and restricting grazing	Opportunity cost only		
Create a shelter-belt by fencing and planting with beech, ash and a conifer nurse crop	280 m fencing £740 1 ha planting £700 (Total £1440)		FC grant at £590 for conifer/broad-leaf mix if shelter-belt is over 30 m wide. Grants from MAFF, DAFS or WOAD if under 30 m wide
Re-establish hedge by planting with hawthorn, hazel, blackthorn and holly	500 m hedge £900		Grant available from CCs, DAFS, MAFF or WOAD
Shelter-belt with assorted broad-leaves and shrubs (420 m x 10 m; 2 m between trees, 1.3 m between shrubs and 2.1 m between rows)	Trees and shrubs £640 300 rabbit spirals £78.30 420 m fencing at £1.40/m Volunteer labour for fencing and planting £588		Grant up to 50% available from Local Authority with assistance from CCs

(Source: Cobham Resource Consultants, 1985, and FWAG Reports)
Abbreviations: CCs: Countryside Commissions; DAFS: Department of Agriculture and Fisheries for Scotland; FC: Forestry Commission; MAFF: Ministry of Agriculture, Fisheries and Food; WOAD: Welsh Office of Agricultural Development

Additional examples of materials costs for a range of options are given in Table 7.1 to give you a broad indication of the sums of money involved. However, to cost the options accurately for your own management plan, you will need to find out current prices from local suppliers.

Assigning priorities for an integrated farm plan

Even if only a small number of options is proposed for your site, it is useful to give them priorities from an integrated landscape, habitat and business perspective. While financial costs and benefits of the options will affect your enthusiasm for them, you can also make your judgements in terms of personal preferences. If you prefer broad-leaved woodland to herb-rich grassland, you can count it as a greater benefit if you wish. However, if your area is well wooded and herb-rich grassland is a rare habitat, other people would probably disagree with this ordering.

In Table 7.2 (overleaf) the conservation options for an arable farm are listed in order of priority according to habitat and landscape values. The revised priority listing in the second column takes account of the farmer's personal preferences and his reaction to the costs and benefits. He was very keen to take up the woodland option to benefit landscape, habitats and game but was discouraged by the cost, even with a 50% grant. This option was moved to the bottom of the list while he investigated the possibility of getting a bigger grant. The pond option was moved to the top of the list, with the qualification that only one pond would be re-instated (the one requiring expensive drain diversion would be left as it was). Planting trees by the farm entrance was moved up the scale — although it gave only a minor landscape benefit for an outsider, it featured very highly in the farmer's perception of his property. The farmer's intention was that all the options, including the expensive woodland planting, would eventually be implemented, in the order shown in the adjusted priority listing.

Where expensive options are proposed, it is sometimes possible to spread the cost over a period of years as shown for the case study in Table 7.5.

For your own land use example:

Assess the cost of the conservation options and also any relevant business options chosen at the end of the previous chapter. Remember to include the cost of labour (even if you are using volunteer labour, they will charge for their overheads and transport).

Write down your options in order of preference and summarise the reasons for this ordering.

Include in the table the cost of each option and adjust the priority ordering if necessary. Options that give a greater benefit for a lower cost are obviously more attractive if there is a limited amount of money to be spent.

Decide on the time-scale for implementing each option.

If necessary, draw a line across the table below the amount you can afford to do now, with the rest being held over until further funds become available.

Alternatively, take a longer-term perspective and explore ways of spreading the cost of the more expensive options over a period of years, as shown for the case study in Table 7.5.

Table 7.2 Priorities among landscape and habitat options for an intensive arable farm

First priority listing	Revised priority listing	Option	Habitat/landscape value	Financial costs/benefits
1	7	Fell some of the dead and senile trees in a small wood (leave some for habitat and landscape value) and re-plant extended area with broad-leaved trees. Create glades near banks of stream.	Very valuable impact for both wildlife and landscape. Some benefit also for game.	Cost £5000 (grant of up to 50% may be available). Value of rental of land taken out of production (i.e. opportunity cost) £500 per annum. Long-term financial benefit from timber.
2	1	Re-instate two farm ponds.	Very few ponds in the area. Very valuable for aquatic wildlife. Little landscape impact.	Low cost: work could be done by farm labour as available. One pond would require expensive drain diversion to avoid pollution.
3	6	Manage tall, overgrown hedge by coppicing on a 10–15 years rotation.	Wildlife and landscape value greatly deteriorated and would increase dramatically if well managed. Some benefit also for game.	Shape-saw contractor rates £10/hour (done in 3 lengths at 5-year intervals at £200 each time).
4	2	Create a new field-corner spinney in an area difficult to cultivate with large machinery.	Will link up with a similar area on the other side of the road and provide a more significant landscape feature. Very small area but quite beneficial to wildlife and game.	Cost £60 (grant aid may be available). Small opportunity cost from area of field lost to cultivation.
5	3	Rationalisation and re-planting of hedgerow trees to avoid shading of crops and to emphasise network of roads in the landscape.	Considerable value for landscape; less for wildlife.	Cost of 200 trees, half with shelters, £250 (50% grant may be available), no felling costs, but no revenue from felled trees. Cost of shading on crops from a large, mature tree, £2–3 per annum.
6	5	Cut road verges only once a year, in autumn.	They are presently mowed twice a year which is inhibiting the regeneration of wild flowers. Moderate wildlife and landscape benefit.	50% saving on present costs.
7	4	Plant ten broad-leaved trees by the entrance to the farm.	Only small wildlife benefit; minor landscape benefit in the longer term.	£15 for trees and protection.

Having costed the options chosen for more detailed consideration at the end of Stage 3, thought about how and when to implement them, and if necessary reordered their priority ranking, you are now ready to summarise your decisions in a formal plan of action.

7.2 Finalising the management plan

Once incorporated into a formal plan of action the options become *management prescriptions*. They should be worded clearly to make it easy to check up on the extent to which they have been implemented, for example 'to fence off 5 hectares of woodland to exclude grazing animals' or 'to allow hedgerow trees to develop at 15 metre intervals'. Where prescriptions are less precisely worded, such as 'to allow hedgerow trees to develop at intervals', it will be more difficult to say whether they have been implemented.

Management prescriptions

In the longer term you also need to check on whether the management prescriptions, when implemented, are helping to achieve the management objectives as expected. This aspect is dealt with in Chapter 8.

Formal records of the management plan should be kept for two different purposes. A summary plan is needed to keep a check on the management prescriptions and make sure they are put into practice. This should be in a simple format, easy to read and short enough to be pinned to the wall in a prominent place. You should also keep a complete record of the planning process in your files, from Stage 1 through Stage 4 to Implementation and beyond. This will serve as a continually evolving diary of the development of the land area and also as a basis for future revisions of the management plan.

Keeping records

To accompany both the summary plan and the long-term record, you should produce a map of your land area based on the example in Figure 6.1, indicating the key areas mentioned in the management plan and, where possible, actions to be taken (see also Plates 15 and 16).

Annotated maps

Different people and organisations involved in land use management planning have developed a wide range of formats for presenting the summary plan and the complete management plan record. As you become more practised at management planning you will devise your own personal variation on the theme. If you have followed all the stages of management planning described here, you should be able to understand someone else's plan even if it is worded differently from your own. You should also be able to comment constructively on its style and content.

Summary management plans

The summary plan should include, as a minimum: a brief description, based on the integrated assessment, of each area to be managed wholly or partly for conservation (Stage 1); the relevant management objectives for the area (Stage 2); the management prescriptions for the area (Stages 3 and 4); an indication of the cost of implementing the prescriptions (Stage 4); and a map showing the position of each area on the site.

Two examples of summary plans are given here. The first, in Figure 7.2 and Tables 7.3 and 7.4 (see pp. 142–147), was produced by an adviser from the Farming and Wildlife Advisory Groups for a farm in south-west England. The second is the summary management plan for the case study in Section 7.3.

> Study both examples and produce a summary management plan for your own site.

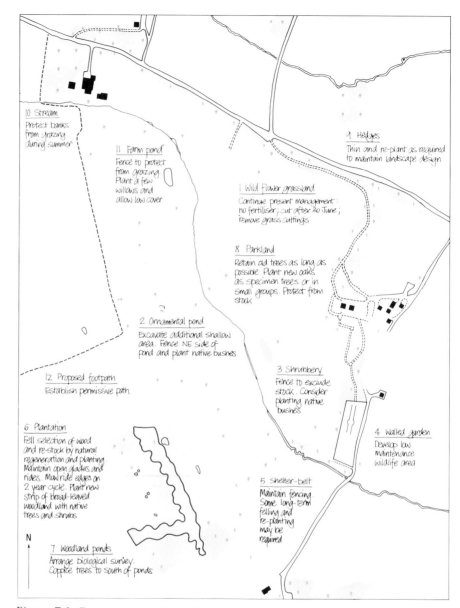

10 Stream
Protect banks
from grazing
during summer

11 Farm pond
Fence to protect
from grazing.
Plant a few
willows and
allow low cover

9 Hedges
Thin and re-plant as required
to maintain landscape design

1 Wild flower grassland
Continue present management:
no fertiliser; cut after 30 June;
remove grass cuttings

8 Parkland
Retain old trees as long as
possible. Plant new oaks
as specimen trees or in
small groups. Protect from
stock

2 Ornamental pond
Excavate additional shallow
area. Fence NE side of
pond and plant native bushes

12 Proposed footpath
Establish permissive path

3 Shrubbery
Fence to exclude
stock. Consider
planting native
bushes

6 Plantation
Fell selection of wood
and re-stock by natural
regeneration and planting.
Maintain open glades and
rides. Mow ride edges on
2 year cycle. Plant new
strip of broad-leaved
woodland with native
trees and shrubs

4 Walled garden
Develop low
maintenance
wildlife area

5 Shelter-belt
Maintain fencing.
Some long-term
felling and
re-planting
may be
required

N

7 Woodland ponds
Arrange biological survey.
Coppice trees to south of ponds

Figure 7.2 Farm conservation plan: site map

Table 7.3 Farm conservation: summary plan

Area description (sites as numbered on Figure 7.2)	Integrated assessment	Management objectives	Management prescription
1 Wild flower grassland	Herb-rich grassland, probably seeded about 1900; important botanically with a high species diversity, including fritillary; tall grass attracts insects which provide food for game.	To retain and if possible improve the species diversity.	Avoid use of fertiliser. Protect from grazing during spring and early summer. Mow and rake in early July.
2 Ornamental pond	Wildlife interest limited by steep banks; attracts duck to give game interest; also stocked with 200 rainbow trout.	To enhance the value of the pond for wildlife and encourage wildfowl while still maintaining a supply of trout.	Extend the pond to form a shallow area to support aquatic vegetation. Fence off an area on the north-east side to protect from grazing to allow some cover to develop for wildlife. (For landscape reasons it may be better to develop this bushy area on the west side.) Cut half of the resulting rough cover on a 3-year rotation and plant the other half with native bushes (guelder rose, alder buckthorn, hawthorn, alder and willow). Keep the stocking rate of trout as low as possible to minimise the impact of fish on the invertebrate community.
3 Shrubbery	A derelict plantation. Diseased elms have been felled but some beeches remain. At present unfenced so no regeneration is taking place and the understorey has been heavily browsed. Potentially good game cover.	To maintain the shrubbery as a screen for landscape reasons and to provide berries and nesting areas for birds and small mammals.	Fence the area to protect it from grazing. Re-plant with native trees and shrubs (hawthorn, spindle, field maple, and hazel). Plant occasional trees (oak, wild cherry).
4 Walled garden	Contains some fruit trees along the wall but the central area is mainly populated by nettles and thistles. Sheltered and a good refuge for butterflies and other insects. The old walls provide nesting holes for birds.	To create a wildlife area that is easy to manage and provides an abundance of food and cover for birds and insects.	Leave the old fruit trees and plant additional old-fashioned varieties of apple, cherry and pear, and also honeysuckle around the edge of the garden. Plant flowering and fruiting shrubs to provide food and cover for birds and insects (privet, buddleia, alder buckthorn, rowan, burberry). Create a varied vegetation structure by cutting areas on 2-year and 3-year rotations. Mow a path round the garden regularly to allow the owners to enjoy it.

Table 7.3 continued overleaf

Table 7.3 continued

5 Shelter-belt	Contains a mixture of Turkey oak, English oak and cherry. A landscape feature planted as part of the layout of the estate. Useful corridor for wildlife and game between the main plantation (6) and the garden area (4).	To maintain a mixed shelter-belt and to provide a wildlife corridor.	Fence the area to exclude stock. Allow natural regeneration in the large gaps at the eastern end. Fell and re-plant groups of trees along the outside of the shelter-belt.
6 Plantation	Mixture of Turkey oak, ash and English oak, planted as a hilltop landscape feature. Even-aged, very dense canopy and restricted ground flora. No open areas to encourage species diversity at the woodland edge.	To maintain and enhance the plantation for amenity, timber and conservation purposes and to diversify its age structure.	Obtain permission from the Forestry Commission to fell trees to form a wide ride running north-west to south-east (in three instalments). Scallop the edges of the ride to increase the edge effect. Make another clearing running east to west. Create a new plantation of oak, ash and cherry to the east of the present area to maintain the continuity of the shelter-belt. Maintain the ride by regular mowing and cut the edge vegetation on a staggered 2-year rotation (one side each year). Encourage natural regeneration of ash and re-plant English oak.
7 Woodland ponds	Very shaded and tend to be covered by fallen leaves. They may contain unusual species found only in shady places. Northern pond will be opened to light when the woodland is felled.	To obtain expert assessment on the value of the ponds and maintain them as recommended.	Ask a member of the local naturalists' trust to survey ponds. If there is nothing of interest in the southern pond, fell trees to the south side and coppice on a 5-year rotation.
8 Parkland	Old trees provide roosting sites for birds and bats and support many invertebrates, fungi and lichens. Also provide shade for game.	To maintain parkland landscape and retain old trees for wildlife conservation purposes.	Plant young oak at 3.5 m spacing, protected by stock-proof fence and by plastic growing tubes. Avoid felling old trees. Avoid ploughing close to the roots of trees (keep beyond the edge of the canopy).
9 Hedges	Many of the hedges have been fenced on both sides and have grown out to form a thick wildlife corridor. Also provide habitat for a number of woodland species and for pheasants and partridges.	To maintain stock-proof hedges as wildlife habitat and corridors, to produce food for birds and small mammals and to grow trees for wildlife and landscape reasons.	Cut hedges on a 3-year staggered rotation to allow bushes to fruit. Carry out all hedge trimming as late in the year as possible. Manage some hedges on a 15-year rotation. Allow hedgerow trees to develop at 15 m intervals.

Table 7.3 continued

10	Stream	Wildlife corridor and refuge for aquatic and river-bank plants. Potential nesting cover.	To enhance the value of the stream for wildlife by allowing more cover to develop and wild plants to flower and set seed.	Use temporary electric fencing to protect banks from grazing animals to allow plants to flower and set seed. Remove fence at 1-year or 2-year intervals to allow stock to graze the vegetation back.
11	Farm pond	Relatively little value at present.	To increase its wildlife value.	Fence 50% of the banks to protect from grazing. Enclose an area to the north of the pond and plant with bushes.
12	Proposed footpath	Existing hedgerow acts as wildlife corridor.	Encourage development of permitted path to enable local people to enjoy the scenery without disturbance to wildlife or the owners. Arrange so that the path can be closed at any time at the discretion of the owners.	Establish a grassed route along the hedgerow and mow the edge of the track on a 2-year rotation. If public use is not heavy, mow the central track as necessary. Install and maintain stiles and signs.

Table 7.4 Estimated costs for conservation work at selected sites on Figure 7.2 (1987 prices)

Plantation (site 6)

(a) *New broad-leaved plantation*

Area 0.5 ha

Fencing 225 m at £2/m (labour and materials)   £450

Plant forest transplants at 3 m spacing, leaving a wide ride

Species	%	Number	Price	Sub-total	
Oak	30	156	33p	£ 51.48	
Ash	20	104	18p	£ 18.72	
Cherry	40	208	23p	£ 47.84	
Bushes	10	52	30p	£ 15.60	
(hazel, hawthorn, bullace, spindle, rowan)					
Tree shelters for oak and ash		260	75p	£195.00	
Netlon guards for cherry and bushes		260	45p	£117.00	£ 446
Labour (preparation and planting)				£140.00	
(weeding for 3 years)				£ 75.00	£ 215
				Total	£1111

Forestry Commission Broadleaved Woodland Grant Scheme £600 paid in three instalments

Table 7.4 continued overleaf

Table 7.4 continued

(b) *Area to be cleared and re-planted*

An area of 0.5 ha is to be felled and re-stocked with a combination of natural regeneration and re-planting

Re-planting (0.25 ha)
Use forest transplants at 3 m spacing
Plant oak in tree shelters and cherry with Netlon guards

Species	Number	Price	Sub-total	
Oak	125	33p	£ 41.25	
Cherry	125	23p	£ 28.75	
Tree shelters	125	75p	£ 93.75	
Netlon guards	125	45p	£ 56.25	£ 220
Labour (preparation and planting)			£ 70.00	
(weeding for three years)			£ 38.00	£ 108

Natural regeneration (0.25 ha)
Preparation of ground
Weeding and removal of sycamore and turkey oak
Thinning ash

Labour (approx. 12 days' work)				£ 300
			Total	£ 628

Forestry Commission Broadleaved Woodland Grant Scheme
Re-planting   £300 (70% paid on completion of planting and the rest in two 5-year instalments subject to successful establishment)
Natural regeneration £300 (60% paid on completion of approved work and the next instalment when adequate stocking has been achieved. Final instalment 5 years later)
Some income from sale of timber

Ornamental pond (site 2)

Excavate additional shallow area and remove soil Hymac £12.50/hour; 2 days' work + cost of machine transport and removal of soil				£ 400
Fencing 150 m at £2/m (materials and labour)				£ 300
Bushes (Plant as 60−90 cm forest whips)				

	Number	Price	Sub-total	
Alder	20	40p/tree	£ 8	
Willow sets	40	no cost		
Bushes	120	50p	£ 60	
Spiral rabbit guards 180 at 25p/guard			£ 45	
Labour			£ 45	£ 158
			Total	£ 858

Eligible for Countryside Commission Landscape Conservation Grant (max. 50%, usually 30%)

Table 7.4 continued

Shrubbery (site 3)				
Fencing 100 m at £2/m (materials and labour)				£ 200
Trees (Plant as 60–90 cm whips)	Number	Price	Sub-total	
Oak	5	60p	£ 3.00	
Cherry	5	50p	£ 2.50	
Hawthorn	20	30p	£ 6.00	
Field maple	10	50p	£ 5.00	
Hazel	10	50p	£ 5.00	
Rowan	10	30p	£ 3.00	
Spiral rabbit guards 60 at 25p			£ 15.00	
Labour			£ 15.00	£ 55
			Total	£ 255

Eligible for Countryside Commission Landscape Conservation Grant (max. 50%, usually 30%)

Parkland trees (site 8)	
Tree and tree shelter	£ 1.10
Individual timber tree guard or	£ 30–£ 40
post and rail fence 3.5 m square with strand of barbed wire or	£ 98
forest fencing: 50 m to enclose 9 trees at 3.5 m spacing	£100

Eligible to apply for Countryside Commission Landscape Conservation Grant (max. 50%, usually 30%)
Country Landowners' Association tree planting scheme (Monument Trust), subject to public access (50–75%)

A complete record of the planning process

If you have been doing all the stages of management planning for your own area of land, you will already have a record of the planning process that is almost complete. For the case study the record would include the following:

Landscape assessment (Section 2.5)
Wildlife and habitat assessment (Section 3.8)
Business assessment (Section 4.6)
Identifying objectives and constraints (Section 5.6)
Exploring and choosing options (Section 6.7)
Drafting the formal plan of action (Section 7.3)

Your equivalent exercises will be your own record.

All that remains is to ensure the long-term implementation of your plans and to devise ways of checking that your management prescriptions are indeed helping to achieve your strategic and management objectives, as described in Chapter 8.

7.3 Case study: Drafting the formal plan of action

Costs and benefits of diversification options

Some preliminary enquiries about the options for diversifying sources of income (see Section 6.7) provided the following information.

1 *Pick-your-own firewood.* A trial advertisement in the post office of the nearby town had failed to raise much interest, but this was in the early autumn before the market for fuel had begun to pick up. The farmer intended to try again in a few months' time. In the meantime, he had negotiated an arrangement with a nearby three-star hotel that had a large open fireplace, where the manager was prepared to pay a premium for 'good-looking' logs sawn to fit in his log basket.

The farmer already has the tractor, winch and chainsaw needed to do the work, and will employ casual labour. The labour cost of extraction and conversion to log size was calculated at £10 per cubic metre. The premium price of logs, collected at the roadside, to be paid by the hotel, is £18 per cubic metre. The hotel expects to take 60 cubic metres per annum, collected at intervals, mainly in winter, giving an annual net income of £480. If a market for the non-premium logs can be established, these will probably sell for around £15 per cubic metre.

2 *Exotic Christmas trees.* There are two major towns within 20 miles of the farm, providing a good likely market for premium quality trees. Visits to potential outlets bearing photographs of Norway spruce and noble fir and Scots pine for comparison indicated that a 20% premium would be likely on noble fir or Scots pine. (Noble fir would probably grow 15% faster than the other species under this farm's conditions.)

Further inquiries to the Forestry Commission indicated that the original idea of planting mixed broad-leaved trees and Christmas trees should be revised. Christmas trees grow better when concentrated at a high density and the biggest demand is for fairly small trees, around 1.5 metres tall. In addition, a broad-leaved planting would only be eligible for the full Broadleaved Woodland Grant from the Forestry Commission if planted without conifers.

The farmer decided that it would be preferable to grow Christmas trees separately from the broad-leaved trees, perhaps on some of the areas currently susceptible to soil erosion and to replace felled woodland with pure broad-leaved stands. He also decided on Scots pine, as a native species, in preference to noble fir.

The number of plants required at 1 metre spacing on 0.25 hectare is 2500. At £150 per thousand, the total cost will be £375. The labour requirement is one worker-day per 50 trees sold, i.e. 50 worker-days in total for a 0.25 hectare crop; the total cost would be £2400.

Assuming the trees grow quickly and are harvested at 6−8 years old, when they will be approximately 1.5 metres high, fetching a premium price of £2.90 each, the total revenue is likely to be £7250. If some trees are harvested earlier, the price will be correspondingly lower.

The profit, using the above calculations, is £4475 from 0.25 hectares over 6−8 years. With no allowance for fencing costs, VAT or tax deductions, this preliminary calculation suggests an idea worth further investigation.

3 *Organic potatoes*. The farmer contacted an organic grower with a view to letting some land to him. He was unable to take up the offer but made a number of suggestions that resulted in the farmer letting the land for conventional potato growing at a much better rent than previously.

4 *Letting fields for grazing by horses*. An arrangement with a local vet was already being negotiated, likely to bring in an income of £500 per annum. (Horses have a serious tendency to bark trees so great care will need to be taken if they are grazed in any of the fields with parkland trees.)

5 *Sheep dairying*. Preliminary inquiries showed that expansion into sheep dairying would be a major undertaking, involving buying new special breeds of ewe, providing housing at night during winter, and converting old buildings into a dairying unit that satisfies the Food Hygiene Regulations.

Breeding ewes cost £200−400 each, with a lactation of 7−8 months, a yield of 400−500 litres of milk and an average flock life of six years. The milk is very high in total solids which makes it excellent for processing into yoghurt, cheese or ice cream (4−5 litres will make 1 kg of hard cheese). It will also keep for up to four months in a deep freezer. The gross margin per ewe can range from £140 to £180 per lactation, including the value of wool and lamb sold for meat consumption.

The farmer intended to make further inquiries about the legal and regulatory situation with a view to considering the idea further at some time in the future. In the meantime it seemed like too big an investment.

In summary, consideration of the opportunities for diversification of farm income in conservation-friendly ways had proved an interesting and very fruitful exercise for the farmer. It had stimulated him to take greater control over the activities of the game syndicate. It had also resulted in several concrete opportunities to increase farm income in ways that would have little direct impact on habitat and landscape conservation, but would make it easier to afford to implement some of the purely conservation options (better rent for the potato land, growing Christmas trees on arable areas susceptible to soil erosion, letting fields for horse pasture). The main business opportunities that would have a direct impact on habitats and landscape are the felling of mature coniferous woodland and its replacement with pure broad-leaved stands, or a mixture of broad-leaved trees and conifers, and the 'pick-your-own' firewood option.

Costs and benefits of conservation options

Of the conservation options proposed in Section 6.7 for the case study farm, some were shelved by the farmer because they seemed too expensive or time consuming (see 5 and 9 below). Of the remainder, the following would have significant costs, in some cases with partial compensation from the Countryside Commission for Scotland (CCS) or the Nature Conservancy Council (NCC).

1 *Ponds* (site 1 on Figure 7.3)
Removing 2 rows of conifers from the edge of the western pond: Forestry
labour, 8 hours at £7/hour   Gross cost £56
(No grant aid available)

Native species will re-establish naturally at the pond edge at no cost, although in future years there will probably be a need for coppicing, requiring a labour input.

149

To open up the eastern pond, two areas, each 10 square metres to be cleared of willow carr: Farm labour, 8 hours at £2.50/hour   Gross cost £20

(No grant aid available)

To coppice birch wood by eastern pond, three areas, each 10 square metres: Farm labour, 12 hours at £2.50/hour   Gross cost £30

(No grant aid available)

2 *Wet corner in arable field* (site 3 on Figure 7.3)

Fence off wet corner of field: 60 m stock-proof fencing at £1.50/m + Contract labour, £0.60/m   £126

Shrub planting: 20 willow, £2.00; 10 alder, £2.00; Netlon guards and canes, £9.00; farm labour, £5.00   £18

Gross cost £144

(Up to 50% grant may be available from CCS)

3 *Shelter-belt* (site 6 on Figure 7.3)

Fence and re-stock shelter-belt with oak, ash, gean and a few conifers: 100 m stock-proof fence at £2.10/m (including labour), £210; 60 trees in guards, £60; farm labour for planting, £10   Gross cost £280

(Up to 50% grant may be available from CCS)

4 *Mixed woodland strip* (site 8 on Figure 7.3)

Clear rhododendrons, stack and burn vegetation and apply Roundup to stumps: Farm labour (24 hours), £60; 1 litre herbicide, £18   Gross cost £78

(No grant available)

Plant trees: 50 trees (oak and conifers) in guards at £1 each, £50; farm labour, £8.50

Plant shrubs: 30 hazel, £6.00; 30 sloe, £3.00; 20 juniper, £20; 20 holly, £20; 100 Netlon guards and canes, £30; farm labour, £17.50   Gross cost £155

(Up to 50% grant may be available from CCS)

5 *Woodland areas* (sites 9, 10, 11 and 12 on Figure 7.3)

These options were deferred for further consideration in a few years' time as the farmer did not feel he could cope with them. When work is done on any of these areas in future the opportunity will be taken to increase the species diversity by planting a higher proportion of native broad-leaved species than exists at present.

6 *Mature trees, isolated and in small groups* (site 14 on Figure 7.3)

Re-instate parkland trees in groups: 1000 m stock-proof fence at £2.10/m (including labour), £2100
Plant 1000 trees (oak, ash, birch, Scots pine) with tree guards at 5 m spacing, £1/tree, £1000; farm labour (65 hours), £163   Gross cost £3263

(Up to 50% grant may be available from CCS)

7 *Field boundary trees* (site 15 on Figure 7.3)

Re-instate field boundary trees using oak and ash: 165 trees + guards at £1 each, £165; farm labour, £30; 2-metre square enclosures stock-proof fencing at £2.50/m including labour (i.e. 8 m/tree), £3300   Gross cost £3495

(Up to 50% grant may be available from CCS)

8 *Hedgerows* (sites 16, 17 and 18 on Figure 7.3)

Fill in gaps in hedgerows using sloe, holly and crab apple: 20 sloe, £2; 10 holly, £10; 10 crab apple, £2; 40 Netlon guards + canes, £12.40; farm labour, £5
                                                                        Gross cost £31

(Up to 50% grant may be available from CCS)

9 *Damp, low-lying area* (site 23 on Figure 7.3)

The option of planting broad-leaved trees for timber was shelved.

To create 2 ponds, each 12 m x 12 m, with a varied depth up to 2 m, uneven edges, and one with a small island: contract labour £20/hour for 16 hours, £320.

To plant shrubs: 35 willow, £3.50; 30 alder £6.00; 35 hawthorn, £8.75; guards + canes, £31; farm labour, £12.50.
                                                                        Gross cost £382

(Up to 50% grant may be available from NCC)

10 *Drystone dykes (walls)* (see Figure 7.3)

Re-build 240 m drystone wall using contract labour at £10/m
                                                                        Gross cost £2400

(Up to 60% grant may be available from the Department of Agriculture and Fisheries for Scotland)

Table 7.5 shows how the cost of these management prescriptions could be spread over a period of five years so that total expenditure in any one year was about £1000, based on the somewhat optimistic assumption that full grant aid would be paid for relevant activities. As this is unlikely to be the case, it was important to assign priorities among the various options that would require significant sums of money, as shown in Table 7.6 (see p 153). These altered priorities, and the links to business diversification options, as shown in Table 7.7, will reduce the overall cost and spread it over a much longer period than five years.

Table 7.5 Five year conservation work programme and cost implications for the case study farm

(The aim of this work programme is to bring the total annual expenditure to approximately £1000, assuming any grants available are paid in full)

Description of area	Site no. (as in Figure 7.3)	Job description	Gross cost	Net cost (assuming full grant aid)*
Year 1				
Mature trees, isolated and in small groups	14	Re-instate parkland trees in groups (20% of total estimated)	£653	£327
Field boundary trees	15	Plant 33 trees in guards	£700	£350
Drystone dykes (walls)		Re-build 60 metres	£600	£240
Hedgerows	16, 17, 18	Plant sloe, holly and crab apple	£31	£10
Mixed woodland strip	8	Control rhododendrons	£78	£78
		Total for Year 1		£1011

Table 7.5 continued overleaf

Table 7.5 continued

Year 2				
Mature trees, isolated and in small groups	14	Re-instate parkland trees in groups (20% of total estimated)	£653	£327
Field boundary trees	15	Plant 33 trees in guards	£700	£350
Drystone dykes (walls)		Re-build 60 metres	£600	£240
Mixed woodland strip	8	Plant trees and shrubs	£155	£78
			Total for Year 2	£995

Year 3				
Mature trees, isolated and in small groups	14	Re-instate parkland trees in groups (20% of total estimated)	£653	£327
Field boundary trees	15	Plant 33 trees in guards	£700	£350
Drystone dykes (walls)		Re-build 60 metres	£600	£240
Ponds	1	Remove conifers around pond	£56	£56
			Total for Year 3	£973

Year 4				
Mature trees, isolated and in small groups	14	Re-instate parkland trees in groups (20% of total estimated)	£653	£327
Field boundary trees	15	Plant 33 trees in guards	£700	£350
Drystone dykes (walls)		Re-build 60 metres	£600	£240
Wet corner in arable field	3	Fence off and plant shrubs	£144	£72
Ponds	1	Clear 2 areas willow carr	£20	£20
			Total for Year 4	£1009

Year 5				
Mature trees, isolated and in small groups	14	Re-instate parkland trees in groups (20% of total estimated)	£653	£327
Field boundary trees	15	Plant 33 trees in guards	£700	£350
Ponds	1	Coppice birch by eastern pond	£30	£30
Damp, low-lying area	23	Dig two ponds and plant shrubs	£382	£191
Shelter-belt	6	Re-stock with oak, ash and gean (wild cherry)	£280	£140
			Total for Year 5	£1038

* Note: the assumption that the full potential grant would be paid on all these projects is very optimistic. It is also important that no work is begun before the grant is applied for.

Table 7.6 Priorities among the most expensive landscape and habitat options for the case study farm

Priority	Management site (no.)	Justification
1	Field boundary trees (15)	The existing trees are the main landscape feature in the arable land area (see Figure 2.6). Their loss, without replacements would have a major landscape impact.
1	Ponds (1)	These are very useful wildlife areas, the options are cheap to implement and will help to increase the habitat diversity. Removing conifers and coppicing birch will link with the 'pick-your-own firewood' business option.
1	Mixed woodland strip (8)	This borders the main driveway to the house and therefore gives visitors their first impression of the land. It is also very visible to the farmer and his family so an increase in its diversity would give them a great deal of pleasure.
2	Wet corner in arable field (3)	The farmer decided to give a high priority to fencing off this area and to encourage the spread of diverse meadow vegetation which is relatively rare on this farm, but not to plant any trees.
2	Damp, low-lying area (23)	Creating ponds in this area will be relatively cheap to implement and will benefit wildlife. The area will be kept as a wildlife refuge, not open to the game syndicate.
2	Shelter-belt (6)	The suggested options will greatly improve the habitat value of the area and will provide both timber and firewood for sale.
3	Hedgerows (16, 17, 18)	Fairly low priority because there are not many gaps in the hedges and they do not need to be stock-proof. It is more important to cut in rotation than to plant up the gaps.
3	Mature trees, isolated and in small groups (14)	Replacement of these trees is very desirable from a landscape point of view but very expensive. At best the work will be spread over much more than 5 years, up to 20 or 30 years, beginning with the most senile trees.
4	Drystone dykes (walls)	Their re-building would have a favourable landscape impact in the same area as the field boundary trees, but they would be less conspicuous from a distance. This, and the cost of the option, gives it a low priority. It would be given a higher priority if it could be done by volunteer labour.

The summary management plan

Table 7.7 and the map in Figure 7.3 (see pp 154–156) form the summary management plan for the case study farm. The sheets should be pinned to the wall in the farm office and checked regularly to make sure that the prescriptions have been implemented at the right time.

Table 7.7 Five year summary management programme and record

Landscape zone/ habitat (no. on Figure 7.3)	Management prescription(s)	Priority	Time-scale	Comments
Hill land				
Heather moorland with scattered tree cover (25)	Continue present light grazing regime; check annually on the state of the heather and consider burning if necessary	1	Continuous, over 5 years	
Arable land				
Track, ditch and field verges (19)	Where not grazed, cut and remove vegetation annually in late summer	1	Continuous, over 5 years	
	Continue reduced pesticide application to field headlands; check for any effect on yields			
Drystone dykes (walls)	Re-build 240 m in total, beginning with stretches of greatest agricultural value	4	In sections, spread over 5 years	
Wet corner in arable field (3)	Fence to keep out stock	2	Year 2 (spring)	
	Transplant 6 turfs from a species-rich area elsewhere on the farm			
Field boundary trees (15)	Remove dead elms and sell for firewood	1	In stages, spread over 5 years	
	Plant 165 oak and ash with guards in 2 m square stock-proof enclosures			
Knoll and grassy bank (21 and 22)	Continue current management; avoid fertiliser application; graze in winter to remove any accumulated vegetation	1	Continuous over 5 years	
Arable fields	Plant 10.25 ha Scots pine on the area most subject to soil erosion at 1 m spacing, as an experimental plot growing Christmas trees commercially	2	Year 2 (late autumn)	
Woods, pasture and parkland				
Ponds (1)	Remove two rows of conifers from the edge of western pond and sell for firewood; allow native species to establish themselves and coppice at 5–10 year intervals, depending on rate of growth.	1	Year 1	
	Clear 2 areas, each 10 m², in willow carr near the eastern pond; stack scrub in piles at the edge of the pond	1	Years 1 and 2	

	Coppice birch wood by the eastern pond, 3 areas each 10 m^2; remove timber for firewood; stack brash in piles	1	Years 1, 2 and 3
Fen (2) and marsh (4)	Continue present light grazing regime in autumn and winter; keep fertiliser application on the catchment to the minimum compatible with the grazing regime	1	Continuous over 5 years
	If herbicides are used to control soft rush and tussock grass in the marsh area, use a weed-wiper bar		
Mixed woodland strip (8)	Cut, stack and burn rhododendrons; paint herbicide on stumps	1	Year 1
	Plant 50 oaks and conifers in guards	1	Year 2
	Plant 100 shrubs, hazel, sloe, juniper and holly in guards	1	Year 2
SSSI (7)	No management except in consultation with NCC where the aim should be to enhance its quality for conservation	1	–
Mature trees, isolated and in small groups (14)	Plant 1000 trees (oak, ash, birch, Scots pine) in groups with 5 m spacing between trees, with tree guards, enclosed in stock-proof fence	3	Beginning in year 4, spread over 20–30 years
Shelter-belt	Fell mature trees for sale as timber; coppice dead elms for sale as firewood	2	Year 2
	Surround with a stock-proof fence (100 m); re-stock with 60 trees (oak, ash, gean and a few evergreen conifers)	2	Year 3
	In the long term, plant shrubs (with protection from rabbits) to provide vegetation in the understorey	3	Year 5 or later
Hedgerows (16, 17, 18)	Trim in winter on a 3-year, staggered rotation	1	Continuous over 5 years
	Allow strong saplings to grow into trees at approx. 15 m intervals	1	Continuous over 5 years
	Fill in gaps in hedgerows with 40 sloe, holly and crab apple with tree guards	3	Year 4 or 5
Damp, low-lying area (23)	Create 2 ponds, each 12 m^2 with a varied depth up to 2 m, uneven edges, and a small island in one pond	2	Year 2
	Plant 100 shrubs, willow, alder and hawthorn in areas to the north and east of each pond	2	Year 3
Small stream	Maintain stock-proof fencing; avoid contamination of water by chemical inputs	1	Continuous over 5 years

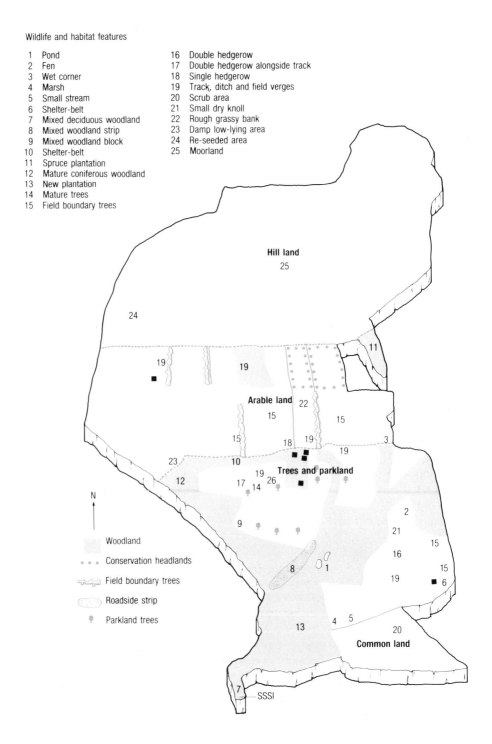

Wildlife and habitat features

1   Pond
2   Fen
3   Wet corner
4   Marsh
5   Small stream
6   Shelter-belt
7   Mixed deciduous woodland
8   Mixed woodland strip
9   Mixed woodland block
10 Shelter-belt
11 Spruce plantation
12 Mature coniferous woodland
13 New plantation
14 Mature trees
15 Field boundary trees

16 Double hedgerow
17 Double hedgerow alongside track
18 Single hedgerow
19 Track, ditch and field verges
20 Scrub area
21 Small dry knoll
22 Rough grassy bank
23 Damp low-lying area
24 Re-seeded area
25 Moorland

Woodland

Conservation headlands

Field boundary trees

Roadside strip

Parkland trees

Figure 7.3 Summary management plan

Chapter 8

IMPLEMENTING THE PLAN AND MONITORING PROGRESS

Summary

This final chapter discusses the processes of implementing the management prescriptions and of checking to make sure that they are indeed helping to achieve your strategic and management objectives. The latter leads naturally to the closing of the management planning cycle. Some management prescriptions will show an obvious conservation benefit more rapidly than others, but they should not be chosen for this reason. There will also always be the chance of unexpected outcomes and you should be ready to take remedial action if necessary.

8.1 Implementing the management prescriptions

As wildlife and landscape conservation increasingly become part of our everyday management of the countryside, more and more people will find themselves involved in the process in a variety of different roles. There will be land managers (who could be land owners, tenants, managers working for a public body or a commercial company), advisers and consultants, employees, teachers or trainers and their students, voluntary workers and other members of the public. If you are a manager, you may only ever work with one plan, but you will be revising it regularly over the years. If you are an adviser or consultant, you will find yourself preparing tens or hundreds of management plans, often under time pressure, when you will have to cut corners and do some stages less thoroughly than you would like.

The management plan is the key to the integration of all these roles, providing a record of the landscape and habitat quality of the land, and a means of explaining and understanding the strategic and management objectives of the land use, how they relate to the manager's preferences and prejudices, and how conservation will integrate with these. The plan will also help to keep track of progress in implementing the management prescriptions and to revise the objectives and options where necessary.

8.2 Checking your progress

Stage 5 of management planning will thus take years rather than months to put into practice, and you will need to keep track of your progress, to check how well and how quickly the landscape and habitats are improving, or, if appropriate, make sure they are not deteriorating.

This is where the cycle of management planning illustrated in Figure 1.2 is closed. You are, in effect, returning to Stage 1 of the next cycle, i.e. carrying out an integrated assessment of your land area after you have implemented the management prescriptions. Comparing this second assessment with the first will give you a measure of your progress.

Unless you have a strong personal interest in some aspect of wildlife conservation, such as birdwatching or studying insects, you will not want to spend a lot of time counting the numbers of various species on your land from season to season. What you will need, as described in Chapters 2 and 3, are simple, straightforward ways of checking your progress.

Monitoring

Detailed monitoring would be much more time-consuming and, if it is to be worth doing at all, would have to be kept up consistently over a period of years. Few working managers will have this degree of commitment, unless they happen to have a conservation-related hobby. Where more detailed monitoring is needed, perhaps because a habitat has been recognised as particularly vulnerable, you may be able to enlist expert help from a local school or college, or through a conservation or wildlife organisation.

Reviewing developments

At the simplest level of record keeping, you will only need to update the notes on a single sheet of paper from time to time. A series of photographs, taken from the same position under similar conditions over a period of years can also be very interesting and useful. The important point is that you keep some records and do not rely on your memory from one year to another. It is easy to preside over a gradual deterioration in the conservation value of a piece of land without being aware of it or to have major improvements taking place in your own back yard without deriving the satisfaction that you deserve.

Some things happen more quickly than others

Remember that you will see the benefit of some conservation options very rapidly while others will take generations to achieve their full potential. Conservation plans should always have a long time-scale and recognise our responsibility to care for habitats and landscapes for the benefit of future generations. If you have incorporated a few options that give a rapid response, it will help to reinforce your sense of achievement in the short term. However, this should not be done for its own sake — only if site assessment and objectives indicate that it is desirable.

Ponds

Creating a new pond or improving an existing one will usually give a rapid response. In the past, when the British environment could still be described as 'natural', ponds would have been fairly short-lived features, created by natural obstructions on low-lying land, being gradually filled by debris and silt and eventually invaded by woodland adapted to wet conditions (carr) (see Chapter 3). The animals and plants that exploited wetlands therefore had to have good powers of dispersal so that they could move to suitable new habitats when the old one changed its character. The result is that when a new pond is created and a few of the appropriate water plants introduced, a diverse range of other aquatic species will probably follow of their own accord within a period of three or four years.

Woodland rides

Improving the maintenance of glades and rides or, where appropriate, creating new ones, can also be very satisfying. Very often an enormous number of wild flowers has been lying dormant in the shade and the access of some light is all that is needed to transform the woodland floor completely. This new habitat will attract large numbers of insects and birds, giving the whole area a feeling of thriving vitality.

Planting woods and hedges and restoring herb-rich grassland or heather moorland are options that will take longer to have a noticeable effect on habitats or landscapes. However, they will also have a more permanent impact in the long run and will nicely complement the speedier options.

Where your integrated assessment has indicated that this is appropriate, management plans should incorporate options that will have an impact over a varying time-scale, both to spread the workload in putting them into practice and maintaining them and to give the manager satisfaction in the long term.

Some things do not happen as planned

Inevitably, some things will not go according to plan when you begin to put your chosen options into practice. Monitoring and reviewing your progress will alert you to the need to modify your plans or to take remedial action on the ground. This will generally be because you failed to take an important factor (or constraint) into account, but even the experts can sometimes be caught unawares.

An example of such a problem occurred at one of the Countryside Commission demonstration farms. Here it was decided that, to encourage wildlife conservation in an area of derelict lime woodland, a coppice rotation would be introduced, even although clear felling and re-planting would be the most financially attractive option. The first section to be coppiced, instead of developing a diverse and attractive ground flora, became inundated with bramble bushes that also retarded the new growth from the coppiced stools. *Brambles* (In the first year, 73% of the ground cover was bramble and in the second year, 92%.) Even though bramble had been one of the three main species in the understorey before coppicing, it was not expected to take over in this way. The management prescription for this woodland has now been revised and coppicing is restricted to the edges of rides. The rest of the wood will be encouraged to develop into high forest with careful felling and re-stocking of small coupes of about 0.25–0.5 hectares. This, incidentally, will have a better benefit/cost ratio than coppicing.

Doesn't look like anything's colonised this pond, yet, Kevin..... Kevin ?

Sometimes woodland is felled and re-planted, or an area is fenced off and planted with trees, only to be taken over by rapid natural regeneration of trees and shrubs. If the planted trees are being grown for timber, this natural regeneration is likely to be viewed as a weed infestation that will need to be controlled. However, if the primary intention is to create an area with wildlife and landscape benefits, and perhaps yielding a little firewood, the money spent on planting and protecting new trees will have been wasted. Under circumstances like that, it would have been enough to fence off the area concerned, perhaps scarify the ground a little to give tree seedlings a chance to establish themselves, and sit back and wait for nature to take its course. If you are monitoring regularly, you can modify your plans in later years to save on seedling establishment and labour costs.

Sometimes, after checking a new pond regularly for a period of about 4–5 years, you may find that it is still relatively lifeless. If this is the case, consider whether the water could be polluted, perhaps by fertiliser run-off from nearby fields, or from rubbish dumped in the pond. Contaminated drainage water can be a very difficult problem to control without cutting back on inputs to crops, as any attempt to divert the contaminated water would probably dry up the pond. The best solution in the long run may be to fill in the pond and plant tree species that are tolerant of moist soils such as alder or willow.

Another common source of frustration is the failure of tree plantations. This can happen for a variety of reasons, such as planting trees on the wrong soil type, drought or browsing by animals. Regular checking can sometimes help you to avoid the problem; for example, watering drought-stricken trees can help if an unusually dry spell of weather is the cause, but this would not be realistic if you had planted the trees on too thin and shallow a soil in the first place. If you notice damage by browsing animals in time, you could fence off the area to keep them out. Where you made the wrong choice of tree species, or tried to plant trees in an unsuitable place, your best course of action may be to begin again with a different type of habitat.

These are only a few of the unexpected outcomes that regular monitoring can pick up. Each habitat will have its own set of potential problems and solutions to them, but successes are much more common than failures overall. The chief reason for monitoring and reviewing your progress will still be the pleasure you get from watching your achievements grow and flourish.

Annual fluctuations and seasonality

The progress of your site will be more obvious at some times of the year than others, and your monitoring plans should take account of this. Late spring is probably the best time to see the variety of plant, bird and insect life in woodlands and hedgerows. In spring you should expect to see tadpoles in a healthy pond. Later in the summer you may see at least one or two species of dragonfly. Around June and July is the best time to record the species diversity in herb-rich pastures.

In all habitats there will naturally be quite a bit of fluctuation in wildlife populations from one year to the next, as described in Chapter 3. It can take several years for bird populations to recover from a particularly hard winter, and a cold, wet summer with few insects can affect the breeding success of some bird species. Such natural catastrophes or trends will be common to a region and there is little that you can do about them, apart from providing the best possible conditions for survival and recovery of the wildlife on your land when conditions improve. If there is a persistent population decline in an important species or group of species, and it is peculiar to your site, it may be caused by something in your own land management regime. If so, there may be something you can do about it.

8.3 *The management planning cycle*

This book has attempted to give you a taste of what management planning is really like, rather than presenting an idealised, sanitised version for public consumption. However, despite these good intentions we have had to compromise and, for the sake of clarity, we have probably over-emphasised the distinctions between the various stages. In practice they will merge into one another much more. There will also, in real life, be much more back-tracking to earlier stages, to make minor or even major adjustments in your analysis, in the light of new information or second thoughts about a particular point.

As you become more expert you will find yourself varying the order in which you approach the stages of management planning. This does not mean that the logic underlying the stages is any less valid, but merely that you are beginning to make very rapid intuitive assumptions about some aspects of the analysis. This will enable you to jump ahead and look at their implications, knowing that you will have to come back and think about them in more detail later.

Once a management plan has been prepared and summarised as described here, it becomes a valuable long-term asset. Use it as a basis for monitoring and reviewing your progress; update it in a small way from year to year; and give it a thorough review at least once every five years (or more often if it seems necessary).

Management planning is, however, not an end in itself and producing the plan is only a prelude to doing something practical. Landscape and habitat conservation require long-term commitment from the manager and a willingness to work in an adaptable way with nature. The result can be a lifetime of discovery and satisfaction.

FURTHER READING

The following list includes books we would recommend as further reading. Those marked with an asterisk were used as sources when writing this book. At the end there is a short list of books to help with the identification of wildlife species.

Blunden, J, Curry, N (eds) (1985) *The Changing Countryside*. Croom Helm, London

Bryson, T (1986) *Farm Wildlife Conservation Manual*. TVS Community Unit, Maidstone, Kent

*Cobham Resource Consultants (1984) *Landscape and Wildlife Conservation on Farms*. Cobham Resource Consultants on behalf of the Countryside Commission for Scotland, the East of Scotland College of Agriculture and the Nature Conservancy Council, Oxford

*Cobham Resource Consultants (1985) *Landscape and Wildlife Conservation on Farms. A Further Study*. Cobham Resource Consultants on behalf of the Countryside Commission for Scotland, the East of Scotland College of Agriculture and the Nature Conservancy Council, Oxford.

Countryside Commission (1984) *Agricultural Landscapes: An Approach to their Improvement*, CCP 169. Countryside Commission, Cheltenham, Glos.

*Countryside Commission (1986) *Management Plans*, CCP 206. Countryside Commission, Cheltenham, Glos.

*Countryside Commission (1986) *Demonstration Farms Project Kingston Hill Farm. Farming with Conservation*, CCP 210. Countryside Commission, Cheltenham, Glos.

*Countryside Commission (1987) *Landscape Assessment. A Countryside Commission Approach*, CCD 18. Countryside Commission, Cheltenham, Glos.

*Countryside Commission (1987) *New Opportunities for the Countryside*, CCP 224. Countryside Commission, Cheltenham, Glos.

*Countryside Commission (1987) *Conservation Monitoring and Management*, CCP 231. Countryside Commission, Cheltenham, Glos.

*Countryside Commission for Scotland (1986) *Countryside Conservation. A Guide for Farmers*. Countryside Commission for Scotland, Battleby, Perth

*Crowther, R E, Low, A J (1986) Advice on establishment and tending of trees. In: *Forestry Commission Bulletin 14, Forestry Practice* (10th edn). Hibberd, B G (ed). Her Majesty's Stationery Office, London

*Darvill, T (1987) *Ancient Monuments in the Countryside: an Archaeological Management Review*. Historic Buildings and Monuments Commission for England, London

*Forestry Commission Environment Branch (1986) Design of streams and water courses. Forestry Commission, Edinburgh (unpublished)

Garner, J F, Jones, G L (1987) *Countryside Law*. Shaw and Sons, London

*Green, B (1985) *Countryside Conservation* (2nd edn). George Allen & Unwin, London

*Hamilton, E (1985) *Tree Planting*. The Woodland Trust, Grantham, Lincs.

*Hudson, P J (1984) Some effects of sheep management on heather moorlands in northern England. In: *Agriculture and the Environment*, pp 143 149. Jenkins, D (ed). Institute of Terrestrial Ecology/Natural Environment Research Council, Cambridge

MacEwen, A, MacEwen, M (1987) *Greenprints for the Countryside: The Story of Britain's National Parks*. Allen & Unwin, London

*Miles, J (1979) *Vegetation Dynamics*. Chapman and Hall, London

*Moore, N (1987) *The Bird of Time*. Cambridge University Press, Cambridge

*Morris, P (ed) (1980) *Natural History of the British Isles*. Country Life Books, Richmond

*Nature Conservancy Council (1984) *Nature Conservation and Afforestation in Britain*. Nature Conservancy Council, Peterborough

*Nature Conservancy Council (1984) *Nature Conservation in Great Britain*. Nature Conservancy Council, Peterborough

*Nature Conservancy Council (1988) *Site Management Plans for Nature Conservation*. Nature Conservancy Council, Peterborough

*Nix, J, Hill, P, Williams, N (1987) *Land and Estate Management*. Packard, Chichester, West Sussex

*Perring, F H, Walters, S M (eds) (1962) *Atlas of the British Flora*. Thomas Nelson, Walton-on-Thames

*Potts, G R (1986) *The Partridge: Pesticides, Predation and Conservation*. Collins, London

*The Game Conservancy (1987) *The Red Grouse, King of Gamebirds*. The Game Conservancy, Fordingbridge, Hampshire

*The National Trust (1985) The preparation of management plans. Guidelines for research teams. The National Trust, Cheltenham (internal paper)

*The National Trust (1986) Forestry subject paper. The National Trust, Cheltenham (internal paper)

*The National Trust (1988) The preparation of management plans. Guidelines for managing agents and regional management teams. The National Trust, Cirencester (internal paper)

*The Open University (1986) S326 Ecology. Third level undergraduate course texts. Open University Press, Milton Keynes

Tittensor, R, Tittensor, A (1986) *Nature Conservation for Busy Farmers*. Countryside Management Consultancy, Arundel, West Sussex.

Usher, M (ed) (1986) *Wildlife Conservation Evaluation*. Chapman and Hall, London

Wildlife Identification

There are numerous books on the market to help with the identification of plants and animals in Great Britain. The following list gives some examples.

Collins Field Guides

Arnold, E N, Burton, J A, Overden, D W (1978) *The Reptiles and Amphibians of Britain and Europe*

Bang, P, Dahlstrom, P (1974) *Animal Tracks and Signs*

Barret, J, Younge, C M (1958) *The Sea Shore*

Chinery, M (1976) *The Insects of Britain and Northern Europe*

Fitter, R, Fitter, A, Blamey, M (1978) *The Wild Flowers of Britain and Northern Europe*

Kerney, M P, Cameron, R A D, Riley, G (1979) *The Land Snails of Britain and North West Europe*

Large, M, Hora, F B (1965) *Mushrooms and Toadstools*

Mitchell, A (1978) *The Trees of Britain and Northern Europe*

Peterson, R, Mountfort, G, Hallam, P A D (1974) *The Birds of Britain and Europe*

Mitchell Beazley Pocket Guides

Hayman, P (1979) *Birds*

Moore, P D (1980) *Wild Flowers*

Rushford, K (1980) *Trees*

Pan Books

Hammond, N, Everet, M (1980) *Birds of Britain and Europe*

Phillips, R (1977) *Wild Flowers of Britain*

Phillips, R (1978) *Trees in Britain*

Phillips, R (1980) *Grasses, Ferns, Mosses and Lichens of Great Britain and Ireland*

Phillips, R (1981) *Mushrooms*

Appendix II
GLOSSARY

Acidic This term refers to soils, and the plant communities they support, with a low pH, e.g. acidic grassland.

Alkaline This term refers to soils, and the plant communities they support, of a calcareous nature and a high pH, e.g. chalk grassland.

Agroforestry The cultivation of mixtures of tree and herbaceous crops on the same ground, as widely spaced trees (grown for timber, fuel or tree crop products) with arable crops or grassland.

Area of Outstanding Natural Beauty (AONB) Areas of particular landscape beauty designated by the Countryside Commission, smaller in size than National Parks and without a managing authority.

Bogs Areas of acid, wet, spongy ground consisting of vegetation in a state of arrested decomposition. The four main categories are basin, blanket, raised and valley bogs.

Cairn A mound of stones erected as a memorial or marker.

Calcareous Made of, or containing, calcium carbonate and therefore alkaline.

Canopy layer The tallest tree layer in a wood.

Carbohydrates These are organic compounds consisting of carbon, hydrogen and oxygen that play an essential part in the metabolism of all organisms, e.g. sugars, starch, cellulose.

Carnivore An animal that eats other animals, i.e. flesh-eating.

Carr Shrub or woodland communities growing in water-logged ground.

Climax community The end-point of an undisturbed succession under the prevailing climatic and soil conditions. Natural events or human activities can cause arrested climax communities by influencing the succession.

Conservation headlands The practice of reducing or eliminating the use of pesticides and/or fertiliser on the headlands of fields.

Constraints Factors that limit the ability to achieve objectives.

Coppicing The process of cutting trees or bushes close to the ground to allow new shoots to grow from the stump, on a rotational basis.

Copse A thicket or dense growth of small trees or bushes.

Coupes Blocks or areas of woodland or forest to be harvested at one time.

Covert A thicket or woodland providing shelter for game.

Croft A small enclosed plot of land, adjoining a house, worked by the occupants (in Scotland).

Culvert A drain or covered channel.

Detritus Organic debris from decomposing plants and animals.

Diversity The variety of species within a particular habitat or the variety of habitats within an area.

Dyke A ditch or water course; a bank made of earth beside a ditch; a drystone wall (Scotland).

Earthworks Soil-covered archaeological remains visible as undulations on the land surface.

Ecology Study of the relations of animals and plants, particularly communities of them, to one another and to their surroundings, both living and non-living.

Environment The external surroundings, both living and non-living, in which plants or animals live, which influence their development and behaviour.

Environmentally Sensitive Area (ESA) Area designated by the Ministry of Agriculture, Fisheries and Food, the Department of Agriculture and Fisheries for Scotland or the Welsh Office of Agricultural Development where it is deemed desirable to conserve and enhance the natural beauty of the area, conserve the flora or fauna or geological or physiographical features of the area, or protect buildings or other objects of archaeological, architectural or historical interest in the area.

Eutrophic Water rich in organic and mineral nutrients and supporting an abundant plant life.

Extensive Low input, low output production practised over a large area, i.e. extensive land use.

Fen Low-lying flat land that is marshy.

Food chain A figure of speech for the dependence for food of organisms upon others in a series, beginning with plants and ending with the largest carnivores.

Food web Interactions among the food chains in a community.

Fossil pollen Pollen that has been preserved in soil or bogs.

Generalist species Species adapted to a wide range of conditions and habitats.

Glade A clearing or open place in a forest.

Ground layer The lowest layer of vegetation in a wood.

Habitat A place with a characteristic environment inhabited by organisms.

Harrow An implement used to level the ground, break up clods, or destroy weeds.

Heathland A large open area, usually with sandy soil and scrubby vegetation, especially heather, normally at lower altitudes.

Herbivore An animal that eats living plants.

Herb layer The herbaceous plant layer in a wood.

Host plant A species of plant on which a particular organism feeds, in particular insects.

Humus Partially decomposed organic matter in the soil.

Improved grassland Grassland that has been treated with fertiliser and sometimes pesticides in order to boost productivity.

Inorganic Of mineral origin; not containing carbon and not produced by living organisms.

Intensive High input, high output production, i.e. intensive land use.

Knoll A small rounded hill.

Landform The physical character of a piece of ground.

Land use capability A land classification scheme based on the uses to which a piece of land can be put given the wetness, gradient, climate, soil and potential erosion.

Larva An immature form of an insect that develops into an adult by metamorphosis.

Leaching The removal of minerals by percolating water.

Less Favoured Area (LFA) Area designated by the Ministry of Agriculture, Fisheries and Food, the Department of Agriculture and Fisheries for Scotland or the Welsh Office of Agricultural Development under an EEC directive which is in danger of de-population and where the conservation of the countryside is necessary. Such areas have to exhibit infertility, a poor economic situation and a low or dwindling population dependent on agriculture.

Levee An embankment alongside a river to prevent flooding.

Lichens Small plants formed by the symbiotic association of a fungus and an alga.

Lynchet A terrace or ridge formed in prehistoric or medieval times by ploughing a hillside.

Management agreement An agreement whereby a landowner or manager avoids environmentally harmful practices in return for financial recompense.

Marsh Low, undrained land that is sometimes flooded and often lies at the edge of lakes or the sea (saltmarsh).

Moorland An upland area of open, unenclosed ground usually covered with heather, coarse grasses, bracken and moss.

National Scenic Area (NSA) Area of particular landscape beauty designated by the Countryside Commission for Scotland.

National Park Area designated by reason of natural beauty and opportunities afforded to the public for open air recreation that has its own planning and management arrangements.

Naturalness The extent to which a habitat has been free from human interference.

Neutral Soil or water that is neither acid nor alkaline.

Niche The status of a plant or animal within its community, which determines its activities and relationships with other organisms and its environment.

Objectives Outcomes or goals to be achieved.

Oligotrophic Water poor in nutrients and plant life and rich in oxygen.

Omnivore An animal that feeds on many different kinds of plant and animal food.

Option The means available to achieve an objective.

Organic material Compounds containing carbon that are produced by living plants and animals.

pH A quantitative expression for the acidity or alkalinity of a solution or soil. The scale ranges from 0 to 14: pH 7 is neutral, less than 7 acid, more than 7 alkaline.

Parasite An animal or plant that lives in or on another (the host) from which it obtains nourishment.

Photosynthesis The synthesis, in plants, of organic compounds from carbon dioxide and water using light energy absorbed by chlorophyll.

Pioneer A plant species that first colonises bare ground in a succession.

Poach To catch game illegally by trespassing; to break up land into wet muddy patches.

Potentially Damaging Operations (PDOs) Operations specified in the designation of an SSSI which could damage the site, and for which prior approval is needed before they can be carried out.

Predator An animal that captures and feeds on other animals (prey).

Prescription Actions to be undertaken, as specified in a written statement.

Primary producers Plants that produce organic materials by photosynthesis.

Primary woodland (ancient woodland) Woodland that has had a continuous tree cover since 1600.

Proteins Complex organic compounds of amino acids.

Pupa An insect at the immobile, non-feeding stage of development between larva and adult.

Ramparts The surrounding embankments of a fort.

Rarity Refers to species with relatively small populations within a defined area.

Ride A pathway or track in woodland, often for horseriding.

Secondary woodland Woodland growing on land that has previously been used for some other purpose.

Scarified Loosened or broken up to a shallow depth (soil).

Semi-natural Used to describe an assemblage of native species that is apparently natural but has been significantly modified by human activities.

Site of Special Scientific Interest (SSSI) Area designated by the NCC as of special interest, because of its flora, fauna, geology or physiography, outside nature reserves.

Shrub layer (see understorey) The tall bushes and small trees below the canopy layer in a wood.

Specialist species A species adapted to particular conditions in one habitat.

Species The lowest unit of classification normally used for plants and animals.

Stand A small block of (usually) mature trees.

Standards Mature trees with an upright trunk free of branches.

Succession The replacement of one kind of community by another, shown by the progressive changes in vegetation and animal life that may culminate in a climax community. Successions developing on new surfaces are primary successions, those on disturbed surfaces, secondary successions.

Sward A grassy land surface or green turf.

Transect A line or path taken across an area of land used to survey vegetation and other wildlife.

Tree Preservation Order (TPO) An order made by a local authority to protect a single tree, a group of trees or an area of woodland in the interests of landscape and amenity.

Tundra A treeless zone lying between the ice cap and timber line with a permanently frozen sub-soil.

Understorey The plant layer below the tree canopy.

Unimproved grassland Grassland that has not been re-seeded, treated with chemical fertiliser or pesticides and is a rich wildlife habitat.

Appendix III

REPRESENTATIVE PLANT SPECIES IN MAJOR HABITAT TYPES

The following lists are intended to give an impression of the sorts of plants to be found in certain typical habitats. They have been compiled so that as you read across the page the soil type becomes increasingly wet and down the page the species graduate from pioneer species of open ground to plants associated with climax woodland community. The habitats are divided into three categories based on soil type — alkaline, neutral or acid.

By first identifying the soil type and then finding the correct type of wetness and the stage of development of the community (open, scrub or wood) the typical species of that habitat can be identified. Few localities will contain all of those species mentioned and the list is not comprehensive, but they may be regarded as representative species.

Reading down the columns, as the habitats become more wooded, the species are divided into groups. Species from one group may often appear in later groups. In addition, species in one column are likely to appear in the soil types in the adjacent column(s).

Alkaline soils

	Dry — Rocks	Moist — Grassland	Wet — Fen
Open	Sticky catchfly	Wild candytuft	Marsh pea
	Whitlow grasses	Autumn gentian	Marsh valerian
	Rock stonecrop		Marsh helleborine
	Wallflower	Rock-roses	Early marsh orchid
	Dark red helleborine	Clustered bellflower	Milk parsley
		Common spotted orchid	Common comfrey
		Pyramidal orchid	Marsh cinquefoil
			Greater spearwort
	Spring sandwort	Fragrant orchid	Fen orchid
	Alpine penny-cress	Bee orchid	Marsh bedstraw
	Spiked speedwell	Salad burnet	Yellow loosestrife
	Hairy rock-cress	Horseshoe vetch	Water chickweed
	Stone bramble	Hairy violet	
		Greater hawkbit	
		Dwarf thistle	
Scrub	Traveller's joy	Hawthorn	Alder buckthorn
	Hazel	Dogwood	Buckthorn
	Blackthorn	Wayfaring tree	Grey willow
		Wild privet	Goat willow
		Spindle tree	Guelder rose
		Sweet briar	Blackcurrant

Dry — Rocks	Moist — Grassland	Wet — Fen
Wood Whitebeams	Beech	Alder
Yew	Ash	Birches
Wych elm	Lime	Hawthorn
	Crab apple	
	Wild cherry	
	Field maple	
Herb robert	Spurge laurel	Hedge bindweed
Wall lettuce	Dog's mercury	Tufted vetch
Jacob's ladder	Sanicle	Yellow iris
Enchanter's	Woodruff	Dewberry
nightshade	Wood dog violet	Comfrey
Herb bennet	Fly orchid	Hop
Wild strawberry	Birdsnest orchid	Hemp agrimony
Broad-leaved	White helleborine	
willowherb	Hellebores	
	Wood sorrel	

Neutral soils

Dry — Waste ground	Moist — Grassland	Wet — Marsh
Open Red dead-nettle	Birdsfoot trefoil	Broad-leaved
Broad-leaved dock	Great burnet	pondweed
Common field	Pepper saxifrage	Water-lilies
speedwell	Dyer's greenweed	Amphibious bistort
Groundsel	Saw-wort	
Shepherd's purse	Greater butterfly	Marsh marigold
Dandelions	orchid	Branched bur-reed
Common stitchwort	Common mouse-ear	Yellow iris
Poppies	Knapweeds	Purple loosestrife
Fumitories	Meadow buttercup	Meadowsweet
Charlock	Ribwort plantain	Water forget-me-nots
Hoary cinquefoil	Yarrow	Lesser spearwort
		Great willow-herb
Scrub Goat willow	Hazel	Goat willow
Elder	Midland hawthorn	Grey willow
	Holly	
	Blackthorn	
Wood Common oak	Sessile oak	Black poplar
	Wych elm	Crack willow
	Wild service tree	White willow
	Field maple	Alder
Nettle	Bugle	Cuckoo flower
Barren strawberry	Wood anemone	Ragged robin
Bramble	Ramson	Water avens
Rosebay willowherb	Primrose	Creeping buttercup
	Common dog violet	Bugle
	Yellow pimpernel	Hedge woundwort
	Red campion	Creeping jenny
	Early purple orchid	Marsh thistle

Acid soils

	Dry — Heath	Moist — Moor	Wet — Bog
Open	Sand spurrey Changing forget-me- not	Shepherd's cress Sheep's sorrel	Bog pondweed Bogbean

	Annual knawel
	Cudweeds
	Thyme
	Harebell
	Petty whin
	Maiden pink
	Tormentil
	Heath milkwort
	Heath dog violet
		Lousewort
		Heath spotted orchid
		Lesser butterfly
		  orchid
		Coralroot orchid
		Foxgloves
		Heath bedstraw
		Dwarf cornel
			Marsh asphodel
			Sundews
			Grass of Parnassus
			Butterworts
			Bog orchids
			Marsh lousewort
			Marsh pennywort
			Marsh St. John's
			  wort
			Marsh violet

Dwarf shrub	Bell heather Gorse Broom Bilberry	Heather Bearberry Crowberry	Cross-leaved heath Bog rosemary Cranberry Bog myrtle Creeping willow
Scrub	Rowan Downy rose	Juniper Aspen	Gorse
Wood	Birches Sessile oak	Scots pine	Norway spruce Birch

	Common cow-wheat
	Lesser stitchwort
	Trailing St. John's
	  wort
	Lesser periwinkle
	Climbing corydalis
		Wintergreens
		Twinflower
		Bitter vetchling
		Cowberry
		Creeping lady's
		  tresses
			Chickweed
			  wintergreen

(Source: adapted from Fitter *et al.* 1978)

SCIENTIFIC NAMES
FOR WILDLIFE SPECIES

Plants

Alder *Alnus glutinosa*
Alder buckthorn *Frangula alnus*
Angelica *Angelica sylvestris*
Ash *Fraxinus excelsior*
Aspen *Populus tremula*
Beech *Fagus sylvatica*
Bell heather *Erica cinerea*
Bilberry *Vaccinium myrtillus*
Birch,
   Downy *Betula pubescens*
   Dwarf *Betula nana*
   Silver *Betula pendula*
Bird cherry *Prunus padus*
Birdsfoot trefoil *Lotus corniculatus*
Black poplar *Populus nigra*
Blackthorn (sloe) *Prunus spinosa*
Bog moss *Sphagnum* spp
Box *Buxus sempervirens*
Bracken *Pteridium aquilinum*
Bramble *Rubus fruticosus*
Broad-leaved dock *Rumex obtusifolius*
Brooklime *Veronica beccabunga*
Broom *Cytisus scoparius*
Bugle *Ajuga reptans*
Bur-reed *Sparganium erectum*
Bush vetch *Vicia sepium*
Chickweed *Stellaria media*
Chickweed wintergreen *Trientalis europaea*
Cocksfoot *Dactylis glomerata*
Common sallow (goat willow) *Salix caprea*
Common sorrel *Rumex acetosa*
Cowberry *Vaccinium vitis-idea*
Cow parsley *Anthriscus sylvestris*
Cowslip *Primula veris*
Cotton grass *Eriophorum vaginatum*

Crab apple *Malus sylvestris*
Creeping thistle *Cirsium arvense*
Cross-leaved heath *Erica tetralix*
Crowberry *Empetrum nigrum*
Daffodil *Narcissus pseudonarcissus*
Dandelion *Taraxacum officinale*
Devil's bit scabious *Succisa pratensis*
Dog-rose *Rosa canina*
Dogwood *Cornus sanguinea*
Dock *Rumex* spp
Douglas fir *Pseudotsuga menziesii*
Eelgrass *Zostera marina*
Elm,
   Common *Ulmus procera*
   Wych *Ulmus glabra*
Elder *Sambucus nigra*
European larch *Larix decidua*
Eyebright *Euphrasia* spp
Fen violet *Viola persicifolia*
Field maple *Acer campestre*
Figwort *Scrophularia nodosa*
Foxglove *Digitalis purpurea*
Gean (wild cherry) *Prunus avium*
Germander speedwell *Veronica chamaedrys*
Glasswort *Salicornia* spp
Gorse *Ulex europeaus*
Gorse, Dwarf *Ulex minor*
Guelder rose *Viburnum opulus*
Hard fern *Blechnum spicant*
Harebell *Companula rotundifolia*
Hazel *Corylus avellana*
Heath bedstraw *Galium saxatile*
Heather (ling) *Calluna vulgaris*
Hawthorn *Crataegus monogyna*
Hogweed *Heracleum sphondylium*
Holly *Ilex aquifolium*
Honeysuckle *Lonicera periclymenun*

Hop trefoil *Trifolium campestre*
Hornbeam *Carpinus betulus*
Horsetail (see Water horsetail)
Iris (see Yellow flag)
Juniper *Juniperus communis*
Knapweed *Centaurea nigra*
Knotgrass *Polygonum aviculare*
Lady orchid *Orchis purpurea*
Lady's bedstraw *Galium verum*
Lady's mantle *Alchemilla alpina*
Lady's smock *Cardamine pratensis*
Larch (see European larch)
Lesser spearwort *Ranunculus flammula*
Lesser stitchwort *Stellaria graminea*
Lime,
    Large-leaved *Tilia platyphyllous*
    Small-leaved *Tilia cordata*
Ling (heather) *Calluna vulgaris*
Lodgepole pine *Pinus contorta*
Male fern *Dryopteris filix-mas*
Marram grass *Ammophila arenaria*
Marsh bedstraw *Galium palustre*
Marsh cinquefoil *Potentilla palustris*
Marsh marigold *Caltha palustris*
Marsh thistle *Cirsium palustre*
Marsh violet *Viola palustris*
Mayweed *Matricaria perforata*
Meadowsweet *Filipendula ulmaria*
Meadow vetchling *Lathyrus pratensis*
Midland hawthorn *Crataegus oxyacanthoides*
Milkwort *Polygala vulgaris*
Monkey flower *Mimulus guttatus*
Mountain avens *Dryas octopetala*
Nettle *Urtica* spp
Noble fir *Abies procera*
Northern marsh orchid *Dactylorhiza purpurella*
Norway spruce *Picea abies*
Oak,
    Common *Quercus robur*
    Holm *Quercus ilex*
    Sessile *Quercus petraea*
    Turkey *Quercus cerris*
Petty whin *Genista angelica*

Pignut *Conopodium majus*
Poplar *Populus* spp
Primrose *Primula vulgaris*
Privet *Ligustrum vulgare*
Purging buckthorn *Rhamnus catharticus*
Ragged robin *Lychnis flos-cuculi*
Red-berried elder *Sambucus racemosa*
Redshank *Polygonum persicaria*
Ribwort plantain *Plantago lanceolata*
Rosebay willowherb *Epilobium angustifolium*
Rowan *Sorbus ancuparia*
Rhododendron *Rhododendron ponticum*
Ryegrass *Lolium perenne*
Scots pine *Pinus sylvestris*
Sedge,
    Bottle *Carex rostrata*
    Carnation *Carex flacca*
    Lesser tussock *Carex appropinquata*
Self-heal *Prunella vulgaris*
Sharp flowered rush *Juncus acutiflorus*
Sitka spruce *Picea sitchensis*
Sloe (blackthorn) *Prunus spinosa*
Sneezewort *Achillea ptarmica*
Snowberry *Symphoricarpos rivularis*
Soft rush *Juncus effusus*
Solomon's seal *Polygonatum multiflorum*
Spindle *Euonymous europaeus*
Stitchwort *Stellaria* spp
Sweet chestnut *Castanea sativa*
Sycamore *Acer pseudoplatanus*
Tormentil *Potentilla erecta*
Thrift *Armeria maritima*
Thyme *Thymus* spp
Timothy *Phleum pratense*
Tufted vetch *Vicia cracca*
Valerian *Valeriana officinalis*
Violet,
    Common dog *Viola riviniana*
    Fen *Viola persicifolia*
    Heath dog *Viola canina*

Marsh *Viola palustris*
Sweet *Viola odorata*
Water horsetail *Equisetum fluviatile*
Wayfaring tree *Viburnum lantana*
Whin (see Gorse)
Whitebeam *Sorbus aria*
White clover *Trifolium repens*
Wild cherry (gean) *Prunus avium*
Wild raspberry *Rubus idaeus*
Wild service tree *Sorbus torminalis*
Willow,
    Bay *Salix petandra*

Crack *Salix fragilis*
Goat *Salix caprea*
Grey *Salix cinerea*
White *Salix alba*
Wood anemone *Anemone nemorosa*
Yarrow *Achillea millefolium*
Yellow flag *Iris pseudacorus*
Yellow-horned poppy *Glaucium flavum*
Yew *Taxus baccata*

Animals

Badger *Meles meles*
Barn owl *Tyto alba*
Black hairstreak butterfly *Strymonidia pruni*
Blue tit *Parus caeruleus*
Bumble-bee *Bombus* spp
Buzzard *Buteo buteo*
Canada goose *Branta canadiensis*
Carp *Cyprinus carpio*
Carrion crow *Corvus corone*
Collared dove *Streptopelia decaocto*
Common frog *Rana temporaria*
Coot *Fulcia atra*
Corncrake *Crex crex*
Curlew *Numenius arquata*
Elm bark beetle *Scolytus scolytus* and *S. multistriatus*
Fallow deer *Cervus dama*
Fox *Vulpes vulpes*
Grey partridge *Perdix perdix*
Grey squirrel *Neosciurus carolinensis*
Hare *Lepus capensis*
Hen harrier *Circus cyaneus*
High brown fritillary *Fabriciana adippe*
Lapwing *Vanellus vanellus*
Mallard *Anas platyrhynchos*
Meadow brown butterfly *Maniola jurtina*
Mistle thrush *Turdus viscivorus*

Mole *Talpa europea*
Moorhen *Gallinula chloropus*
Newt *Triturus vulgaris*
Otter *Lutra lutra*
Pearl bordered fritillary *Clossiana euphrosyne*
Peregrine *Falco peregrinus*
Pheasant *Phasianus colchicus*
Rabbit *Oryctolagus cuniculus*
Red grouse *Lagopus lagopus*
Red squirrel *Sciurus vulgaris*
Roe deer *Capreolus capreolus*
Short-eared owl *Asio flammeus*
Shrew *Sorex* spp
Silver washed fritillary *Argynnis paphia*
Small pearl bordered fritillary *Clossiana selene*
Small tortoiseshell *Aglais urticae*
Sparrowhawk *Accipiter nisus*
Stoat *Mustela erminea*
Tawny owl *Strix aluco*
Toad *Buto buto*
Trout *Salmo* spp
Tufted duck *Aythya fuligula*
Two spot ladybird *Adalia bipunctata*
Wheatear *Oenanthe oenanthe*
Wild cat *Felix catus*
Winter moth *Operophtera brumata*

Acknowledgements

The Open University course team is greatly indebted to the many people, with a wide range of experience of countryside management, who have contributed to the development of this teaching programme.

First, we must acknowledge the very generous financial support of the Nature Conservancy Council, along with the Esmée Fairbairn Charitable Trust, the Ernest Cook Trust and British Gas plc.

We are also grateful to our Steering Committee for the many hours devoted to discussions and to reading successive drafts:

M Banham (British Trust for Conservation Volunteers)

D Brown (Department of the Environment)

T Bryson (Wye College, University of London)

A Cade (Nature Conservancy Council)

P Gilder (Countryside Commission)

R Grant (Countryside Commission for Scotland)

E Hammond (Nature Conservancy Council)

J Harvey (National Trust)

A Horsefield (Agricultural Training Board)

K B C Jones (Ministry of Agriculture, Fisheries and Food)

G Kerby (Agricultural Training Board)

R Loomes (Nature Conservancy Council, England)

R MacMullen (Farming and Wildlife Advisory Group)

C Mattheson (National Trust)

C Newbold (Nature Conservancy Council)

W Martin (Nature Conservancy Council, Wales)

R Potts (Game Conservancy)

T Reed (Nature Conservancy Council)

R Robinson (Nature Conservancy Council, Scotland)

We also value the comments and the support of the external assessor, Dr Bryn Green, The Sir Cyril Kleinwort Professor of Countryside Management, Wye College, University of London.

We would like to thank the many other people who provided source material for the book or read and commented on preliminary drafts:

J Andrews (Royal Society for the Protection of Birds)

S Bell (Forestry Commission)

I Bradley (Soil Survey and Land Research Centre)

E Carter (Farming and Wildlife Advisory Group)

E Christie (Farming and Wildlife Advisory Group)

J Howe (Farming and Wildlife Advisory Group)

J Keith (Farming and Wildlife Advisory Group)

C Langton (Forest Manager)

D Lawrence (Farming and Wildlife Advisory Group)

R Lesley (Forestry Commission)

P Mayhew (British Association for Shooting and Conservation)

J McKay (Countryside Commission for Scotland)

175

J Meredith (Countryside Commission)
N Moore (formerly Nature Conservancy Council)
P Palmes (Farming and Wildlife Advisory Group)
P Ramsay (Farmer)
V Wood (Farming and Wildlife Advisory Group)
D Yellowlees (Farmer)

Grateful acknowledgement is made to the following sources for permission to use material in this book:

Figures

Figure 1.3: *Countryside Conservation: A Guide for Farmers*, 1986, Countryside Commission for Scotland; *Figures 2.2, 2.4 and Box 4.3*: *Demonstration Farms Project: Kingston Hill Farm*, 1986, Countryside Commission; *Figures 3.5 and 6.2*: Potts, G. R. *The Partridge: Pesticides, Predation and Conservation*, 1986, Collins; *Figure 3.7*: Perring, F. H. and Walters, S. M. *Atlas of the British Flora*, 1962, A & C Black; *Figure 4.2*: *Conservation Monitoring and Management*, 1987, Countryside Commission; *Figure 5.1*: *Management Plans: A Guide to Their Preparation and Use*, 1986, Countryside Commission; *Figure 6.1*: Severn–Trent Water Authority; *Figure 6.3*: Forestry Commission.

Tables

Table 3.1: *Countryside Conservation: A Guide for Farmers*, 1986, Countryside Commission for Scotland; *Table 6.2*: Hamilton, E. *Tree Planting*, 1985, The Woodland Trust.

Plates

Plate 5: Soil Survey of England and Wales, Crown copyright; *Plate 6*: Cambridge University Collection: copyright reserved; *Plate 11*: Royal Society for the Protection of Birds; *Plate 12*: by courtesy of the British Museum (Natural History); *Plate 16*: Ministry of Agriculture, Fisheries and Food, Crown copyright.

Index

I

Ice Age *39, 40*
ice house *33, 69*
identification of species *58, 164*
imaginative approach *121, 128*
implementation *10, 12, 157–61*
insects *43, 44, 115;* rare *72*
integrated assessment *12, 13, 14, 70–87;* and constraints and objectives *10, 88–9;* exercises *80;* hill farms *73;* land use management *70–1;* summary *156–61 see also* business, habitat and landscape assessments; options, and individual entries
integrated farm plan: priorities *139–40;* site map *142;* summary plan *143–5*
intensive land use *see* land use

K

Kingston Hill Farm profile *78*

L

Lake District *20*
lakes and tree planting *73, 74*
land manager *70, 80, 83, 84, 91*
land use: capability *77;* case study *62, 63, 83, 84;* changes *19, 24, 40, 122;* and conservation objectives *93–7;* designated *8;* diversification *97, 98;* extensive *73–5;* intensive *73–5;* management planning *89;* non-conservation *73;* primary *84*
landform *14, 15, 20, 23, 26*
landscape: cultural associations *14;* diversity *19;* and economy *22;* features *21, 27, 34, 127;* and habitat value *71–2;* naturalness *19, 54;* perception *28;* and structures *71;* unstable *17;* wildlife interaction *71;* zones *23, 37 see also* land use; landscape assessment; vegetation
landscape assessment *14–37, 70;* case study *31–7;* equipment *29–30;* and local history *24;* maintenance *89;* non-intervention *104;* personal criteria/perception *118–19, 35;* recording data *26–8;* and recreation *74;* statutory designations *24, 33;* view-points *24–5, 33, 35–7 see also* business, habitat, and integrated assessments; landscape; options, and individual entries
landscape value *71, 72, 140*
legal criteria *24, 33, 92*
Less Favoured Area *13, 73, 77, 80, 86*
local history *24*
lynchets *18*

M

management agreements *85*
management options *see* options
management planning *7–8, 90, 147, 159–61;* business *73–6;* cycle *161;* and land use *11;* process of *10–13;* public access *22, 147 see also* forestry management; habitat and integrates assessments; options
management prescriptions *123–4, 132–3, 141, 159;* implementation *157–61 see also* options
maps: business assessment *81;* farm conservation *142;* habitat distribution *57;* wildlife assessment *58*
marshes *51;* case study *65, 125;* management *107–8;* wildlife value *55 see also* bogs; fens; wetlands
meadows *see* grassland; pasture
Ministry of Agriculture, Fisheries and Food (MAFF) *138*
moorland *42;* bracken control *107;* case study *61, 62, 68;* as habitat *49, 52–3;* replacement *75 see also* heather moorland
mowing *72, 105*

N

National Scenic Area *23*
National Trust *93, 95*
naturalness *19, 54*
Nature Conservancy Council *85, 92*
niche *39;* grey partridge *46*
nitrogen cycle *41*
nutrient replacement *41–2*
nutrients *41–2*

O

objectives *10, 12, 79;* case study *100–2;* conservation *93;* farmed land *93, 98–9;* flexibility *91;* identifying *88–9, 100;* large scale forestry *98;* management *90, 93;* strategic *90, 93, 98;* tactical *90, 98 see also* options
objective trees *89–91, 97;* case study *97–8, 101–2, 124*
oligotrophic environment *51–2*
omnivores *39*
options *10, 12, 97;* benefits *140;* brainstorming *121, 128, 129;* case study *125–32;* choosing and exploring *10, 103–33;* conservation *139;* costing *134–9, 145–7, 148–52;* definition *103;* forestry *119;* habitat *104, 124, 125;* habitat value *140;* imaginative approach *121, 128;* landscape value *140;* management *10;* and objectives *103;* selection *130;* using other knowledge *130*
organic farming *128, 149*
Ottercops farm *73, 75*

P

parasites *44*
parkland *21, 53, 77;* case study *37, 67, 126*
pasture: case study *68, 127;* permanent *13, 67, 126 see also* grassland
peat bogs *51;* wildlife value *55*
personal criteria/perception *18–19, 35*
pesticides *81, 104, 111, 113*
photosynthesis *41*
pigs, free range *131*
pioneer species *47*
pollution *74, 75, 108, 111, 160*
ponds *49, 92, 94, 143, 158, 159;* adverse features *71–2;* case study *65, 125;* commercial *122;* costing *135–7, 149–50;* dredging *109;* management *94, 108–9 see also* integrated assessment, water, wetlands
population dynamics *44–7*
Potentially Damaging Operations *92*
predators *44, 76, 85;* control *75*
prescriptions *see* management
primary producers *42*
protected species *75 see also* species
public access *22, 94*
public relations *87, 94*

R

rabbits   20, 68, 81, 86, 113, 114
Raechester Farm   73, 75
ramparts   18, 32
rarity   54, 56
recreation: and public access   87,
   94; and wildlife habitats   74,
   75
red grouse   38, 106; profitability
   76
reproductive strategy   44
rhododendrons   15, 85, 107, 115
rights of way   22, 33, 87, 94,
   120, 145
rivers   109; and archaeological
   sites   111; bank management
   110, 111; and shade   111
roadside verges see boundary
   habitats
rock types   14, 31
rough shooting   131 see also
   game shooting

S

salt marsh   53
sand dunes   53
scarification   111
Scotland   13, 20, 23
Scottish Agricultural Colleges   9
scrub   47, 105; case study   68,
   85; control   107, 108; and
   wildlife   107, 120
seminatural habitats   54, 98
sheep   76, 82, 84, 106; dairying
   130, 131, 149
shelterbelt   66, 126, 150
shrub layer   51, 115
Sites of Special Scientific Interest
   85, 92
soil: acid   53; alkaline   15;
   calcareous   56; characteristics
   15, 16; erosion   81, 86, 105,
   106, 148; inorganic   52;
   urban   54
sounds and smells   20, 28
species: dispersal and distribution
   40, 48–9; encouragement
   104; generalist   38; identification   58, 164; protected   75;
   rarity   54, 56, 104; specialist
   38, 76
squirrels   39
stand   23, 114
stream scouring   74
streams see rivers; water
structures   17, 23–4, 34;
   preservation   120; and wildlife   120 see also archaeological
   sites; buildings
succession   39, 47–8, 72;
   grassland   105; heather
   moorland   76

T

tenants   91
tidiness   72
timber production   23, 97, 122
Tree Preservation Order   23
trees: case study   37; field
   boundary   150; felling   92,
   118; hedgerow   113, 138; and
   insect population   43; and
   landscape value   72; pioneer
   species   47; plantation failure
   160; properties and requirements   114, 116–17; and red
   grouse   76; and soil types   15
   see also forestry, woodland
tundra   39
turtle dove   39